Ever since it was first published, Leonard's *Guide to the European Union* has played an invaluable role in unravelling these mysteries and complexities [of the European Union]. It is especially valuable, and rare, for doing so in a sober, meticulous and non-partisan way . . . No one could be better qualified to produce an updated, authoritative and highly readable guide than Leonard and Taylor.

Bill Emmott, Editor-in-Chief of The Economist *1993–2006.*

The Routledge Guide to the EU is the best book I know that explains clearly the complexities of the EU to the intelligent layman . . . Curious voters will find this book a useful source of objective information about the EU, and I have no doubt that it will be respected as such by both defenders and critics of the EU. In the longer run many students, business people or politicians that need to deal with the Brussels institutions will feel that they should own this book.

Charles Grant, Director of the influential think-tank, the Centre for European Reform (CER).

Dick Leonard's *Guide to the European Union* has long had a deserved reputation for clarity and reliability. His new, updated edition comes at an important moment in the history of European integration and will be a valuable aid to the public debate in Britain and throughout the European Union.

John Palmer, former European Editor of The Guardian *and former Political Director of the European Policy Centre.*

The Routledge Guide to the European Union

Written by experts, this long-established and definitive guide to the workings of the European Union provides comprehensive, straightforward and readable coverage of this sometimes misunderstood and complex institution. It explains not only what happens but also why, and analyses the EU's strengths and weaknesses, as well as opportunities for it to be more effective. With the EU's very existence under pressure due to fiscal crises and the eurozone, migration and borders, and Euroscepticism, it specifically outlines:

- How it works: the institutions, the mechanisms.
- Every area of EU competence from agriculture to workers' rights.
- The effects of the single market and the single currency and the successes and stresses of the eurozone.
- The impact of the enlargement of the EU and the prospects for further enlargement and for closer political integration.
- The EU under strain – the 2008 recession and after.
- 'Britain in or out'.
- Fully updated and revised material with new data, statistics, examples and non-partisan coverage.

The Routledge Guide to the European Union is well-established as the clearest and most comprehensive guide to how the EU operates. This new edition brings you up to date at a crucial stage in its history at a time when, arguably, it has never been under greater threat, but conversely is perhaps more important than ever.

Dick Leonard is a journalist, author and former Labour MP. He was Assistant Editor of *The Economist* for 12 years, and has also worked for *The Observer*, the BBC, the Fabian Society, the Centre for European Policy Studies and the Publishers Association.

Robert Taylor runs European Research Associates, a Brussels consultancy specialising in European public policy. For more than 30 years, he worked as a journalist and foreign correspondent, covering the European Union, reporting on its performance, policies and personalities.

The Routledge Guide to the European Union

Previously known as *The Economist Guide to the European Union*

Dick Leonard and Robert Taylor

Routledge
Taylor & Francis Group

LONDON AND NEW YORK

First edition published 2016
by Routledge
2 Park Square, Milton Park, Abingdon, Oxon, OX14 4RN

and by Routledge
711 Third Avenue, New York, NY 10017

Routledge is an imprint of the Taylor & Francis Group, an informa business

© 2016 Dick Leonard and Robert Taylor

The right of Dick Leonard and Robert Taylor to be identified as authors of this work has been asserted by them in accordance with sections 77 and 78 of the Copyright, Designs and Patents Act 1988.

Previously known as *The Economist Guide to the European Union*
First edition published by The Economist - Blackwell 1988
Tenth edition published by The Economist - Profile Books Ltd. 2010

British Library Cataloguing in Publication Data
A catalogue record for this book is available from the British Library

Library of Congress Cataloging in Publication Data
A catalog record for this book has been requested

ISBN: 978-1-138-67038-9 (hbk)
ISBN: 978-1-138-67039-6 (pbk)
ISBN: 978-1-315-61765-7 (ebk)

Typeset in Bembo
by Sunrise Setting Ltd, Brixham, UK

In memory of Dr Gertrud Heidelberger, my mother-in-law, an indomitable lady who represented all that is best in European culture – DL

Contents

Illustrations

Figure

Tables

About the Authors

Dick Leonard

Courtesy of Mark Leonard

Dick Leonard is a journalist, author and former Labour MP. He worked in Brussels for 30 years, writing, primarily, about the European Union, for leading newspapers around the world. A former Assistant Editor of *The Economist,* he is the author of the best-selling *Economist Guide to the European Union,* and is the author or part-author of over 20 other books, including most recently, *A History of British Prime Ministers: Walpole to Cameron.* This contains short biographies and reassessments of all of the 53 British prime ministers. He has also worked for *The Observer,* the BBC, the Fabian Society, the Centre for European Policy Studies and the Publishers Association. He has taught at the Universities of Essex and Brussels (ULB) and has made five lecture tours to leading American and Canadian universities, including Harvard, Yale, Stanford, Princeton, Columbia, Cornell, the University of California and Queen's University, Ontario.

Also by Dick Leonard:
A History of British Prime Ministers: Walpole to Cameron
The Great Rivalry: Gladstone-Disraeli – a dual biography, Elections in Britain

Paying for Party Politics
Crosland and New Labour (edited)
The Pro-European Reader (edited with Mark Leonard)
World Atlas of Elections (edited with Richard Natkiel)
The Backbencher and Parliament (edited with Val Herman).

Robert Taylor

As a journalist and foreign correspondent, Robert (Bob) Taylor has covered the European Union for more than 30 years, reporting on its performance, policies and personalities. He headed the Reuters Brussels bureau before becoming correspondent there for *The Economist*. He has edited a number of books on EU themes for the International Chamber of Commerce in Paris, European Quality Publications (Montreux, Switzerland) and Oxford University Press. He began his career at the overseas service of the Swiss Broadcasting Corporation and reported from Brussels for the BBC's European

Courtesy of Thomas Boon

service. He also managed EU-funded reconstruction and development projects in broadcasting and telecommunications in the Balkans and the Middle East (Lebanon, Jordan and Syria). He was an international member of the broadcasting and telecoms regulatory authority in Bosnia-Herzegovina from 2000 to 2004. He has written and edited a number of books on EU-related themes and he now runs European Research Associates, a Brussels consultancy specialising in European public policy.

Also by Robert Taylor:
From EEC To European Union
Unity In Diversity (edited)
The New Europe In The World Economy (edited with Lionel Walsh)
E-Commerce In Action (edited)
Agenda for a Growing Europe (editorial coordinator)

Map of the European Union

European Union members and candidates

Membership (by year of entry)				Applications for membership
1958	Belgium	2004	Cyprus	Turkey
	France		Czech Republic	Macedonia
	Germany[1]		Estonia	Montenegro
	Italy		Hungary	Albania
	Luxembourg		Latvia	Serbia
	Netherlands		Lithuania	Bosnia-Herzegovina
1973	Denmark		Malta	Switzerland[2]
	Ireland		Poland	
	United Kingdom		Slovakia	
1981	Greece		Slovenia	
1986	Portugal	2007	Bulgaria	
	Spain		Romania	
1995	Austria	2013	Croatia	
	Finland			
	Sweden			

Map courtesy of the University of Texas Libraries, The University of Texas at Austin.

Notes:
[1] East Germany joined as part of a united Germany in 1990.
[2] The Swiss application was suspended indefinitely in 1993.

Introduction

This book is both old and new. Previously known as *The Economist Guide to the European Union*, it achieved 'best seller' status, going through 10 editions and being translated into 11 languages. It has been widely hailed as the most authoritative and reliable account of how the European Union works. It has been extensively used as a text book by students of politics, international affairs and economics, and – not least – by candidates hoping to be employed by the European Commission and other international organisations.

It has now been completely rewritten and updated with a new publisher and a new co-author – Robert Taylor – who has been primarily responsible for producing this new eleventh edition. It is fully up to date, and is brim-full of background information for UK residents still pondering how to cast their votes in the coming 'in/out' referendum.

Many excellent books have been written about the EU. The majority have been addressed to specialists, or are concerned with one particular aspect of the Union. The purpose of this book is rather different. It is addressed specifically to lay people, and is intended to give a simple account of the origin, history, institutions and functions of the Union in a form accessible to the intelligent reader with no previous knowledge of the EU.

The book is divided into four parts. Part 1 recounts the origins of the European Community (EC; later the EU), followed by a historical narrative of its development up to the beginning of 2016. Part 2 describes in some detail the institutions of the EU, such as the Council of Ministers, the European Commission, the European Parliament, the Court of Justice and so on. Part 3 deals with the EU's responsibilities in policy areas from agriculture to research and innovation. Part 4 considers some specific problems, including enlargement and the UK's continuing difficulties in reconciling itself to EU membership. It concludes with a brief assessment of the EU's future in the wake of the euro-crisis and the

2015–16 tidal wave of refugees from Syria, both of which have shaken EU core values like the single currency and frontier-free mobility to their limits. A series of appendices provide reference material on the Union and its institutions. Lastly, there are suggestions for further reading for those keen to learn more.

The source of most of the figures and much of the factual information contained in this book is the European Commission. Permission to reproduce this information is gratefully acknowledged.

Dick Leonard and Robert Taylor
February 15th 2016

Part I
The background

1　The origins

Hitler was the catalyst

Adolf Hitler was the main catalyst of the European Economic Community (EEC), although none of its leaders would readily admit him as a founding father. Like Charlemagne and Napoleon before him, Hitler brought together, by the sword, virtually the entire land area of the original EEC, destroying in the process the self-confidence of the nation states from which it sprang.

These were recreated in 1945, but no longer saw themselves as autonomous actors on the world stage. The governments of the three smallest – Belgium, the Netherlands and Luxembourg – decided in 1944, before the liberation of their territories was completed, that their economic futures were inextricably intertwined. The Benelux Union came into force on January 1st 1948 as a customs union, with the intention of progressing to a full economic union at a later stage.

The Marshall Plan

The United States and the Soviet Union each gave the nations of western Europe a strong shove in the direction of unity; one with apparently benign, the other with malign intentions. The Organisation for European Economic Cooperation (OEEC) was set up in 1947 to divide up among its member states the flow of US aid under the Marshall Plan. The aid programme was completed over three years, but the OEEC continued as a forum for promoting economic cooperation and free trade among west European countries. It later widened its membership to include all the advanced industrialised nations of the non-communist world, and changed its name in 1961 to the Organisation for Economic Cooperation and Development (OECD).

Fear of the Soviet Union

If the United States, partly no doubt through self-interest, had contributed hope, the Soviet Union contributed fear. Its brutal suppression of the countries of eastern Europe, culminating in the communist takeover of Czechoslovakia in February 1948, forced several west European countries to come together for self-preservation. As early as March 17th 1948, the Treaty of Brussels was signed, providing for a 50-year agreement between the UK, France, Belgium, the Netherlands and Luxembourg known as the Western European Union (WEU). This provided for 'collaboration in economic, social and cultural matters and for collective self-defence'. In practice, the WEU was largely superseded by NATO in 1949. West Germany and Italy joined the WEU in 1954. The first significant step to bring west European nations closer together was the creation of the Council of Europe in Strasbourg in 1949. But British wariness of closer involvement in Europe ensured that it was, and remains, an intergovernmental body with no shared responsibility except for human rights.

And fear of Germany

Fear of the Soviet Union in the immediate post-war years was matched by fear of Germany, which had tried to overrun western Europe in World War II, and had fought three ferocious wars with France over a period of 70 years. How to prevent a recurrence of these wars in the future occupied many minds in western Europe, as elsewhere in the world. Two possible solutions presented themselves; the first was to ensure that Germany should not only remain divided (which in the context of rising east–west tensions it did anyway) but that it should also be reduced to a permanent state of economic backwardness. Apart from intrinsic improbability, this solution had the serious disadvantage of conflicting with another west European priority: resisting the advance of Soviet communism. This pointed to the need not only for a German military contribution to western defence, but also for a strong economy which would help to satisfy the rapidly rising material expectations of west Europeans. It was this consideration which tipped the balance decisively towards the second solution to 'the German problem'. This was that Germany (or West Germany at least) should be linked so organically with its neighbours, and that this link should appear so evidently in the self-interest of both Germans and all the other nationalities, that another war between the nations of western Europe would become impossible.

Monnet's decisive role

The continental country most resistant to this concept was France, and it was fortunate that the most clear-sighted and persuasive advocate of this approach was a Frenchman, Jean Monnet. If Hitler provided the impetus towards European unity, Monnet was indisputably its principal architect. He had a remarkable career, almost all of it devoted to international cooperation of a genuinely practical kind. Originally a salesman in the UK for his family firm of brandy distillers, he spent World War I as a temporary civil servant coordinating the contributions of the French and UK economies to the joint war effort. Between the wars he acted as deputy secretary-general of the League of Nations, but in 1939, he was recalled to resume his role as an Anglo-French coordinator. It was his plan for a Franco-UK Union which Churchill put forward in 1940 in a vain attempt to forestall the French surrender to the Germans. Monnet spent the rest of the war years in London and Washington, once again coordinating the economic warfare of the allied nations.

He returned to France as a member of de Gaulle's government, and subsequently became head of the French planning organisation. In 1950 his moment of destiny came: it was his proposal that paved the way for the Franco-West German reconciliation which has been the essential condition for all subsequent progress towards European integration. The occasion was the Franco-West German dispute over the Saarland, which was largely fuelled by French fears that, if its iron and coal industry was integrated with those of the rest of West Germany, it would once again dominate the economy of Europe. France had tried unsuccessfully to annex the Saarland, which was overwhelmingly German in population, and, as in the post-1919 period, this attempt had poisoned relations between the two countries.

The Schuman Plan

Monnet captured the ear of the French foreign minister, Robert Schuman, a man whose personal history (as an Alsatian born in Luxembourg) had predisposed him to the advantages of European integration. Monnet's proposal, which was put forward by the French government as the Schuman Plan, was that the West German and French coal and steel industries should be placed under a single High Authority which should supervise their development. 'The solidarity between the two countries established by joint production will show that a war between France and Germany becomes not only unthinkable but materially impossible', Schuman said, in launching his plan on May 9th 1950.

Other European countries were invited to join the plan. It was instantly accepted by Chancellor Konrad Adenauer on behalf of the West German government which rightly saw it as a way to rejoin the European comity of nations on equal terms. Italy and the Benelux countries also quickly responded, and the Treaty of Paris, signed on April 18th 1951, formally established the European Coal and Steel Community (ECSC), which came into being on August 10th 1952. Jean Monnet was the first president.

The UK stands aloof

Today's European Union would no doubt look very different had two notable absentees taken part in setting up the ECSC and (five years later) the EEC. Stout wardens of national sovereignty, neither would have accepted their supra-national elements. Despite being invited by the others, the UK declined to participate. The second absentee was de Gaulle, who had led France's first post-war government but who spent his 'wilderness years' from 1947 to 1958 in self-imposed political exile. When he returned to power in 1958, the ECSC and the EEC were *faits accomplis*. Britain's decision to stay aloof was shared by Labour and Conservative governments at the time. The UK did not then regard itself primarily as a European nation. It adopted a superior attitude to the new organisation, as evidenced by the private remark of Winston Churchill to his doctor in January 1952: 'I love France and Belgium, but we must not allow ourselves to be pulled down to that level.'[1]

The absence of the UK facilitated the construction of a community that was different from the many other international organisations set up during this period like the Council of Europe, the North Atlantic Treaty Organisation (NATO) or the General Agreement on Tariffs and Trade (GATT). Each of these bodies established a permanent secretariat: however, there was no question of it having any more than an administrative role. Decision-making was reserved for meetings of representatives from each of the member states. The ECSC was unique in being provided with a supra-national High Authority which was given wide powers to determine the direction of two key industries throughout the member states. There was provision for a Council of Ministers, an Assembly (or indirectly elected parliament) with only advisory powers, and a Court of Justice. But the High Authority was, and was intended to be, the main organ of decision-making.

The constitution of the ECSC, as spelled out in the Treaty of Paris, closely reflected the view of Monnet, who wrote in his memoirs of the need to provide a firm institutional base to give effect to political intentions. 'Nothing is possible without men; nothing is lasting without institutions.'[2] He had intended that the ECSC would be paralleled by a common European defence force, which would supersede national armies and facilitate the rearming of West Germany without creating a specifically West German force. The same six governments – France, West Germany, Italy, Belgium, the Netherlands and Luxembourg – signed a treaty in May 1952 providing for the creation of a European Defence Community (EDC) for this purpose, but the French National Assembly in August 1954 declined to ratify the treaty.

Towards an economic community

The failure of the EDC had two significant consequences. West German rearmament proceeded on a national basis, and West Germany was admitted as a full member of NATO in October 1954. For his part, Monnet concluded that the path towards European unity lay through economic rather than military coordination. When his first term of office as president of the High Authority came to an end in February 1955, he declined a further term. Instead he left to head a high-powered pressure group, the Action Committee for the United States of Europe (ACUSE) which included leading figures from the Socialist, Christian Democratic and Liberal parties of all six member states.

The Action Committee did not wait long for the first fruits of its activities. The foreign ministers of the Six (as the founder members of the Community were known) met at Messina in Italy in June 1955 and appointed a committee under the chairmanship of the Belgian foreign minister, Paul-Henri Spaak, to investigate establishing a common market. The committee produced a report which formed the basis of the Treaty of Rome, signed on March 25th 1957, establishing the European Economic Community (EEC). A separate treaty, signed in Rome on the same day, set up the European Atomic Energy Community (Euratom) to develop the peaceful uses of nuclear energy. All six parliaments ratified the treaties, which came into effect on January 1st 1958, with a West German, Walter Hallstein, as first president of the EEC Commission.

The EEC's constitution paralleled that of the ECSC, but the supra-national element was significantly less. The EEC Commission, which was the counterpart of the High Authority, had substantially less power, and the Council of Ministers significantly more, than under the Treaty of Paris. In the early years of the EEC, this difference was hardly apparent, as the confident and decisive Hallstein dominated the development of the Community. But in 1965–66, his authority was successfully challenged by de Gaulle, back in power as president of France (see p. 12), and he subsequently resigned. None of his successors has wielded as much power as he did, and since his departure the supremacy of the Council of Ministers (made up of representatives of all the member states) over the supra-national commission has been evident.

Amalgamation

The three communities – the ECSC, Euratom and the EEC – were formally amalgamated on July 1st 1967. They became jointly known as the European Community (EC), or sometimes the European Communities, although the abbreviation EEC remained in common use to denote the combined organisation. From November 1993, when the Treaty of Maastricht took effect, the EC became the European Union (EU).

Notes

1 Alfred Grosser, *The Western Alliance: European-American Relations since 1945*, London, Macmillan, 1980, p. 131.
2 Ibid., p. 102.

2 Evolution – 1958–2008

The EEC might have broken up during the first year of operation. On June 1st 1958, five months after its foundation, de Gaulle became prime minister (and subsequently) president of France. His followers had bitterly opposed its creation. Now that it was in place, however, de Gaulle saw the EEC as a useful means of extending French influence, and during his early years in power he encouraged its development.

Three months after coming to power he had a momentous meeting with the West German chancellor Konrad Adenauer, which French historian Alfred Grosser described as a case of 'love at first sight'.[1] Grosser quotes from de Gaulle's memoirs: 'From then until mid-1962, Konrad Adenauer and I were to write to each other on some 40 occasions. We saw each other 15 times . . . we spent more than 100 hours in conversation.' From this mutual attraction sprang an enduring alliance which has proved to be the mainspring of the Community ever since. It was formalised in the Elysée treaty between the two countries on January 22nd 1963, which provided for the coordination of French and West German policies in foreign affairs, defence, communications and culture. For many, the treaty also sealed Germany's post-war rehabilitation.

Franco-German coordination has been spasmodic, but whenever the two countries have acted together within the Union their influence has been enormous and they have generally been able to achieve their objectives. Where they have not done so, the Union has drifted and has found it difficult or impossible to agree on a course of action. For many years West Germany, although the stronger of the two powers economically, was content to play a subordinate role. When West German leaders' views differed from those of France, they were often willing to defer to their partners. Following reunification and the creation of the European single currency, Germany took a more affirmative attitude.

An encouraging start

Against the background of Franco-West German *entente*, strong economic growth in all six members and the enthusiastic encouragement of the United States, the Community got off to a tremendous start in the first years after 1958. Intra-community trade leapt by 28.4 per cent annually during the first ten years of the EEC, and the average increase in imports from outside was 10 per cent

The common market (or customs union) created by the Six included internal free trade whereby goods made in one country moved duty-free to the others, and fixing the same external tariff for everyone so that imports from outside the EEC paid duty in the country of arrival and could circulate freely to other member states thereafter. A step-by-step adjustment process was completed on July 1st 1968 – 18 months ahead of schedule. As it completed the customs union, the EEC worked with the US in the Kennedy Round of global GATT negotiations, which resulted in a further 25 per cent cut in the common external tariff.

The other economic objective spelled out in considerable detail in the Rome treaty was the development of a common agricultural policy (CAP) with EU self-sufficiency rather than open markets as the prime goal. In fact, the two main prongs of the EEC, boosting industrial trade on the one hand and promoting agriculture production on the other were seen as a Franco-German *quid pro quo*: the first for the benefit of German manufacturers and the second for French farmers. Despite the provisions in the Rome treaty, the CAP proved more difficult to launch than the customs union. But in January 1962 after what a commission document[2] described as 'lengthy and often bitter negotiations' and a marathon session of the kind for which the EEC became famous, the Council of Ministers adopted the basic regulations for a common market in agriculture.

Foreign policy gap

The EEC's economic success highlighted the lack of political cooperation among the Six on foreign affairs which had not been included in the Rome treaty. The EEC heads of government agreed at a 1961 summit to set up a political union among the Six. They charged a committee headed by a French politician, Christian Fouchet, with the task. He and his colleagues produced a first Fouchet plan followed by a second. Neither was approved, reflecting a basic difference between the larger countries, particularly Gaullist France, to seek the lead role, and the smaller Benelux countries who fought for a more equal say between big and small. In the end, nothing came of the proposal, except that heads of government agreed to hold regular meetings for general political consultation. Despite this decision, no further summit was held for six years, and it was only in December 1974 when the European Council (see p. 75) was formalised that the heads of government began to meet regularly three times a year. Other European countries quickly became aware of the economic success of the Community. Greece and Turkey both applied to become associated states in 1959. Their respective association treaties (signed in Athens in 1961, and in Ankara in 1963) promised full membership to each in due course. The UK government whose earlier attempt to negotiate a wider free trade area within the OECD had ended in failure, became alarmed at the prospect of being left out in the cold. It took the initiative in organising the European Free Trade Association (EFTA), a looser arrangement involving only internal free trade, along with six small west European states. They became known as the 'outer seven' to distinguish them from the EEC's 'inner Six'. The seven (the UK, Austria, Denmark, Norway, Portugal, Sweden and Switzerland) signed the Stockholm convention establishing EFTA on January 4th 1960.

The UK knocks at the door

Yet no sooner had this convention been signed than the UK Conservative government, led by Harold Macmillan, reappraised its position once again, and decided EFTA was too small a grouping to match its trading interests. The EFTA had a combined population of 90 million compared with the EEC's 190 million. In July 1961 the UK applied for full membership of the EEC. It was followed shortly afterwards by Ireland, Denmark and Norway.

The application was welcomed by five of the Six, but it soon transpired that de Gaulle was lukewarm if not actually hostile to the entry of an 'Anglo-Saxon' nation. Accession negotiations began in November 1961 but soon became bogged down as UK negotiators strove, perhaps ill-advisedly, to achieve a mass of detailed concessions on agriculture, Commonwealth trade (including future tariffs on canned kangaroo-tail soup from Australia) and future relations with previous EFTA partners. De Gaulle bided his time. But in January 1963, following Macmillan's Nassau agreement with President John F. Kennedy on the supply of Polaris nuclear missiles, which confirmed his view that the UK's links with America came before any commitment to Europe, he vetoed the UK application at a press conference in Paris. The other three candidates promptly withdrew their applications.

The other five members were aghast at the French action, but were unwilling to bring matters to a head. The EEC without the UK was a misfortune, in their view; without France it would be an impossibility. So they reluctantly acquiesced in de Gaulle's action. The Franco-German Elysée treaty was signed the following week. Four years later, in May 1967, a UK Labour government under Harold Wilson applied a second time for membership; but following another veto threat from de Gaulle, the application lay inactive until the French president resigned in 1969.

Hallstein versus de Gaulle

At the head of the European Commission for the EEC's first nine years was Professor Walter Hallstein, formerly a close aide of Adenauer. His name was previously associated with the so-called Hallstein doctrine whereby West Germany refused to have diplomatic relations with any government which recognised the East German regime. Hallstein had led the West German delegation to the Schuman Plan conference in 1950. He enjoyed a large fund of French, as well as German, goodwill at the outset of his presidency which greatly helped keep up the momentum of developing the EEC. After several years however, the gap between his own beliefs in a supra-national Europe and the nationalistic tendencies of de Gaulle became more and more apparent, and it was probably only a matter of time before a clash would occur.

The split could have come over foreign policy or the rejection of UK membership. In the event, it was the decision-making process within the Council of Ministers which led to the break. During the early years of the Community, most decisions in the council needed to be taken, under the terms of the Rome treaty, by unanimous vote. From 1966 onwards, when the initial transition period came to an end, a wide range of decisions should have been reached by qualified majority voting. One big country on its own could no longer block a decision backed by the other five. De Gaulle was unwilling to accept the possibility of France being outvoted on major issues. So when in June 1965, France found itself isolated in its opposition to commission proposals for CAP funding, allowing the EEC to have its own financial resources, and giving the European Parliament more budgetary powers, he refused to allow decisions to be taken. For the next six months, France boycotted all meetings of the Council of Ministers. This 'empty chair' policy was only abandoned in January 1966 when the so-called Luxembourg compromise was reached. This effectively gave all member states a right to veto when their 'very important interests' were involved. Not long afterwards, Hallstein, who rightly concluded that the Luxembourg compromise had severely undermined the role of the commission as the principal initiator of policy, submitted his resignation.

The transformation of farming

In the 1960s and 1970s the CAP, with its system of common prices and unlimited production guarantees for farmers, transformed agriculture in the EEC. Not surprisingly, production and productivity shot up, making the Community more than self-sufficient in most temperate products. At the same time, the number of people working on the land fell sharply, from 15.2 million in 1960 to 5.8 million in 1984, in the original six member states. The first plan to curb CAP spending and reform the sector came in the form of the Mansholt Plan, named after Sicco Mansholt, the commissioner in charge of agriculture and later president of the European Commission. This plan, put forward in 1968, would have provided incentives for more people to leave the land, to create larger and more efficient holdings and to take some 5 million hectares of poorer land out of cultivation. A much watered-down programme was eventually approved by the Council of Ministers in 1972, but it did nothing to cure the emerging problem of surplus production nor to reduce the cost to the EEC budget of paying out production guarantees. It would take another 20 years and mountains of surplus butter and beef and lakes of excess milk and wine before real CAP reform got under way.

A new lease of life

Just seven months after de Gaulle's resignation on April 28th 1969, the Six held what was a landmark summit in The Hague on December 1st and 2nd that year. It was both a catch-up process from the past and a commitment to further European integration. The summit settled the issues on CAP financing and EC budget resources that de Gaulle had previously blocked. Led by President Georges Pompidou of France and Chancellor Willy Brandt of West Germany, the summit also agreed to hold direct elections for the European Parliament for all voters across the EC and to expand its budgetary powers. They decided to open entry negotiations with the UK and its fellow candidates the following year. The heads of government launched initiatives on economic and monetary union (EMU) and political cooperation among EC governments on foreign policy issues. Leaders also approved a first approach for creating a regional development fund to transfer resources from the richer to the poorer EEC regions. Proposals for economic and monetary union and for political cooperation quickly took form. The plan for EMU, developed by the then Luxembourg prime minister Pierre Werner, envisaged 1980 as the target date. This proved wildly over-optimistic, as the initiative was stopped in its tracks by external events as early as 1971 when the US unilaterally broke the link between the price of gold and the dollar. This ended the Bretton Woods system of fixed exchange rates put in place after World War II. The report on political cooperation, drafted by a Belgian diplomat, Etienne Davignon, laid the basis for the regular meetings on international issues by foreign ministers which began in 1972.

Enter Denmark, Ireland and the UK

De Gaulle's resignation removed the main obstacles to UK accession. Pompidou was more flexible and Brandt strongly urged him to back enlargement of the Community. Entry negotiations duly began in June 1970 with Denmark, Ireland, Norway and the UK. After much hard bargaining, treaties of accession were signed in Brussels on January 22nd 1972. Norway narrowly rejected the treaty terms in a referendum in September 1972 (by 53 to 47 per cent), but the other three countries formally joined the EC on January 1st 1973.

Denmark and Ireland also held referendums which produced majorities in favour of membership of 83 per cent and 63 per cent respectively. The UK did not initially do so, although the issue of accession was highly divisive. The Conservative prime minister, Edward Heath, pursued the objective of UK membership with great determination, and succeeded in rallying a large majority of his party behind him. The Labour Party, however, was badly split on the issue, with the majority coming down decisively against. A defiant minority of 69 Labour members of parliament led by Roy Jenkins broke party ranks to vote in favour of the terms Heath had negotiated in the House of Commons ratification vote in October 1972. The Labour party subsequently resolved to hold a retrospective referendum on continued UK membership if it won the next general election.

The Labour government of Harold Wilson, which came to power in 1974, fulfilled this undertaking in June 1975 after having 'renegotiated' the original terms of entry. The main change was the institution of a 'corrective mechanism' intended to prevent excessive UK contributions to the Community budget. The mechanism was later to prove inoperative, but the referendum produced a decisive vote (67 per cent) in favour of continued membership, and it seemed the controversy had been laid to rest.

Denmark and the UK left EFTA on joining the Community, but were able to keep their trading links as the remaining EFTA members negotiated industrial free trade agreements with the Community, sharing the benefits of tariff-free trade, except for farm goods.

Problems of enlargement

The 1973 enlargement which increased Community membership from six to nine, and its population from 191 million to 255 million, was expected to invigorate the EC and speed its development during the 1970s. These hopes went largely unfulfilled. This was partly because the enlarged EC lacked a programme for the medium-term. Moreover, the nine members formed a less cohesive grouping than the original six, while the newcomers sometimes found it hard to adjust to the essential process of compromise and give-and-take that characterised the way the Community worked.

The biggest blow to the Community's development at the time was undoubtedly the prolonged economic recession which followed the Yom Kippur war of 1973 and the consequent fourfold rise in oil prices. All member states suffered from mounting inflation and unemployment. Most saw their balance of payments slide into deep deficit. In addition, efforts to coordinate national energy policies proved elusive, as did attempts to find a common economic strategy to haul the Community out of recession. All member governments felt constrained, to varying degrees, to implement austerity policies in their own countries. It became increasingly hard to persuade them to free funding to finance new common policies under the aegis of the Community.

Yet at the Paris summit of December 1974 EC leaders agreed to establish the European Regional Development Fund (ERDF; see Chapter 24). Although the ERDF provided assistance to less-favoured regions in all member states, the main beneficiaries in the first ten years were the UK, Ireland and Italy, then the poorest EC countries.

The European Council

The same summit conference took three other important decisions. The EC heads of government decided to consult among themselves much more frequently and instituted the European Council (see Chapter 7) which should meet three times a year to consider important foreign policy issues as well as Community affairs. They also set 1978 as the year (later postponed to 1979) when elections to the European Parliament by direct universal suffrage should begin. And it appointed the then Belgian prime minister Leo Tindemans to prepare a report on European union by the end of 1975. Tindemans duly reported a year later, proposing a series of measures, including a common foreign policy, economic and monetary union, European social and regional policies, joint industrial policies for growth sectors, policies affecting citizens and a substantial reinforcement of Community institutions. The European Council discussed the report on several occasions but took no action. This was a clear indication of how Community leaders were losing interest in the notion of European union.

The appointment of Roy Jenkins as president of the commission for four years from January 1977 rekindled hope in the EC's future. A senior political figure, who had been deputy leader of the Labour party as well as chancellor of the exchequer and home secretary, he had along with Heath been the most consistent and energetic campaigner for British EC membership. His admirers from many member states hoped his arrival in Brussels would give the Community the added momentum which the enlargement four years earlier had failed to provide.

Jenkins was resourceful and diligent but, partly because of lack of support from the UK government, first under James Callaghan and then Margaret Thatcher, his presidency did not match expectations. He did, however, have one significant achievement to his credit: as one of the architects of the European Monetary System (EMS) which took effect in March 1979.

The European Monetary System

The EMS was a serious bid to relaunch the stalled process of economic and monetary union. Based on the European Currency Unit (the ECU) as a notional currency, it consisted of a fixed exchange rate mechanism for EU currencies along with credit facilities. Proposed by Jenkins in a speech in Florence, it was taken up by West German chancellor Helmut Schmidt who, with strong backing from French president Valéry Giscard d'Estaing, was able to secure its acceptance by the European Council in the course of three successive meetings in 1978. Despite the UK's refusal to join the exchange rate mechanism for the first 11 years, it was credited with limiting currency fluctuations and encouraging cooperation on financial policies among member states.

The EC's trading relations developed throughout the 1970s. The centrepiece was the Tokyo round of GATT negotiations involving the European Community and 99 other participants. Against a background of world recession and rising unemployment (which was to reach 16 million in the EC), the results were remarkable, leading to further cuts in import duties averaging about one third. These came into force in 1980.

In parallel, the EC widened its network of bilateral trade deals with developing countries. In 1975, the EC signed a far-reaching trade and aid convention with the former colonies of member states in the African, Caribbean and Pacific (ACP) regions. The convention, signed in the Togolese capital of Lomé, built on earlier association agreements with former French colonies in Africa (see Chapter 38). Agreements with the

Maghreb countries of North Africa (Tunisia, Algeria and Morocco) were signed in 1976, followed by others with the Mashreq countries (Egypt, Jordan, Syria and Lebanon) in 1977. Agreements were concluded with Israel in 1975 and Yugoslavia in 1980, enabling the EC to implement a global Mediterranean policy.

In Asia, more limited agreements were made with Sri Lanka (1975), Pakistan and Bangladesh (1976) and India (1981), while a cooperation agreement was reached with the five ASEAN countries in 1981. In Latin America, agreements with Uruguay (1973), Mexico (1975) and Brazil (1980) were followed by a cooperation agreement with the five-nation Andean Pact in 1983.

Attempts to create a framework to expand trade with the communist countries of eastern Europe made little headway. Talks with Comecon, the Soviet-dominated organisation for economic cooperation, ran from 1977 to 1980, but no agreement was reached. The dialogue was only resumed in 1986, following Mikhail Gorbachev's rise to power. However, trade agreements were concluded with China and Romania alongside sectoral agreements with some other communist states.

Greece joins the Community

Meanwhile, further enlargements of the EC appeared on the agenda when three countries which had recently emerged from dictatorial or military rule applied to join. Greece tabled its application in 1975; Portugal and Spain in 1977. Negotiations with Greece proceeded relatively smoothly, partly because the Greek government saw EC membership as the best way to consolidate democracy and did not argue over details. It took the view – as the UK had done in its entry negotiations in 1970–71 – that its bargaining power would be greater once inside the Community. Greek membership began on January 1st 1981.

Negotiations with Spain and Portugal were much more difficult, and not only because these two countries took a more robust negotiating stance than Greece. There was far more opposition to their entry from within the Community itself, notably in France. This was because farmers in southern France, as well as some in Italy and Greece, feared the arrival of Spanish competition. There was lively speculation that France could, once again, veto a membership application. This did not happen, although Giscard d'Estaing, who became French president in 1974, actively slowed down the negotiations.

If his role was negative over Spanish entry, Giscard d'Estaing's overall influence on the Community was positive. In his seven years as French president he worked in close partnership with Helmut Schmidt. The two shared many common views despite their different political backgrounds. Using

English as their common language, the two sat side-by-side at meetings of the European Council, where they were often able to steer it in the direction they both wanted it to take. In so far as anyone provided leadership to the Community during these seven years it was Schmidt and Giscard d'Estaing.

In 1981–82 both lost power. Their successors, François Mitterrand and Helmut Kohl, were unable to replicate the Schmidt–Giscard d'Estaing relationship. This led to a vacuum at the apex of the Community, lasting several years. The Community drifted. Problems remained unresolved.

'I want my money back'

The biggest problem of the time, often blocking out all the others, was the fight over the UK's contribution to the EC budget. It was brought to a head by Margaret Thatcher. Shortly after taking office, she bluntly told her fellow EC leaders at a summit in Dublin in 1979: 'I want my money back.' Her combativeness came as an unwelcome revelation to the other heads of government. It made an already intractable problem worse. The fact that the UK's contribution was set to rise significantly once its initial transitional period of membership was over had come to light in the closing months of the previous Labour government. The basic reason was that agriculture still accounted for the lion's share of the budget despite indications given during the UK's negotiations and renegotiations that farm spending would fall as a percentage of the budget. Left unaltered, the UK, as a big food importer, was paying a disproportionally high amount in import levies into the budget. But as a small food producer it only got a small share back in the form of support payments for its farmers.

The search for a lasting solution went on until 1984, practically monopolising several meetings of the European Council before a settlement was reached which, in the opinion of many, could have been achieved much earlier had cooler counsels prevailed. One by-product of Thatcher's hard-hitting campaign was to rekindle anti-EC feeling within the Labour party which passed a resolution at its 1980 conference calling for UK withdrawal from the EC. This was incorporated into the Labour manifesto for the 1983 election – which Labour lost.

A maze of problems

Although dominant, the crisis over the UK budget contribution was linked to a series of other pressing problems. These concerned:

- the threat of EC resources running out, allied to the need to cut the amount spent on the CAP;

- the need to reform EC institutions to speed up decision-taking and make them more accountable;
- the need to respond to the technological challenge posed by the US and Japan if Europe was not to become an industrial backwater;
- the need to remove technical and administrative barriers to trade within the Community;
- the completion of the entry negotiations with Spain and Portugal.

The link between UK payments to the EC and the looming crisis over insufficient budget funding (the EC's 'own resources' in Community jargon) is obvious. The latter were becoming too small to meet the many demands on the budget. The proceeds of customs duties and agricultural import levies were falling each year. The day was approaching when the EC's only other resource – a maximum take equal to 1 per cent of value-added tax (VAT) across the Community – would be exhausted. The EU member states were divided. Some wanted to raise the VAT limit. Others, particularly the UK, were more interested in budget-cutting, especially of the 70 per cent devoted to agriculture.

Towards a single market

Those seeking to increase spending supported the commission in its call for a big rise in financial support for technological research and innovation so that EC firms could compete in world markets where the US and Japan were poised to become dominant suppliers of goods for the 'third industrial revolution'. In parallel came a growing realisation that, in order to compete at all, Europe needed to turn itself into the truly common market it was supposed to be. Although tariffs and quotas had gone, other barriers – technical, administrative, regulatory and political – still hindered internal free trade 25 years after the Community had been established.

Progress on removing these barriers was being thwarted by the failure of the Council of Ministers to adopt a vast number of proposals for liberalisation tabled by the European Commission over the years. The backlog, stemming largely from the council's unwillingness to apply the majority voting rules foreseen in the Rome treaty, stimulated demands for faster and more democratic decision-making which emanated particularly from the European Parliament. Lastly, frustration was growing dangerously in Spain and Portugal at delays in their entry negotiations. This led to a widespread feeling within the Community itself that these newly democratic countries were not receiving the encouragement they deserved.

Mitterrand's initiative

Like previous French presidents, François Mitterrand eventually made his own considerable mark on the EC. After the pending problems had been argued back and forth to no avail for several years, he evidently decided that the French presidency of the Council of Ministers in the first half of 1984 was the time for action. Accordingly, and rising above narrow French interests on occasion, he brokered agreements at a summit in Fontainebleau in May on the UK budget issue, on increasing the Community's own resources, on curbing agricultural spending and removing obstacles to Spanish and Portuguese entry.

The settlement for the UK was based on a yearly rebate of 66 per cent of the difference between its VAT contribution and its share of EC expenditure. In exchange for this, Thatcher agreed that the general limit of VAT contributions should be raised from 1 per cent to 1.4 per cent. It was also agreed that future farm spending would rise each year at a lower rate than the overall increase in EU spending, so that the percentage of the budget spent on agriculture would fall year by year.

The 1992 programme

A year later at a summit in Milan, progress was made on two other issues: a seven-year timetable was agreed for removing 300 identified barriers restricting the internal market (see Chapter 17). The EC leaders also decided to hold an intergovernmental conference (IGC) to discuss amendments to the Rome treaty and other ways to speed up and democratise decision-making. This led to the Single European Act, adopted in December 1985 and implemented after ratification by all 12 national parliaments (involving referendums in Denmark and Ireland) in July 1987. As the single market involved the free movement of people as well as of goods, services and capital, five of the then ten member states (Germany, France and the Benelux countries) signed an agreement in the Luxembourg town of Schengen on June 14th 1985 as a first step towards passport-free travel within the EU.

The programme to complete the internal market became known as 'the 1992 programme' from the target date for completion which was December 31st 1992. The single market programme was the brainchild of Jacques Delors who took over as commission president in 1985. But credit for its detailed planning and the enthusiasm surrounding its launch should go to his UK colleague Lord Cockfield, then commissioner in charge of internal market affairs. Despite initial scepticism, it soon became clear that the programme was on track to be completed on time and would bring economic benefits to all member states. Beyond this, it gave a new sense of purpose to the Community, helping to create a mood in which further initiatives to widen and deepen the EC appeared both practical and desirable. By the end of 1992, almost 95 per cent of the single market programme had in fact been legislated.

Meanwhile, agreement was reached to launch several R&D programmes (see Chapter 22), as well as the Eureka programme which involved several non-EC European countries, although the budgets agreed by ministers were considerably lower than proposed by the commission. Thus the EC showed itself capable of dealing effectively with difficult issues.

The next budget crisis

No sooner had Spain and Portugal joined than the Fontainebleau budget deal began to come unstuck. Because of falling world food prices, and the steep decline in the value of the dollar in 1986 and 1987, the cost to the EC budget of subsidies on farm exports rose dramatically, making it politically impossible to stick to the agreed curbs on agricultural spending. Within a year of raising the VAT limit from 1 per cent to 1.4 per cent, the available funds for the EC budget again ran out. In early 1987 it was clear the EC would face a budget deficit for the year of 5 billion to 6 billion ecus, with vast overspending on agriculture and no prospect of remaining within the agreed budgetary framework. With Delors in charge, the commission then produced what became known as the 'Delors package' designed to put Community funding on a sounder footing. This entailed reinforced controls over farm spending and freeing up resources for priority objectives including R&D programmes and the expansion of the so-called structural fund (the regional and social funds and part of the agricultural fund – the EAGGF[3]), which the commission argued should be doubled in real terms by 1992.

A new beginning

It took three meetings of the European Council to agree the Delors package. This was in part due to Thatcher's reluctance to accept budget controls she considered to be less than watertight. It also reflected her determination to make sure that no future budget settlement would undermine the Fontainebleau terms agreed for the UK rebate. However, at an emergency summit in Brussels in February 1988, she finally agreed with the other 11 national leaders on proposals largely based on those put forward by Delors a year earlier.

The Brussels agreement meant that the Community could make a fresh start. A new budget limit was set at 1.2 per cent of the total GNP of the Community member states, equivalent to 1.9–2.0 per cent of VAT contributions as calculated the old way. The new formula enabled a budget of 43.8 billion ecus to be adopted for 1988, compared with actual expenditure of 37 billion ecus for the previous year. By 1991 the budget had increased to 55.6 billion ecus. Under the new agreement, a fourth resource based directly on the national share of EC GNP was added to the three existing sources of revenue. The Fontainebleau formula, securing the UK's 66 per cent refund on its net contribution, was written into the deal.

The other main features of the agreement included a doubling of the structural funds in real terms by 1993, with more focus on economically backward areas, while much stricter controls were to be applied to agricultural spending. In future, this was not to grow by more than 74 per cent of the annual GNP growth rate, and so-called 'stabilisers' would be applied progressively to surplus products. Moreover, farmers would receive 'set-aside' payments if they took less fertile land out of production.

EMU back on the agenda

Encouraged by the settlement of these long-standing problems, EC leaders dusted down the project for economic and monetary union. At a summit in Hanover in June 1988, heads of government set up a committee under Delors to study and report on ways to prepare for monetary union. The summit confirmed the progress made towards completing the internal market on time by 1992 and noted the success of the Single European Act in speeding up decision-making. To underpin the social aspects of the single market programme, the Delors commission made proposals for a Community charter of social rights. It hoped to have it approved by heads of government at their Madrid summit in June 1989. In the meantime, the Community witnessed yet another example of UK reluctance to commit itself to closer European integration. This came in Thatcher's strident attack on the European Commission for alleged power-grabbing intentions in a highly publicised speech at the College of Europe in Bruges in September 1988.

The speech (widely characterised as 'Gaullist') was followed by a period when the UK systematically set out to nit-pick over commission proposals. This was ill-received in other member states, but also in the UK when the government's negative attitude was perceived at times to go against UK interests as a beneficiary of EC-funded programmes. The narrow national attitude of the Conservative government reached a high-point in the party's campaign for the June 1989 elections for the European Parliament. The party did not do well. The strong support for candidates from Labour and the Green Party sent a message to Thatcher, which she seemed to have taken on board if the Madrid summit, which took place a week later, is anything to go by. The main agenda item was the report on monetary union from Delors and his committee. The committee, which included the central bankers of all 12 member states, proposed a three-stage process leading to a full currency union and a European system of central banks. The summit agreed that the first stage, which involved all 12 member states joining the exchange rate mechanism (ERM) of the EMS, would begin on July 1st 1990, while an intergovernmental conference would be called to prepare the two subsequent stages and agree the necessary amendments to the Rome treaty. Despite her reluctance, she accepted the idea of the conference, and confirmed that the UK would join the exchange rate mechanism once certain conditions had been met. She declined, however, to endorse the Social Charter approved by the 11 other leaders, who went on to sign it without her later that year.

Downfall of communism

Meanwhile, momentous changes were taking place in eastern Europe, which were to have a profound impact on the Community. By the summer of 1989, Poland and Hungary were completing a peaceful transition from communism to democracy. In the following months, communist rule crumbled in East Germany, Czechoslovakia, Bulgaria and, after violent but short resistance, in Romania. The new democracies instinctively looked to the Community as a source of economic assistance and a potential guarantor of their democratic development.

The Community responded with grants and aid for economic development and institutional reform for Poland and Hungary. This programme was extended later to include Czechoslovakia, Bulgaria, Romania and Yugoslavia. All these countries signed trade and cooperation agreements with the EC as did the Soviet Union itself in December 1989.

A similar agreement was negotiated with the German Democratic Republic (East Germany) but Germany was reunited on October 3rd 1990, before it could take effect. Six months previously, EC heads of government had agreed at an emergency summit in Dublin that the former GDR should be incorporated into the EC without requiring any revision of the Rome treaty as soon as reunification was legally established. As a result, East Germany joined the EC as part of the Federal Republic with a minimum of formalities, no fanfare, and no ratification procedures, less than a year after the fall of the Berlin wall.

Central and eastern Europe

No such favourable treatment awaited the other countries of central and eastern Europe, although all their leaders, including those of Yugoslavia and Albania, declared EC membership as their long-term objective. Instead, ten-year association agreements involving trade concessions, financial assistance and wide-ranging cooperation were signed with Poland, Hungary and Czechoslovakia in December 1991. These agreements specifically acknowledged that each country would eventually be eligible to join the EC. Similar agreement followed with Romania, Bulgaria, Albania and the three Baltic states of Estonia, Latvia and Lithuania, whose independence was recognised in September 1991. By early 1994 so-called Europe Agreements had been signed with each of these countries as well as with the now separate Czech Republic and Slovakia, replacing the previous agreement reached with Czechoslovakia.

Ukraine signed a partnership agreement with the European Union (the Community's new name under the 1992 Maastricht treaty) in 1994, by which time the EU was negotiating similar agreements with Russia and the former Soviet republics of Belarus, Kazakhstan and Kyrgyzstan. Unlike the agreements with central and eastern European countries, the agreements with the former Soviet republics did not include the prospect of eventual EU membership. By contrast, future membership was indeed implicit in a trade and economic cooperation agreement signed with Slovenia in April 1993.

The EU was involved from the outset in trying to prevent the warfare that broke out in former Yugoslavia after Slovenia and Croatia declared their independence in June 1991. The EU immediately sent a team of foreign ministers to broker a ceasefire. As a result, a peace conference opened in The Hague under EU auspices in September 1991. Monitors from the EU were sent to see that the ceasefire was being respected. It held in Slovenia but not in Croatia where it took UN intervention and a large UN peace-keeping force in March 1992 to stop the fighting. In the meantime a third of the country was overrun by Serb forces and the federal Yugoslav army. It was the first time the EU had attempted to play a mediator role beyond its own frontiers. It was not up to the task. Later in 1992 a similar scenario was played out in Bosnia-Herzegovina although the EU role there was more marginal and the UN intervened, if ineffectively, at an earlier stage. At the UN's request, the main effort to contain the conflict fell to NATO. It was only after NATO air strikes against Bosnian Serbs in August 1995 that hostilities ended, leading to the Dayton peace accords later that year. The EU assumed a predominant role in providing post-conflict reconstruction funds and technical assistance. Similarly, following the Kosovo conflict in 1999, the EU undertook the major responsibility for rebuilding the shattered territory, establishing the European Agency for Reconstruction for this purpose.

The Community also became involved in western efforts to provide material assistance to the former Soviet Union. In December 1990 it put together programmes of 750 million ecus for food and 400 million for technical assistance during 1991. After the failed coup by Moscow hardliners in August 1991 and the dissolution of the Soviet Union, the EC aid effort was extended not only to Russia but to the other former Soviet republics. A number of these claim to be European states, and therefore declared an interest in eventual membership of the EU – Armenia, Azerbaijan, Belarus, Georgia, Moldova and Ukraine – but then, as now, the EC considered them to be close neighbours and partners rather than potential members. In any case, their economies and political structures were far below levels required for EC membership.

More than just EMU

The swift incorporation of East Germany into the EU clearly betokened confidence on the part of fellow EU members in Germany's lasting commitment to the EU and its democratic institutions. This was confirmed by Chancellor Helmut Kohl who believed the place of unified Germany was at the heart of a more democratised Community with a reinforced political component. Supported by France, he pushed for a second intergovernmental conference to be held in parallel to the one on monetary union. Its task would be to recommend treaty changes required to put the EC firmly on the road to political union. In June 1990, EU heads of government agreed to launch both conferences in parallel in Rome in December 1990 with a view to completing their work in time for ratification by member states before the end of 1992.

Although all Community members agreed to set up the two IGCs, the reluctance of Margaret Thatcher's government was evident. She did not like the turn the EC was taking, and the far-reaching proposals for change which other member states, headed by Germany and France, were putting forward with increasing urgency. Although Thatcher finally agreed in early October 1990 to let sterling join the ERM, more than 11 years after it was set up, her hostility to monetary union remained unabated. Three weeks later, at a summit in Rome she was outvoted 11 to 1 on the starting date for the second stage of EMU. Her intemperate reaction to the rebuff triggered the challenge within her own Conservative government which led to her replacement as prime minister by John Major.

Major quickly mended fences with fellow EC leaders at the second Rome summit which followed on December 14th and 15th 1990. It was then the two IGCs, involving, respectively, the finance and foreign ministers of the 12 member states, were formally convened. Compromise was in the air: progress towards EMU would be slower than originally planned, while the moves toward political union would be much less radical than Germany and France had been seeking.

Maastricht treaty

So it proved when the European Council met at Maastricht in December 1991 to consider a draft treaty based on the work of the two IGCs. After two days of hard bargaining, the Treaty on European Union was approved, but only after Major had obtained two important opt-outs for the UK on the single currency and social legislation. Clearly the UK, or at least its Conservative government, was still not reconciled to European integration. The Maastricht treaty is described in some detail in Appendix 8, and is discussed in Chapters 19, 23 and 39. It represented the most important development in the EC's history since the Treaty of Rome in 1957. It not only set the detailed count-down to economic and monetary union, by 1999 at the latest, and created the framework for common foreign and defence policies, it also introduced a new concept of EC institutions. A protocol signed by 11 member states, but not the UK, opened the way to implement Social Charter legislation in those 11 countries. Lastly Maastricht committed the EU to hold another IGC in 1996 to review progress since Maastricht, and set ground rules for the EU into the coming century.

Ratifying the Maastricht treaty, which was signed in February 1992, caused problems. It was narrowly rejected in a referendum in Denmark in June 1992, although approved comfortably by Irish voters later that month. In France, the Socialist government of François Mitterrand called a referendum, which was not legally required, ostensibly to refurbish its European credentials. But the intention back-fired as opinion polls showed voters would use the referendum to voice opposition to an unpopular government. An alarming prospect arose that France, a co-founder of the EC, could reject Maastricht. In the event, a narrow majority (51.05 to 48.95 per cent) approved the treaty in September 1992.

Parliamentary ratification in the UK also proved difficult. Major ran into stiff opposition within his Conservative Party. And because he opted out of the Social Charter legislation, he could not count on the consistent support of the opposition Labour Party and the Liberal Democrats to get the treaty through the complex ratification process in the House of Commons. After wrangling for several months, parliament finally approved the treaty in July 1993, and the instruments of ratification were deposited the following month.

In the meantime, Denmark was offered an opt-out on the single currency, on the same basis as the UK, as well as other largely cosmetic interpretations of the treaty. This enabled Danes to reverse their earlier rejection in a second referendum in May 1993, when they backed the treaty by 56.7 to 43.3 per cent. Uncharacteristically, Germany was the last country to ratify Maastricht. The process was delayed by opponents to the treaty who sought a formal ruling declaring it incompatible with the German constitution, although the German parliament had already adopted it by an overwhelming majority. The German Constitutional Court rejected the request on October 12th 1993, and the German instruments of ratification were deposited the same day. The treaty came into force on November 1st 1993, ten months behindhand. Since then the EC has been generally known as the European Union.

The ratification difficulties in Denmark, France, the UK and Germany brought home to EU governments how much they were moving ahead of public opinion in their top-down approach to European integration. Thatcher had called Maastricht 'a treaty too far'. There was some force in this criticism. Public knowledge of Maastricht and its impact was not extensive and government information campaigns had been extremely limited. But three other factors were probably more responsible:

- Economic recession had hit all EU countries to varying degrees between 1990 and 1994.
- Turmoil in currency markets forced Italy and the UK out of the exchange rate mechanism in 1992.
- There was dismay at the EU's poor record in trying to bring peace to former Yugoslavia.

New enlargement

In January 1995, three EFTA countries – Austria, Finland and Sweden – became members of the EU. This was the culmination of a process to associate the EFTA members as closely as possible with the benefits of the single market. All seven EFTA countries were keen to share the expected benefits. On the initiative of Jacques Delors, the EC offered to negotiate the creation of a European Economic Area (EEA) which would enable

EFTA countries to join the EU's 1992 programme at the price of accepting many of the obligations of the EC member states. The EEA treaty was signed in 1992 but was rejected by Swiss voters in a referendum. By the time it came into force in January 1994, four EFTA countries, Austria, Finland, Sweden and Norway had applied to join the EU, leaving Iceland on its own. The door was left open for Liechtenstein. Switzerland had also applied for EC membership but its application was held in abeyance following the vote against the EEA. The four other applicants completed negotiations in March 1994 and the results were ratified by referendums in Austria, Finland and Sweden later that year. In a re-run of 1972, the referendum in Norway produced a negative result. It remains, however, a member of the EEA.

No sooner were negotiations concluded with the EFTA countries than the enlargement focus pivoted eastward; 12 applicants wanted in. Hungary and Poland came first, followed over the next two years by Romania, Bulgaria, Slovakia, the Czech Republic, Slovenia and the three Baltic states. Cyprus and Malta had already applied. The EU heads of government agreed in December 1995 to open entry negotiations with each of the 12.

In May 1995, the commission issued a white paper setting out detailed guidelines for applicant states concerning necessary changes in their economies and their legal and administrative systems. These included the introduction of a free market and firm guarantees of democratic and human rights. On this basis, the commission proposed in summer 1997 that negotiations should begin the following March with six candidates – Cyprus, the Czech Republic, Estonia, Hungary, Poland and Slovenia. The remaining applicants, said the commission, did not yet meet membership criteria. Their position would be kept under permanent review. A summit in Luxembourg in December 1997 accepted the commission recommendations, but decided all applicants (plus Turkey) should be invited to annual European conferences, the first to take place in March 1998. The Turkish government, whose EU application dated from 1987, was offended that, unlike the other candidates, it had not been given an assurance of eventual membership and boycotted the conference.

Negotiations with the favoured six duly began in March 1998 and with the others (including Malta which had temporarily withdrawn its application) in February 2000. At a Helsinki summit in December 1999, Turkey was fully recognised as a valid candidate. Its negotiations with the EU began in 2005. By the summer of 2002 negotiations were nearing completion with 10 of the 12 active candidates, with May 1st 2004 as their tentative entry date.

Turin intergovernmental conference

The intergovernmental conference to review the Maastricht treaty began in Turin in March 1996. But well before the conference met it was clear its agenda would have to be broadened. This IGC would have to revise the institutional arrangement initially conceived for 6 members, now enlarged to 15, with the likelihood of reaching 27 or more in the next decade. Serious questions were at stake:

- Should there be more majority voting in the Council of Ministers, given the increasing difficulty of getting unanimous agreement with an ever-increasing membership?
- Should votes in the council be reweighted between big and small countries to avoid the possibility of the larger member states being outvoted by the ever rising number of small countries whose combined population was far smaller? In particular should it become easier or more difficult to form a blocking minority?
- Should the size of the European Commission be limited or should each member state, however small, still be entitled to nominate a commissioner?
- Should justice and home affairs continue to be handled on an intergovernmental basis or come under normal EU institutional rules?
- How could the intergovernmental framework of the common foreign and security policy be made to work better?

As the IGC got under way, it was clear member states were divided on all issues, especially where interests differed between large and small countries. Most were, however, prepared to compromise – but not the UK, which had set itself against any increase whatsoever in the EU's powers and was hostile to any extension of majority voting. Instead of concluding as expected in spring 1997, the IGC stalled. Sensibly, the other EU members agreed informally to wait for the coming UK election on May 1st to see whether a new government might be more amenable to compromise.

Labour ends UK isolation

The UK's uncooperative attitude at the IGC reflected a series of events which had progressively alienated the UK from the European mainstream. This started in the Thatcher period and, despite early hopes that Major's government would heal the rift, the reverse happened. Stung by the hostility within his own party towards ratifying the Maastricht treaty, he set out to appease the growing number of Eurosceptics in its ranks by taking a hard line with his EU partners. This was a serious misjudgement. Every concession he made to their demands only whetted their appetite for more. In turn, this attitude undermined the influence the UK could exert within the EU. In April 1996, Major adopted a policy in the Council of Ministers reminiscent of de Gaulle's 'empty chair' tactic 30 years earlier. His ministers vetoed virtually every proposal under consideration – even those the UK had put forward. This was a vain bid to force the EU to lift a health ban on British beef exports at the time of the outbreak of mad cow disease in the UK. Major abandoned this self-defeating tactic after six weeks, but the government maintained its negative position towards the EU, until it crashed to a heavy electoral defeat at the hands of the Labour Party in May 1997. The new Labour government announced a fresh start in relations with the EU, enabling the IGC to conclude amicably, although the most difficult decisions were postponed. Its recommendations were adopted at the Amsterdam European Council in June 1997. It took another IGC in 2000 to agree on how to weight votes in the Council of Ministers, how to extend majority voting and how many members the commission should have. These matters were finalised at a lengthy and ill-tempered summit at Nice in December 2000.

Towards the single currency

By this time, economic and monetary union with the creation of a single currency was becoming reality. The third stage which launched the single currency was set to start as planned on January 1st 1999. It was also clear that a majority of member states would participate. It had been agreed at a Madrid summit in 1995 that the new currency would be called the euro. It would have the same value as the EU's reference currency, the ECU, which was based on a basket of national currencies used, *inter alia*, to calculate payments within the EU budget. A year later, a stability pact was agreed to ensure that countries qualifying to use the euro would continue to do so thereafter. Finally, as described on p. 153, a special Brussels summit on May 1st and 2nd 1998 agreed that 11 of the 15 members would join stage three and adopt the single currency. Greece was excluded because it failed to meet the Maastricht criteria for membership, while the other three – the UK, Denmark and Sweden – excluded themselves, for essentially political reasons. The UK indicated that, in principle, it favoured the single currency but would only join 'when the conditions are right'. The summit also appointed former Dutch central banker Wim Duisenberg as the first president of the European Central Bank (ECB), which was set up on June 1st 1998.

On December 31st 1998, EU finance ministers agreed the fixed rates of exchange against the euro for the 11 participating national currencies.

From January 1st 1999 the euro became operational for accounting and banking transactions. Greece became the twelfth euro zone country in January 2001. The introduction of euro notes and coins on January 1st 2002 and the progressive withdrawal of national currencies that followed was handled with exceptional care. Overall, the operation was a great success, passing off with hardly a hitch (see p. 154).

The Santer Commission resigns

In December 1998, a row broke out between the European Parliament and the commission. It led to the resignation of the commission, headed at the time by Jacques Santer, a former Luxembourg prime minister, four months later. The parliament refused to approve the final accounts of the EU budget for 1996 because of concerns of fraud, mismanagement and cronyism, allegedly involving several commissioners, notably Edith Cresson, a former French premier, who was in charge of research and education. To head off a vote of censure by parliament, which would result in the sacking of the whole commission, Santer agreed to the appointment of a five-person independent committee to audit the commission's work. Their report to parliament five weeks later strongly criticised Cresson for appointing a dentist friend to a fictitious job and for her lax management of the Leonardo vocational training programme. But it made only minor criticisms of other commissioners. It also turned up little in the way of corruption. The report, however, contained the stinging phrase 'it is becoming difficult to find anybody who has even the slightest sense of responsibility'.

Parliament cannot censure individual commissioners and Cresson refused to resign or, indeed, offer any sign of contrition; nor did Santer demand her resignation. Within days, it was clear that there was the two-thirds majority in parliament needed to dismiss the entire commission. To avoid this humiliation, all 20 members of the commission resigned on March 11th 1999. Two weeks later, the European Council meeting in Berlin nominated former Italian prime minister Renato Prodi to succeed Santer. The Prodi Commission, formally appointed the following September, included only four survivors from Santer's team.

The budget guidelines

The other main business of the Berlin summit was to set EU budget guidelines ('perspectives' in EU jargon) for the seven years 2000–06. The newly elected German chancellor Gerhard Schröder made a pitch for a big cut in Germany's contribution to the EU budget which was far in excess of any other member. But he settled for only marginal relief, and the UK budget rebate (which came under strong attack from other EU members) survived intact (see pp. 118–20). The financial guidelines agreed in Berlin allowed for a modest extension of EU activities during the seven-year period. It also provided a financial package to support candidate countries in central and eastern Europe in the run-up to membership in 2004.

The convention and constitutional treaty

The Nice summit, badly handled by French president Jacques Chirac, produced a set of messy conclusions on the weighting of votes in the Council of Ministers and on the size of the European Commission: was every member state entitled to nominate a commissioner? This confusion was said to be partly to blame for the rejection of the Nice treaty by Irish voters in a referendum in June 2001. The EU governments were also concerned at the growing indifference, if not disenchantment, about the EU on the part of their citizens as evidenced, *inter alia*, by the record low turnout in the elections for the European Parliament in 1999. It was time for another IGC to revitalise the Union and put it back on track. Largely at German behest, one was convened for 2004. It would consider a wide range of reforms, including a constitution which would replace, or supplement, the Treaty of Rome and the subsequent amending treaties. It would be a simplified document, clearly-worded for ordinary citizens to understand.

The Laeken summit in Belgium in December 2001 decided the IGC should be preceded by a convention which would seek input from a range of stakeholders and draw up a preparatory text. Its 105 members, under the chairmanship of former French president Valéry Giscard d'Estaing, included EU governments, members of national parliaments and MEPs, representatives from the 12 candidate countries as well as Turkey, and other EU institutions. Voluntary organisations were also able to feed ideas to the convention.

It started work in February 2002, and produced a text, approved almost unanimously, which was presented to heads of government at the Thessalonica summit in June 2003. It was in the form of a draft constitution, replacing all previous EU treaties (save for the Euratom treaty) but incorporating and consolidating most of their provisions. It also set out with more clarity the policy areas coming under EU responsibility, those remaining under national control, and those where responsibility was shared by the EU and the member states. It proposed the appointment of a full-time president of the European Council and of an EU foreign minister who would chair meetings of the Council of EU foreign ministers, and who would also be a vice-president of the European Commission. The constitutional document took the essential step of replacing the fiendishly complex system of qualified majority voting contained in the Nice treaty with a simpler and more transparent formula based on a 'double majority' of member states and of the overall population of the Union. Heads of government handed on the draft to the IGC, made up of their foreign ministers. The latter succeeded in producing a slightly watered-down text, but retained about 95 per cent of the convention's proposals. This was put to a summit in Brussels in December 2003 for approval. Agreement was blocked by Spain and Poland – two countries who were given far more votes than they were entitled to by the Nice treaty and who refused to give ground. The IGC could do little. But the right-wing Spanish government lost the March 2004 national elections to a socialist administration which proved ready to compromise. This left the Poles isolated. But they soon gave way, enabling the document to be agreed at a June 2004 summit. The new constitutional treaty did envisage a limited increase in EU responsibilities, but it was far from the blueprint for a European super-state as claimed by the Eurosceptic press, particularly in the UK (see Chapter 39). It went beyond the 'tidying-up exercise' the UK government portrayed it to be, although it still left the member states clearly in charge of sensitive areas like foreign policy, defence, taxation, criminal law, social security and education, where unanimity in decision-making was still required.

The Treaty establishing a Constitution for Europe (TCE) should have come into force in October 2006 after ratification by the European Parliament and by all 25 member states. By June 2005, ten countries had ratified it. But its rejection by voters in referendums in the Netherlands and France left it in limbo.

Enlargement to 25 – and then 27

In December 2002, accession negotiations were successfully concluded with ten candidates – Cyprus, the Czech Republic, Estonia, Hungary, Latvia, Lithuania, Malta, Poland, Slovakia and Slovenia – who would join the EU on May 1st 2004. The target entry date for Bulgaria and Romania, whose negotiations were still ongoing, was reset for 2007. At the same time, EU heads of government agreed to review the question of Turkish membership at the end of 2004 with a view to launching entry negotiations the following year.

During 2003, accession treaties with the ten new members were ratified by EU governments, the European Parliament and the ten applicants, nine of which held national referendums to approve the entry conditions. The exception was the divided island of Cyprus. The Greek-Cypriot Republic of Cyprus, recognised by the EU, ratified the accession treaty. A UN plan for the reunification of the island which would have enabled both parts to enter as a federalised state, was put to a referendum in both the republic and the Turkish-controlled northern part of Cyprus. The Turkish community approved the UN plan by a two-to-one majority. But Greek Cypriots rejected it by a majority of three-to-one – to the fury of the EU. Therefore only the Greek-Cypriot state joined the Union on May 1st 2004. This enlargement, the biggest in EU history, raised membership from 15 to 25.

Negotiations with Bulgaria and Romania were completed by the end of 2004 and they became the EU's 26th and 27th members on January 1st 2007. Meanwhile Croatia and the former Yugoslav republic of Macedonia applied to join. Negotiations with Croatia began in 2005 and it became the EU's 28th member on July 1st 2013. Entry talks with Macedonia have not yet taken place, having been blocked by Greece because Macedonia takes the same name as its own northern province, implying (in the eyes of Athens) a claim to Greek territory.

Barroso Commission

In June 2004, the European Council met to nominate a successor to Prodi at the head of the commission, whose mandate expired on October 31st. But a dispute arose among member states which resulted in the rejection of both leading candidates – former Belgian premier Guy Verhofstadt (too federal for the British) and the UK commissioner for external relations, Chris Patten (too British for some EU governments). An emergency meeting of the European Council ten days later unanimously nominated José Manuel Barroso, Portugal's centre-right prime minister, as commission president. Barroso was to serve two five-year terms.

Under the Nice treaty, the new commission was to have 25 members, one from each member country. In consultation with Barroso, national governments each made their own nominations, which after agreement from the Council of Ministers were submitted for approval by the European Parliament. It had the right to approve or reject the whole commission, but not each commissioner individually. This did not stop it vetting each incoming commissioner. In several instances, the parliamentary vetting committee raised objection, notably on Ricco Buttiglione, a right-wing Italian catholic who had been given the justice and home affairs portfolio by Barroso. Buttiglione upset many MEPs by making disparaging remarks about gay people and women, declaring homosexuality to be a 'sin'. They demanded his nomination be withdrawn, or at least that he be given a less sensitive portfolio. Barroso resisted but when it became clear parliament was ready to sack the whole commission, he sought a delay in the parliamentary vote. The Italian government then swiftly withdrew Buttiglione as nominee, offering instead its foreign minister Franco Frattini. Barroso also replaced a Latvian nominee allegedly involved in a party-funding scandal and switched one portfolio between nominees to satisfy parliament. The chain of events heartened MEPs as another sign of their growing influence. This had already been demonstrated by the European People's Party which had won most seats in the 2004 elections. It insisted that the new commission should reflect the election outcome and that the new commission president should come from the centre-right. The European Council took the hint, declining to consider the claims of several well-qualified socialist candidates, including former prime ministers.

Towards the Lisbon treaty

A short time into the Barroso Commission, the EU was shocked by the rejection by Dutch and French voters in June 2005 of the Treaty establishing a Constitution for Europe. Despite a swathe of national ratifications, including two extremely favourable referendum results in Spain and Luxembourg, the TCE was dead. Recovering from the shock, EU leaders, headed by German Chancellor Angela Merkel, decided to salvage what they could from the wreckage. The idea was to draft a less ambitious treaty, which would, however, retain most of the institutional reforms contained in the TCE. But it would leave aside some of the constitutional trimmings so as to avoid giving the misguided impression that the EU would convert into a 'super-state'. To avoid more referendums when popular sentiment is sometimes directed more against an unpopular government or other extraneous factors rather than against the issue at hand, EU leaders opted to ratify the new treaty via national parliaments if possible. Only Ireland was to hold a referendum after being advised that it was a legal requirement under the Irish constitution. There were shrill calls for a referendum in the UK from elements in the opposition Conservative Party, egged on by the majority of the Eurosceptic popular press. A referendum, they claimed, had been promised on the TCE. The Labour government saw off the challenge on the ground that the proposed treaty and the TCE were different documents. In no other member state was there a significant demand for a referendum to be held.

A summit in June 2007, under German presidency, duly convened an IGC composed of their 27 foreign ministers to draft a new treaty. This was approved by the European Council in Lisbon in October 2007 and signed in the Portuguese capital on December 13th 2007. It took the first member state – Hungary – only three days to ratify the Lisbon treaty. The forecast date of implementation was autumn 2008. Then the inevitable accident happened. Irish voters rejected the treaty by 53.4 to 46.6 per cent in a referendum on June 12th 2008. Other EU governments quickly agreed they would not be put off by the Irish rejection and duly continued the ratification process. The UK parliament did so six days after the Irish vote. Most of the others followed suit.

A post-mortem by the Irish government and subsequent opinion polls showed that, apart from resistance to the idea that Ireland would lose its automatic representation in the European Commission, other concerns were not linked to the new treaty. They were related to general issues like Irish neutrality, taxation, workers' rights and social matters, particularly abortion. The then Irish premier, Brian Cowen, brought these concerns to the European Council, where a deal was struck in December 2008. By that time a number of other EU governments had also concluded that perhaps losing a national representative in the European Commission was not such a good idea after all. They all agreed to use the Lisbon treaty rules to bring back the principle of one commissioner per member state. They also agreed, provided Ireland held another referendum by October 2009, to provide 'binding guarantees' that the treaty would not affect Irish sovereignty in three key areas: taxation, neutrality and family-related and ethical issues. Bolstered by these assurances, Irish voters duly backed the Lisbon treaty in a second referendum on October 2009 by 67.1 to 32.9 per cent. The Lisbon treaty came into force on December 1st 2009.

Notes

1 Grosser, *The Western Alliance*, p. 189.
2 Steps to European Unity, European Documentation, 1985.
3 The EAGGF, the European Agricultural Guarantee and Guidance Fund, contained a small component for structural measures.

3 The EU under strain
2008–

A new watershed

Some analysts wondered at the time whether the Maastricht summit in December 1991 and its eponymous treaty might represent the high-water mark of European integration. Its reach was Olympian. It capped eight years of effort to consolidate the EU's 1992 single market programme and set the 1999 deadline and timetable for the single currency. At the same time, the treaty opened the door for the EU's biggest-ever enlargement and enshrined the principle of the borderless and passport-free Schengen area. The euro, introduced in 1999, led what in retrospect was a charmed life for the first ten years. This was a period where, for instance, a shaky Greek government could borrow money at virtually the same cost as rock-solid Germany. The single currency was introduced at a rate of one euro for US$1.17. It dipped below the dollar in 2000, reaching a low of US$0.82 on October 26th that year before rising again beyond dollar parity in December 2002. The euro touched a record high of US$1.60 on July 16th 2008, just weeks before the global crisis erupted, after which it eased back.

A financial tsunami

All member states of the Union were hit by the worldwide recession sparked by the subprime mortgages crisis in the United States and the collapse of Lehmann Brothers on September 25th 2008. Some were worse affected than others. The worst hit were to be eurozone countries Greece, Ireland, Cyprus, Portugal and Spain. Coping with the crisis, and especially Greece's near-bankruptcy, dominated EU activity in the years that followed. In their instinctive first crisis response, member states acted to bail out their banks and to stimulate their national economies. These separate efforts were pulled together at a meeting of the European

Council on December 11th and 12th 2008 into a grandly titled European Economic Recovery Plan. It was worth €200 billion, including €35 billion of EU money. In the meantime, three new non-euro member states, Hungary, Latvia and Romania, suffered big fund outflows and were bailed out by the IMF, with EU support, in late 2008 and early 2009.

It soon became clear, however, that Union member states as a whole, and especially those in the eurozone, were ill-equipped to cope with the asymmetric shocks which hit its members with different intensity. First of all, there was no political union to provide a framework for common action, as some Maastricht architects had postulated. Then there was no economic component in the economic and monetary union to force member states to coordinate economic policies. If this were not enough, the half-finished nature of the euro project was exposed. There was no provision for a common debt pool as in standard currency areas. There was no lender of last resort for commercial banks – a function usually attributed to central banks, but not to the ECB. Nor was there a transfer mechanism for redistributing fiscal resources from rich to poor regions as in other currency unions (like the US for instance) save for the meagre, and totally inadequate, EU budget. Weak eurozone economies with high unemployment and high costs could not devalue to recoup some lost competitivity. The euro's many critics (principally outside the eurozone) forecast wrongly, yet almost on a daily basis at the height of the crisis, the imminent demise of the single currency. They underestimated the depth of commitment to the euro among participant countries, starting with Germany, and the centrality of the single currency to the process of European integration. Rash investors who bet on the euro's disappearance lost money. Greece's survival in the eurozone turned out to be more touch-and-go.

But problems seldom come alone. The period since 2008 has also seen the other iconic EU achievement – its frontier-free and passport-free Schengen area – come under unprecedented threat as hundreds of thousands of refugees and migrants from the Middle East and Africa and beyond sought to enter the EU. The movement accelerated after the Arab Spring in 2011 and the resulting violence and chaos, especially in Libya and Syria. Together, Schengen and the euro symbolised what Europe meant for many citizens: the space where you can travel without a passport and without changing money. It was the carefully crafted, but complex, rules for processing and handling migrants and asylum-seekers which underpinned Schengen that fell apart under the sheer weight of numbers. It also became blindingly clear that its mechanisms for controlling entry across its external frontiers, land and sea, were woefully inadequate.

For its part, the common foreign and security policy has also faltered, despite the appointment of a high representative for external relations, over Ukraine and the disastrous aftermath to the Arab Spring. These crises opened fissures between and among member states – north–south over the Greek bailout, east–west over refugees and asylum-seekers, and every which way over Ukraine and the Middle East.

Business as usual

Until the financial crisis broke out in the autumn, 2008 was devoted to EU business-as-usual. The highlight was EU mediation in the conflict between Georgia and Russia which broke out in August 2008. Succumbing to Russian provocations, the impetuous president of Georgia, Mikheil Saakashvili, attacked the breakaway region of South Ossetia where Russian troops were stationed on August 7th. His forces were quickly driven back and Russian units occupied parts of Georgian territory. President Nicolas Sarkozy of France, whose country held the rotating EU presidency, undertook lightning visits to Moscow and Tbilisi, brokering a ceasefire five days later. Russia withdrew its forces in October 2008. The ceasefire left South Ossetia and Georgia's other breakaway region, Abkhazia, in Russian hands; but even if only partly implemented by Russia, Sarkozy's ceasefire prevented further bloodshed. His relative success, which many in Brussels believed would not have been possible if a smaller EU member had held the EU presidency, reinforced support for the provision in the Lisbon treaty for a permanent president of the European Council.

New appointments

In anticipation of Lisbon's final ratification, EU heads of government proceeded to appoint in October 2009 the president of the European Council and the high representative for external relations, who would double up as a vice-president of the commission. The first post went to former Belgian premier Herman Van Rompuy, a consensus figure, who had impressed his peers by the way he had just steered his linguistically divided country through its umpteenth political crisis. He was a compromise candidate, strongly backed by Germany and France. Unsuccessful front-runners had included former UK Labour premier Tony Blair (although he never openly declared his candidacy) and Jean-Claude Juncker, prime minister of Luxembourg. Blair lost for a number of reasons. He was not from the centre-right where the majority of EU leaders came from at the time. He was also opposed by many for his active part in the invasion of Iraq, while others did not want a president from a country whose commitment to the EU was shaky at best. Juncker lost on the understandable ground that a number of EU countries did not want someone from one of their smallest members as the first EU president. But his day was still to come. Juncker overcame a hostile campaign and personal attacks from UK Prime Minister David Cameron and leading members of his Conservative Party (who claimed he was bent on creating the by-now mythical EU super-state) to succeed Barroso as commission president in November 2014.

The function of EU foreign affairs supremo, now called the High Representative of the Union for Foreign and Security Affairs, was reserved for a figure from Europe's centre-left in the interests of political balance. For that reason, and as a consolation prize to the UK, the job went to Catherine Ashton, who had briefly served in the outgoing Barroso Commission with responsibility for trade policy. As high representative, she was also the head of the EU's new European External Action Service (EEAS). Both Van Rompuy and Ashton were appointed for a 2.5-year term from December 1st 2009, but their mandates were later extended to a full five years. As for Barroso himself, following elections for the European Parliament in June 2009 in which the centre-right European People's Party remained the largest group, he was appointed commission president for a second five-year term in September 2009.

Faced with an oncoming recession, the ECB reduced interest rates four times between January and May 2009 bringing them close to zero. In March the Council of Ministers issued a warning to Greece and several other countries, under the Excessive Deficit Procedure. In October, the newly elected Greek socialist government under George Papandreou announced that its budget deficit for 2009 would be more than 12 per cent of GDP, while government debt was set to exceed €300 billion, making it a higher percentage of GDP than even Italy. The eurozone financial crisis was about to start. It would test the Union as no other event in its 55-year history. The financial and economic implications for the rest of the world were huge.

The first battle

In 2010, the EU began a desperate search for ways to save the euro, prevent Greek bankruptcy and bail out other overstretched governments, with very few tools to hand. It counter-attacked on two fronts. One priority was to put in place a credible policy and regulatory structure, including adequate means of intervention, to enable the euro to survive. The other was to devise and oversee rescue packages capable of bailing out deeply indebted – or in the case of Greece, near bankrupt – governments in the eurozone. The eurozone countries at greatest risk were relatively small (Greece, Ireland, Portugal and Cyprus) except for Spain, which is the EU's fifth largest economy, although its problems were less acute than the others. But there were always nagging fears that, if the contagion spread, the next victim after Spain would be Italy, the most fragile of the major EU economies and widely recognised as 'too big to save'. What then?

The EU put together a Troika, consisting of the European Commission, the ECB and the IMF to coordinate and draw up rescue packages with each of the countries concerned. The Greek parliament started in 2010 by adopting two austerity packages in quick succession, on February 9th and March 3rd. These included public sector wage freezes followed by cuts, an increase in VAT, higher taxes on fuel, tobacco and alcohol and labour market reform. Yet in Papandreou's own words, Greece was still floundering. Eurozone leaders and the IMF agreed a first bailout for Greece on May 2nd worth €110 billion over a three-year period. Eurozone countries would lend the money, but at non-concessionary rates, thereby helping to push Greek debt to unsustainable levels. The bailout imposed a draconian deficit-reduction programme over three years – hard to do for a country in deep recession. It required *inter alia* public sector job reductions, pensions reform and the privatisation of state assets. The bailout was linked to the adoption and implementation of further austerity measures. Three days later violent protest demonstrations rocked Athens and other centres. Three died in the Greek capital.

Building a firewall

On May 8th 2010, eurozone heads of government took action to protect the euro from further market turmoil after the Greek bailout by creating mechanisms for greater budgetary surveillance, and more economic coordination. They also set up the European Financial Stability Facility (EFSF) and the European Financial Stabilisation Mechanism (EFSM) as part of a support package worth €750 billion. Tensions eased until the autumn. Then on November 28th eurozone leaders had to put in place a second bailout, this time for Ireland. The Irish government had rescued its banks, which lost billions after a property bubble burst. As a result, the Irish budget deficit soared, raising fears for the country's solvency. The EU finance ministers agreed a €67.5 billion aid package on December 7th. The principal sources of bailout funding were the EFSF and the EFSM. Although not eurozone members, the UK, Sweden and Denmark chipped in with bilateral loans to Ireland. The Irish rescue operation was followed on May 5th 2011 by a €78 billion bailout for Portugal whose long-underperforming economy took the full brunt of the recession. Like Ireland, Portugal drew heavily on the EFSF.

The use of the EFSF and the EFSM facilities rekindled questions as to their compatibility with EU legislation which did not allow for bailouts. The German government, fearing possible strictures from its constitutional court, was particularly concerned. Consequently, the European Council agreed on December 17th 2010 to seek a two-line amendment to article 136 of the Lisbon treaty to bring these operations under EU law. It was duly incorporated into the treaty after approval by the European Council on March 25th 2011 by a simplified procedure which avoided national referendums for ratification. After ratification, the euro area member states signed an intergovernmental treaty establishing the European Stability Mechanism (ESM) on February 2nd 2012. It was formally inaugurated the following October. Based in Luxembourg, the ESM is the permanent successor to the EFSF and the EFSM, which were to expire in mid-2013. The ESM would provide a eurozone country with financial aid only if it is considered necessary to ensure the financial stability of the euro area as a whole. Any eurozone member state receiving assistance must implement a macro-economic adjustment programme. The ESM, with a rescue fund of €500 billion, became the central element in the eurozone's protective firewall.

Second Greek bailout

From spring 2011, it became clear that the Greek rescue programme was not working. Criticism of Greece's reluctance or inability to respect its commitments had swelled, particularly in creditor countries like Germany, the Netherlands and Finland. Some of the poorer euro countries in central and eastern Europe also objected at having to put up money to rescue Greece. Suggestions that Greece leave the eurozone became persistent. However, fear of unknown and perhaps huge turmoil in Europe and beyond following a 'Grexit' (Greek exit) easily prevailed. A second bailout of €130 billion was agreed by eurozone governments on July 21st 2011. It eased repayment terms on Greek debt and lowered interest rates. Private sector creditors accepted a 50 per cent haircut on their Greek sovereign bonds as their 'contribution' to the rescue package. Unhappy at the outcome, Papandreou took the surprise decision to submit the second package to a national referendum. Greece had not held a referendum since the 1970s. The EU kept the bailout package in abeyance, until after the referendum. Papandreou ran into stiff opposition within his Socialist party as well as from the opposition. He withdrew the plan for a referendum on November 3rd 2011 and resigned as prime minister six days later. The package was finalised on February 21st 2012.

More high drama

But there was more high drama to come before 2011 was out. It took the form of a veto by UK Prime Minister David Cameron at the European Council of December 8th of the Fiscal Stability treaty[1] which imposed stricter budget discipline on eurozone countries and required them to coordinate their economic policies more closely. The aim was to give more substance to the economic side of economic and monetary union and bolster the eurozone's defences against future crises. Cameron said that without specific guarantees to protect the role of London as a financial centre, the treaty (also known as the fiscal compact) could be used by eurozone members to undermine Britain's interests in the European Single Market. But the great majority of heads of government rejected his demands for:

- a UK veto on any transfer of power from a national to an EU financial regulator;
- a commitment that the European Banking Authority would remain in London;
- rejection of upcoming proposals from the ECB that euro-denominated transactions should take place within the eurozone.

To get round his veto, the European Council repackaged the fiscal stability treaty as an intergovernmental treaty, outside the EU framework, between the signatory countries. The fiscal compact was signed on March 2nd 2012 by all EU member states save the UK and, initially, the Czech Republic. It took effect on January 1st 2013. It is located in Luxembourg. It imposes rules for balanced budgets, with automatic correctives, and requires eurozone members with excessive debt, to cut debt by a fixed amount every year. The treaty specifies that 'to the extent compatible' it will comply with EU treaties and EU law, but that 'It will not encroach upon the competence of the Union to act in the area of economic union.' The treaty commits the signatories to bring it back under EU law as soon as possible within a target period of five years.

Cameron's use of the veto in a vain bid to block the treaty marked a departure in Britain's EU strategy. This had previously been to defend perceived important national interests within the EU framework via opt-outs (as for the single currency) or through special deals (the rebate on its EU budget contribution). For many in Brussels and other EU capitals, Cameron's attitude reflected pressure from colleagues within his Conservative Party to adopt a more robust attitude when defending UK interests. There were fears that the party would lose members (and voters) on its right flank to the anti-EU United Kingdom Independence Party (UKIP) which wanted Britain out of the EU altogether so as to recover elements of UK sovereignty ceded to the EU and to prevent further encroachment. Under its leader, Nigel Farage, UKIP did well in 2009 and again in the 2014 election for the European Parliament when it won the biggest number of British seats with 24, against only 19 for the Conservatives and 20 for Labour. The hardening of British attitudes on Europe must also be seen in the context of the European Union Act 2011 adopted on July 19th that year. The act requires any subsequent modification of EU treaties to be subject to a national referendum. Following on from the Act, Cameron announced in January 2013 that his government intended to seek (at the time) unspecified EU reforms as a prelude to a referendum to be held by the end of 2017 as to whether the UK should stay in the EU or withdraw.

Rumblings from without

The inauguration of the European External Action Service in January 2011 coincided with the start of the Arab Spring in Tunisia. But the new body was unable to hold the EU together when popular protests spread to Libya. In February, France and the UK took the lead in pushing for a UN Security Council resolution to create a no-fly zone to protect civilians against violence from the Gaddafi regime. Resolution 1973 was adopted by the Security Council on March 19th 2011. France and the UK led a coalition of forces, under NATO command and with US support, to implement the no-fly zone. Germany, which abstained in the UN vote, did not participate in military action in Libya. However, earlier, in January, the EU Council of Ministers imposed economic sanctions and a travel ban against Libya. It did the same against Syria on May 9th following the violent crack-down on protestors there by the government forces of president Bashar Al-Assad. These were extended in October.

Mario's magic

Within months of the second bailout in February 2012, it became clear that Greece's austerity medicine was still not working. Europe had entered a double dip recession. The impact on Greece was worse than expected. Its privatisation programme had stalled. The haircut imposed on private investors was seen as too small to be effective, yet big enough to scare the markets. In short, the bailout was badly calibrated and mishandled. Despite abundant liquidity supplied by the ECB, banks stopped lending across borders. Borrowing costs for the most vulnerable member states rose. The fear of debt contagion spreading to Italy came back. Could the euro itself survive the turmoil? Enter Mario Draghi, an Italian central banker who became ECB governor in November 2011. In a speech to a group of investors in London on July 26th 2012 he said the ECB was ready within its mandate 'to do whatever it takes to preserve the euro'. This time those analysts and pundits who were once again forecasting the euro would not last another week or month finally got it: EU governments' commitment to the single currency was for real. For good measure, the ECB introduced on September 6th a programme of conditional bond buying from EU countries requesting help. This was in addition to cheap refinancing facilities for commercial banks introduced earlier in the year. Mario's magic worked; markets took him at his word. Tensions eased, at least temporarily, and fragile countries could again borrow at non-punitive rates. Draghi had saved the euro – but he had not saved Greece.

More fire-fighting

But first there were other fires to douse. In June 2012, Spain signalled to its partners that if would need a bailout following a crisis involving its local savings banks. On July 20th, eurozone governments pledged €100 billion to Spain to save its banks in return for a programme of banking reforms. The Spanish crisis added new impetus to EU efforts to introduce banking supervision at EU level – the first real step towards its proposed European banking union. On December 13th 2012, the European Council agreed to create a single supervisory mechanism (SSM), which puts all eurozone banks under the direct prudential supervision of the European Central Bank. The Council of Ministers adopted the operational regulations for the SSM on October 22nd 2013. A decision to create a Single Resolution Mechanism (SRM) followed in April 2014. The SRM complements the Single Supervisory Mechanism in cases where a bank still faces serious difficulties despite stronger supervision, so that its problems can be settled efficiently with minimal costs to taxpayers and the real economy. However, the third pillar of the banking union, the deposit insurance scheme, involving joint guarantees, was delayed because of German reticence.

By mid-2012, Cyprus had also indicated it would need EU financial support. Cyprus was badly hit by the post-2008 recession affecting tourism, local property values and its big off-shore banking sector much-used by wealthy Russian expatriates. Cyprus banks had also been hit by the Greek crisis. The government could not raise money on international capital markets. It received a short-term emergency loan of €2.5 billion from Russia in 2011. But it soon needed more. The eurozone governments reached a messy rescue deal with the Cyprus government on March 25th 2013. In return for the €10 billion bailout, one of the island's two biggest banks was wound up. The second was restructured. Big depositors took a haircut on their deposits of up to 60 per cent. Small savers (those with less than €100,000 in their bank accounts) had originally been bailed-in to pay a 6.75 per cent 'levy' as their contribution to the rescue operation. This was against the principle of EU-wide guarantees for small savers, and was dropped in the final agreement. The EU negotiators did not handle the Cyprus crisis well. During sometimes ill-tempered meetings, the threat of Cyprus's departure from the eurozone was raised by both sides. Evidently, kicking midget Cyprus out of the eurozone held none of the fears surrounding a 'Grexit' in other eurozone capitals.

A state of grace

Away from the hard reality of successive crises, the EU ended 2012 on a calmer note when on December 10th it received the 2012 Nobel peace prize at a ceremony in Oslo. The citation recognised the EU's contribution over six decades to the promotion of peace and reconciliation, democracy and human rights.

Housekeeping and husbandry

As the debt crises ebbed temporarily, the Union spent time during 2013 to puts its internal finances and policy management in order. A meeting of the European Council in Brussels on February 7th and 8th agreed in principle on the 2014–20 EU budget planning framework. The agreement sets the global EU budget for the period at just under €960 billion. This is slightly less than the ceiling of €974.8 billion for 2007–13. It is the first time the overall budget has fallen from one financing period to the next. Although heads of government reached a political agreement in February, it was only in December, just as the new period was about to begin, that the Council of Ministers agreed the final figures. One reason for the delay stemmed from the difficult efforts to reform – yet again – the Common Agricultural Policy which, with a total spend of €373.2 billion for 2014–20 still represents the biggest single budget component. The reforms agreed will ensure that direct payments to farmers are more fairly distributed and reflect their commitment to manage their land and the surrounding countryside in a sustainable manner; price-support payments and subsidies will be simpler and more flexible; and EU money spent on rural development will focus on increasing competitiveness and promoting innovation. The enabling legislation for the reforms was adopted by agriculture ministers on December 13th 2013.

Trouble next door

By this time, however, trouble was brewing on the EU's very border. It started at a summit meeting of the so-called Eastern Partnership between the EU and its eastern neighbours in the Lithuanian capital of Vilnius on November 28th 2013. In Vilnius, leaders from Georgia and Moldova initialled their association and free trade agreements negotiated with the European Union. Ukrainian president Viktor Yanukovych, who was due formally to sign his country's agreement with the EU, had a last-minute change of heart. Although a direct neighbour and keen to join the EU, Ukraine has never been considered by the Union as a candidate for membership. Its first relationship with the EU after independence was a partnership and cooperation agreement which took effect in 1998. The new agreement which included a 'deep and comprehensive free trade area' was geared to align the Ukraine as closely with EU trade, economic and industrial policies and rules as is possible without full EU membership. Although Ukraine had negotiated and initialled the deal, Yanukovych announced he would not sign unless he received short-term financial support which the EU was unable to provide. He turned to Moscow. On December 17th, President Vladimir Putin offered Yanukovych a $15 billion loan and a 33 per cent reduction in the price Ukraine paid for its imports of Russian gas, in exchange for joining a Russia-led customs union. Yanukovych's about-turn ran into strong popular opposition in Kiev. From November 21st, demonstrators rallied at the main square now dubbed the 'Euromaidan' on a daily basis. Many waved miniature EU flags. They continued for weeks throughout the depth of winter. They were largely peaceful, although at times rough. Real violence erupted on February 20th with dozens of protestors killed. The next day Yanukovych and opposition leaders reached a quick deal to end the violence, form a unity government and hold elections. The agreement was endorsed by German, Polish and French foreign ministers who helped to broker it. The protestors were unimpressed and showed it. Yanukovych fled to Russia on February 22nd.

Unrest continued after his departure especially in the east of Ukraine where ethnic Russians had set up breakaway territories in the Donetsk and Lugansk regions near the Russian border. They were supported by regular and irregular forces from Russia. With Yanukovych gone, the EU and Ukraine representatives signed the political provisions of the stalled association agreement on March 21st 2014. The economic and trade provisions were signed in Brussels on June 27th. Following a Russian takeover and rushed local referendum there on March 16th, Crimea was annexed by Russia two days later. Meanwhile, shelling and violence continued in

48   *The background*

the breakaway regions in Donetsk and Lugansk. Ceasefire and de-escalation agreements were signed in Minsk, the first in September 2014 and the second in February 2015. These confirmed the territorial integrity of Ukraine, but allowed for interim self-government for certain districts of Donetsk and Lugansk.

On March 20th 2014, the European Council strongly condemned the Russian annexation of Crimea and Sebastopol as illegal and called for a first series of economic sanctions against Russia. Following the election of Petro Poroshenko to replace Yanukovych as president on May 25th, the European Council issued a statement reaffirming its commitment to uphold Ukrainian sovereignty and territorial integrity, and calling on the new president to reach out to all regions of the country. Poroshenko is a Ukrainian oligarch, known as the 'chocolate king' because part of his assets were in the confectionery business. The EU imposed a series of economic and diplomatic sanctions on Russia between March 2014 and June 2015. These covered the boycott of goods from Crimea and Sebastopol, a ban on EU investment in Crimea, a travel and visa ban and asset freeze on Russian personalities linked to the situation in eastern Ukraine, a freeze on financial dealings with Russian state banks, energy and defence companies and a ban on exports and technology transfer in transport, telecommunications and energy-related sectors. To the surprise of some, but not all, observers, Poroshenko was slow in implementing some policies, especially on ending corruption.

New style meets old apathy

Away from managing crises and reacting to events, the humdrum exigencies of the EU calendar had to be respected. Elections for the 2014–19 legislature of the European Parliament were held in May 2014. These were followed by the appointment of a new president and members of the European Commission as well as the nomination of the next president of the European Council and the high representative for foreign policy. Building on a new provision in the Lisbon treaty whereby the European Council should designate the commission president 'taking account of the results of the European elections', the parliament put on a roadshow to stir voter interest. This consisted in a series of US-style televised debates between the principal candidates for the presidency of the parliament. In all ten were held, culminating in a debate featuring all candidates on May 15th 2014, just a week before the vote. Made in English, the programme was available to all European public service broadcasters. As a gimmick with relatively low visibility, it may have worked. As a device to motivate apathetic voters, it failed. At best, it helped stabilise turnout, which had fallen with every previous election, at 42.61 per cent, just under the 42.97 per cent of 2009.

Under parliament's formula, the new commission president would be Jean-Claude Juncker as the candidate of the group which won most seats in the parliament, the Christian Democrats. The EU heads of government, allergic to doing the parliament's bidding, feigned to ignore the result and carried out their own post-election consultation with the main parliamentary groups. To no-one's surprise they nominated Juncker on July 27th. Two months later, they appointed the then Polish prime minister, Donald Tusk, to replace Van Rompuy as European Council president and Italian foreign minister Federica Mogherini as the new high representative. On November 1st 2014, the fifth anniversary of the Lisbon treaty, one of its final innovations was implemented. Henceforth decisions in the Council of Ministers are no longer taken by a complex qualified majority formula, but by a simplified 'double majority' system. To be adopted, new items of EU legislation now need the approval of 55 per cent of member states, representing at least 65 per cent of the EU's population.

More trouble ahead

As the EU busied itself with internal housekeeping, it was also setting the scene for two new dramas: the storm over Mediterranean and Middle East (mainly Syrian) refugees and migrants, and the third Greek financial rescue. On October 9th 2014, the Italian interior ministry ended its Mare Nostrum search-and-rescue mission for people fleeing Libya by boat. Although it had rescued 120,000 refugees and migrants in the previous 12 months, it was deemed too expensive for a number of EU countries who co-financed the operation at a cost of €9 million a month. Some felt it only encouraged more migrants to attempt the perilous crossing. It was replaced by a more limited EU-operated mission called Triton with a monthly budget of €3 million. Unlike Mare Nostrum which operated in international waters, its operations were limited to within 30 kilometres of the Italian coast and included a border-protection function with less scope for search-and-rescue.

The third bailout

By the second half of 2014, Greece was clearly not complying with the conditions agreed in exchange for the scheduled programme of transfers under the first two bailout agreements. This caused understandable frustration and exasperation among Greece's creditors in Germany and elsewhere, and their even more sceptical public opinions, now readier than ever to eject Greece from the eurozone. In December 2014, the Troika froze payments, pending full compliance by Greece and to await further developments. Already in June, German finance minister Wolfgang Schäuble warned that Greece 'would have to continue to meet the troika's demands for reforms or risk leaving the eurozone'.[2] Some analysts believe the Greek government was easing up on austerity measures after losing to Syriza, the radical left-wing party led by Alexis Tsipras, in the 2014 European elections. This raised the distinct possibility that Syriza, who had pledged to end the austerity programmes linked to the EU bailouts, could win the next domestic Greek election. The coalition government of Antonis Samaras duly collapsed over the failure by parliament to elect a new Greek president on December 29th. As expected, Alexis Tsipras and his anti-austerity party won the snap election held on January 25th 2015. There followed a six-month tragi-comedy of aggressive, ill-tempered and sullen posturing and negotiating on the part of both Greece and its creditors that did indeed bring Greece to the brink of leaving the eurozone. The aim of the negotiations was to unblock the flow of EU support funding to Greece before it went bankrupt. Frustrations grew on both sides as the Tsipras government submitted a series of proposals, often too vague to be taken seriously. Eurozone ministers met Greek counterparts on a weekly, sometimes daily, basis. In late June, Tsipras finally made a proposal which came close to what Greece's creditors were demanding. He put it to a referendum, hastily called for July 5th.

However, he recommended that voters reject his own proposal – which they duly did with a majority of 61 per cent. It was Tsipras's last stand. A number of eurozone ministers and even Council president Donald Tusk warned him, improbably, that the referendum was in fact a vote on whether Greece should stay in the eurozone or leave. When tension reached its pinnacle just before the third rescue package was finally agreed on July 13th, Schäuble did circulate a plan to boot out the Greeks. He did not table it formally. It would not have worked in any case: a member can choose to leave the eurozone, but it cannot be forced out against its will. The third bailout, worth a total of €86 billion over three years, contained all the eurozone's original conditions, including tax reforms, privatisations and labour market reforms virtually unchanged. There was to be no immediate debt-relief, the top Greek demand. The possibility of debt relief via longer grace and repayment periods was held over for review later in 2015. Having exhausted the options, Tsipras agreed to the deal. Defeated by much greater forces, but with Greece still a euro member, he resigned on August 20th 2015. But he was easily re-elected in the election held on September 20th.

Solidarity: a fragile flower

If solidarity among EU states bent before the Greek crisis, it buckled as they strove to cope with the massive influx of refugees and asylum seekers. From early in 2015, it was becoming clear that the reduced Triton search-and-rescue operation faced rising difficulties as the number of migrants and refugees from Libya surged. Between February and early April more than 1,800 boat people perished as they set out from Libya for the Italian coast in unseaworthy craft operated by people-smugglers. A special session of the European Council in Brussels on April 23rd agreed to make greater efforts to protect asylum-seekers, to act against people-smugglers and to speed up arrangements for sending back illegal economic migrants with no claim to refugee status. They also tripled the Triton budget, bringing it back up to the same level as the Mare Nostrum mission, while individual member states dispatched support vessels to the region.

As advances by ISIS in Syria made a desperate situation for Syrian refugees even worse, hundreds of thousands poured into Europe to seek asylum. They came from Turkey to Greece, some overland, but most by boat from the Turkish mainland to nearby Greek islands. A number had abandoned the Libyan route for the much shorter sea journey via Turkey. The big majority used Greece only as a transit point, as they headed hopefully for Germany and Sweden where they believed prospects for a future life were best. Germany opened its frontiers wide. This created huge problems in Hungary and other transit lands on the refugees' route north, leading to the closure of internal EU borders inside the Schengen area. Unable to cope with the numbers arriving in Greece and Italy, EU governments struggled to revise the rules for processing and registering refugees, distributing them across all member states – by mandatory quotas if necessary. A number, mainly in eastern Europe, refused to take their share. A meeting of the European Council on October 13th sought to reach an agreement with Turkey, whereby in exchange for financial support and other political concession by the EU, Turkey would do more to improve conditions for the two million Syrian refugees it hosted and stop them from crossing into Greece. Russian military intervention in Syria from September onwards brought additional complications.

Notes

1 Formally titled the 'Treaty on stability, coordination and governance in the economic and monetary union'.

2 In an interview with *Focus* magazine on June 1st 2014.

4 Treaties

The Treaty of Rome

The bible of the European Union, which provides the ultimate authority for the greater part of its decisions and responsibilities, is the Treaty of Rome, which created the European Economic Community (EEC). Signed on March 25th 1957 by representatives of Belgium, France, West Germany, Italy, Luxembourg and the Netherlands, it was one of two treaties signed in Rome that day by the same countries. The other established Euratom, the European Atomic Energy Community. Six years earlier on April 18th 1951 the six countries had signed the Treaty of Paris, setting up the European Coal and Steel Community (ECSC).

The Treaty of Rome is a bulky document: 248 articles plus 160 pages of annexes, protocols and conventions. The first four articles quoted here in their entirety, define the purposes of the European Economic Community, and the principal institutions to be created to ensure their achievement.

Article 1 By this Treaty, the HIGH CONTRACTING PARTIES establish among themselves a EUROPEAN ECONOMIC COMMUNITY.

Article 2 The Community shall have as its task, by establishing a common market and progressively approximating the economic policies of Member States, to promote throughout the Community a harmonious development of economic activities, a continuous and balanced expansion, an increase in stability, an accelerated raising of the standard of living and closer relations between the States belonging to it.

Article 3 For the purposes set out in Article 2, the activities of the Community shall include, as provided in this Treaty and in accordance with the timetable set out therein:

a   the elimination, as between Member States, of customs duties and of quantitative restrictions on the import and export of goods, and of all other measures having equivalent effect;

b   the establishment of a common customs tariff and of a common commercial policy towards third countries;

c   the abolition, as between Member States, of obstacles to freedom of movement for persons, services and capital;

d   the adoption of a common policy in the sphere of agriculture;

e   the adoption of a common policy in the sphere of transport;

f   the institution of a system ensuring that competition in the common market is not distorted;

g   the application of procedures by which the economic policies of Member States can be coordinated and disequilibria in their balances of payments remedied;

h   the approximation of the laws of Member States to the extent required for the proper functioning of the common market;

i   the creation of a European Social Fund in order to improve employment opportunities for workers and to contribute to the raising of their standard of living;

j   the establishment of a European Investment Bank to facilitate the economic expansion of the Community by opening up fresh resources;

k   the association of the overseas countries and territories in order to increase trade and to promote jointly economic and social development.

Article 4

1   The tasks entrusted to the Community shall be carried out by the following institutions:

- an ASSEMBLY
- a COUNCIL
- a COMMISSION
- a COURT OF JUSTICE

Each institution shall act within the limits of the powers conferred upon it by this Treaty.

2   The Council and the Commission shall be assisted by an Economic and Social Committee acting in an advisory capacity.

Articles 5–248 These articles deal with the following areas:

- 5–8: setting up the Community during a transitional period of 12 years.
- 9–11: free movement of goods.

- 12–29: the establishment of a customs union.
- 30–37: the elimination of quantitative restrictions.
- 38–47: provisions for agriculture.
- 48–73: the free movement of persons, services and capital.
- 74–84: the requirements for a common transport policy.
- 85–102: competition policy, taxation and the approximation of laws.
- 103–116: economic and trade policy.
- 117–128: social policy.
- 129–130: the establishment of a European Investment Bank.
- 131–136: the association of overseas countries and territories.
- 137–198: the composition and powers of the various Community institutions.
- 199–209: financial provisions.
- 210–248: the legal personality of the Community, the admission of additional members, the setting up of the institutions and various miscellaneous points.

Article 240 states that 'The Treaty is concluded for an unlimited period'. The treaty came into effect on January 1st 1958.

Key updates

The Rome treaty has been modified and updated a number of times down the years by some of the treaties mentioned below. These are amending treaties, which contain agreed changes to the various articles of the Rome treaty. They are unreadable on their own. The Council of the European Union regularly issues consolidated texts of the Treaty of Rome incorporating all valid amendments and modifications into the original document in a coherent read-through version. The most recent dates from January 2015. However, the consolidated texts are published for information and documentation purposes. They have no legal status. The Lisbon treaty retitles the Treaty of Rome as the 'Treaty on the functioning of the European Union' (TFEU). This belatedly recognises the transformation of the EC into the European Union by the Maastricht treaty of 1992. In fact, at Maastricht the European Council separated out a second treaty from the original text which they baptised the Treaty on European Union (TEU). This sets the basic principles and goals of the union and identifies its main policies and the institutions to carry them out. Nearly half its articles (26 out of 55) are devoted to the common foreign and defence policies. The Rome treaty, now retitled the TFEU, is responsible for the detailed policies and decisions as set out in the original text with extra sections *inter alia* on citizenship, the single market, free movement, justice and home affairs, and economic and monetary policy. The two treaties, TEU and TFEU, exist side-by-side. They overlap and contain many cross-references. They both have equal legal validity. A new consolidated version of the Treaty on European Union was also published in January 2015.

The treaties of Maastricht and Lisbon contained the most significant amendments to the Rome treaty. They are among a series of treaties, protocols and conventions signed by the member states over the years, which have also modified the original provisions of the Treaty of Rome.

From Rome to Lisbon via Maastricht, Amsterdam and Nice

1   The first of these, amalgamating the three European Communities (ECSC, EEC and Euratom), was signed in Brussels on April 8th 1965. It is usually known as the merger treaty. When the Paris treaty expired after 50 years in 2002, the residual operational activities of the ECSC were folded into those of the EU.

2   The accession treaties signed for each intake of new members required appropriate changes in the Treaty of Rome. There have been seven to date:

- Denmark, Ireland and the United Kingdom (signed in 1972)
- Greece (1979)
- Spain and Portugal (1985)
- Austria, Finland and Sweden (1994)
- Czech Republic, Estonia, Cyprus, Latvia, Lithuania, Hungary, Malta, Poland, Slovenia and Slovakia (2003)
- Bulgaria and Romania (2005)
- Croatia (2012)

3   The Single European Act, signed in 1986, amended several articles of the Treaty of Rome regarding voting procedures in the Council of Ministers, while somewhat enlarging the legislative powers of the European Parliament. The main objective was to facilitate the adoption of the programme of nearly 300 legislative measures to complete the Community's internal market (see Chapter 17).

4   The Maastricht treaty, agreed in December 1991 and signed in February 1992 was a much more thorough-going revision of the Rome treaty, comprising two major sets of provisions: those aiming to establish economic and monetary union (EMU), at the latest by January 1st 1999; and those defined as steps towards the achievement of a political union, involving common foreign and defence policies.

Other provisions extended or refined the Community's competences in other policy areas and amended the powers of various EC
institutions. It introduced the co-decision procedures giving the
European Parliament more say (along with the Council of Ministers)
in decision-making. The treaty established three pillars for the EU.

- Pillar One embraced the three existing European Communities
  treaties (the ECSC, EC and Euratom)
- Pillar Two contained new provisions on a common foreign and
  security policy (CFSP)
- Pillar Three provided for cooperation between the member
  states on justice and home affairs

Pillars Two and Three were not subject to the EC institutions and were
organised on an intergovernmental basis (see Figure 8.1). This treaty is
summarised in Appendix 8.

5   The Treaty of Amsterdam signed in October 1997 took effect after
    ratification by all the contracting parties on May 1st 1999. This was
    largely a tidying-up exercise, improving the arrangements for the
    Common Foreign and Security Policy, bringing the Protocol on
    Social Policy and the Schengen Agreement into the EC framework,
    extending the powers of the European Parliament and the president
    of the commission, adding employment and 'flexibility' clauses, and
    providing for greater transparency. This treaty is also summarised in
    Appendix 8.
6   The Treaty of Nice, signed in February 2001, only came into effect
    on February 1st 2003. It was rejected by a referendum in Ireland in
    June 2001, but was ultimately approved in a second referendum in
    October 2002, by which time it had been ratified by all the other
    member states. The treaty, which is summarised in Appendix 8, was
    mainly concerned with revising the membership and voting powers
    of the EU institutions to make way for the expected large increase
    in the number of member states during the first decade of the
    twenty-first century.
7   The Treaty establishing a Constitution for Europe (TCE), signed in
    Rome on October 29th 2004, consolidated all previous treaties into
    a single document. It clarified which decisions shall be taken by the
    EU, which by member states and which should be shared; gave a
    greater role in decision-making to national parliaments; revised the
    system of qualified majority voting in the Council of Ministers; gave
    more legislative power to the European Parliament; and extended
    the scope of majority voting, while retaining national vetoes on areas

such as the budget, social security, foreign policy and defence. It provided for the appointment of a president of the European Council and an EU foreign minister, who would also be a vice-president of the commission. It also incorporated a charter of fundamental rights. The treaty was due to come into force on November 1st 2006, after ratification by the European Parliament and all 25 member states. Rejected by referendums in France and the Netherlands in May and June 2005, the treaty was abandoned.

8 The Treaty of Lisbon, signed there on December 13th 2007, finally took effect on December 1st 2009 following ratification problems in Ireland. It conserves most of the content of the TCE, including the voting reforms and the charter of fundamental rights. In line with the TCE, it dismantles the pillar structure brought in under Maastricht and simplifies how power is shared in different policy areas between the EU and the member states. The Lisbon treaty also brings in a simplified procedure for making minor treaty changes, thereby avoiding approval and ratification procedures that could involve referendums in some member states. This procedure was used for the first time in 2011 to create the European Stability Mechanism (see Chapter 15, pp. 159–60). In addition, to secure Irish approval at a re-run referendum, it reinstated the principle (dropped in the original Lisbon text) that every member country has the right to nominate a member of the European Commission.

Part II

The institutions

Under the Treaty of Rome, four main institutions were established to give effect to its provisions. The following is a simple definition of their functions:

- The European Commission initiates policies and implements those already decided upon.
- The Council of Ministers (formally known as the Council of the European Union) decides or legislates, on the basis of proposals brought forward by the commission.
- The European Parliament started with a largely advisory role, but its powers have subsequently been increased and it is now a co-legislator with the Council of Ministers on the bulk of EU law-making.
- The European Court of Justice interprets the Union's decisions and the provisions of the treaty in the event of dispute.

The institutions continue their functions today under the Treaty on European Union (the Maastricht treaty) and the subsequent treaties of Amsterdam, Nice and Lisbon. Since the Maastricht treaty, the former European Community (EC) has become the European Union and has acquired additional powers that are not subject to the institutions of the EU, but are dealt with by member states on an intergovernmental basis. These include a common foreign and security policy (see Chapter 37) and certain aspects of cooperation over judicial, police and immigration issues (see Chapter 30).

Strictly speaking, the EU is now a hybrid organisation consisting of one part whose management and decision-taking are subject to EU procedures with their carefully defined division of powers between its constituent institutions, and an additional intergovernmental component. The first part is sometimes described as the supranational 'community method' of decision-taking in contrast to the intergovernmental approach where member states take their own decisions. A comparison of results in recent years shows that the community method has been more successful in reaching and implementing EU-wide agreements, although this may in part reflect the fact that the intergovernmental approach covers more sensitive policy issues and aspects. In any case, decision by consensus is harder with 28 members than with 6, 9 or even 15.

Part 2 of this book describes in some detail the principal EU institutions.

5   The Commission

The European Commission is the executive organ of the Union. It is often seen as the embodiment of the European idea as its members, although appointed by national governments, are under no obligation to them, and their total loyalty is pledged to the interests of the Community as a whole. Each commissioner, on assuming office, makes the following solemn declaration:

I solemnly undertake:

- to respect the Treaties and the Charter of Fundamental Rights of the European Union in the fulfilment of all my duties;
- to be completely independent in carrying out my responsibilities, in the general interest of the Union;
- in the performance of my tasks, neither to seek nor to take instructions from any Government or from any other institution, body, office or entity;
- to refrain from any action incompatible with my duties or the performance of my tasks.

I formally note the undertaking of each Member State to respect this principle and not to seek to influence Members of the Commission in the performance of their tasks.
I further undertake to respect, both during and after my term of office, the obligation arising therefrom, and in particular the duty to behave with integrity and discretion as regards the acceptance, after I have ceased to hold office, of certain appointments or benefits.

To the extent that the reality falls short of these aspirations, the commissioners will be failing in their allotted role, and the ability of the Union to achieve its purpose will be impaired.

The commissioners

The commission currently consists of 28 members, one from each member state. They are appointed for a five-year term by the Council of Ministers, on the nomination of their own national governments. The appointment of the commission as a whole is approved by the European Parliament. Until 1995 the term was only four years, and until 2004 the five largest member states were entitled to two commission members each. The term of office is renewable, and in the past at the end of each four- or five-year period typically about half of the commissioners have been reappointed, the remainder being replaced by new nominees. Most commissioners are politicians, usually from the governing party (or parties) in the member states. A minority of commissioners have been senior administrators, trade union leaders or businessmen.

The presidency

The president of the commission was originally appointed for a two-year term, although this was extended to four years, virtually automatically. Each commission term is identified by the name of its president; thus, the Delors Commission, the Barroso Commission or the Juncker Commission. The Maastricht treaty changed arrangements for appointing the commission. From January 1st 1995 the mandate of both the commission and the president was extended to five years. The governments of the member states were now required to consult the European Parliament before nominating the president of the commission. They must also consult the president-elect before nominating the other commissioners. The president and other members of the commission are then subject to approval, as a body, by a vote of the European Parliament. Prior to the vote, special parliamentary hearings are held to vet each prospective commissioner.

This procedure applied to the Santer commission, which resigned prematurely in March 1999 (see p. 31), as well as to the subsequent Prodi commission (1999–2004) and the two commissions headed by José Manuel Barroso (2004–09 and 2009–14). The appointment of Jean-Claude Juncker as commission president for 2014–19 was the first which required the European Council to 'take account of the results' of the elections for the European Parliament held in May 2014 which were won by Junckers's group, the centre-right European People's Party (see Chapter 3, pp. 48–9).

The crisis resignation of the Santer commission has helped subsequent presidents consolidate their power. Prodi was able to insist on the right to allocate portfolios and to change them round, if he chose, at a later stage. He also asked for, and obtained, assurances from each of the nominees for commissioner that they would resign, at his request, if he felt that this was in the interests of the EU. These acquired rights were exercised by Barroso and Juncker, who had extra legitimacy by dint of his party's victory in the European elections. In a new departure, and in a bid to strengthen further his power as president, Juncker nominated one of the seven vice-presidents, Frans Timmermans, a former Dutch socialist foreign minister, as his deputy and fixer. Rather than allotting him a specific policy area like the others, Juncker made Timmermans the first vice-president and gave him wide-ranging responsibilities for 'better regulation' and relations with other EU institutions.

With the Treaty of Nice, the larger member states lost their right to a second commissioner as of 2004. The treaty also stipulated that when EU membership got to 27 or more, it would no longer make sense for every member state automatically to nominate a commissioner. There would therefore be fewer commissioners than member countries. They would be appointed on a rotating basis with all states, large or small, taking it in turn to lose a commissioner for five years. However, the Lisbon treaty allows heads of government – acting unanimously – to vary the provisions made by Nice. So in the autumn of 2009 they agreed – as part of a stitch-up with the Irish government in advance of the second referendum on Irish ratification of Lisbon – to extend the system of one commissioner per member state at least until 2014. Thus, it was applied to the Juncker commission, whose mandate runs from November 2014 to October 2019 and which has 28 commissioners. The president would continue to be nominated by the European Council, but in future by qualified majority vote rather than by unanimity.

Responsibilities of commissioners

Commissioners are each allocated an area of responsibility under the treaty, and the relevant supporting staff from the commission's directorates-general (departments) will report directly to them (see Appendix 3 for the current distribution of responsibilities). They also have the assistance of a small cabinet (private office) of half a dozen personal appointees who not only act as advisers but also customarily intervene on their commissioner's behalf at all levels within the commission bureaucracy.

Responsibilities of the commission

Article 155 of the Rome treaty lists the responsibilities of the commission as covering initiative, implementation and supervision.

Initiative

The treaty gives a general responsibility to the commission to ensure that its provisions are carried out, but it also gives it the specific right of initiative to put proposals before the Council of Ministers, which in most circumstances is unable to make decisions in the absence of such a proposal.

Implementation

The commission is entrusted with the implementation of the decisions taken by the council. It also has substantial autonomous powers relating to competition policy and the running of the common agricultural policy. The commission administers the various funds established by the Union (the Agricultural Guidance and Guarantee Fund, Social Fund, Regional Development Fund, Cohesion Fund, and so on). It prepares a draft annual budget for the European Union which must be approved by the council and the European Parliament. It also negotiates international agreements on behalf of the Union, though these can only be concluded by the council.

Supervision

The commission supervises the implementation of EU law by the member states. In this role, the commission is sometimes called the 'guardian of the treaties'. Whenever it concludes that a member state has infringed its treaty obligations the commission is required to deliver an 'opinion' to this effect. In the event of non-compliance by the member state concerned, the commission can take the case to the Court of Justice for a ruling.

Location

The commission is based in Brussels, and occupies the Berlaymont building, a purpose-built glass-fronted edifice in the shape of a cross constructed in 1969 on the site of a former convent. In 1992 the Berlaymont was closed down for a major refit and extensive reconstruction work because of the health risk from the large amounts of asbestos used in the original structure. Decontamination and reconstruction work took until September 2004. Only a minority of commission staff can be accommodated in the building. The remaining staff are housed at more than 30 other locations in the city.

Staff

The commission employs about 24,000 people, one-third of whom are concerned with translating or interpreting between the 24 official languages of the Union (English, French, German, Italian, Dutch, Danish, Greek, Spanish, Portuguese, Swedish, Finnish, Czech, Slovak, Estonian, Latvian, Lithuanian, Maltese, Polish, Hungarian, Slovene, Romanian, Bulgarian, Irish and Croat). The total includes about 5,000 commission employees engaged in scientific research work at Ispra in Italy, Culham in the UK, Petten in the Netherlands, Geel in Belgium and other centres, or working for other EU agencies spread across the member states. The commission staff, part of which is based in Luxembourg, is organised in 44 directorates-general and services, each of which answers to one or more commissioners (see Appendix 4).

Working practices

The commission meets as a body every Wednesday. During sessions of the European Parliament in Strasbourg, the commission meetings take place there. Commission decisions are normally by simple majority vote, with the application of the principle of collective responsibility. Although all official documents are translated, and some meetings involving national officials may be simultaneously interpreted into all 24 languages, most day-to-day business within the commission is conducted in English (now the dominant working language) or French.

6 The Council of Ministers

If the commission as an institution represents the general European interest, the Council of Ministers (formally known as the Council of the
European Union) is where the interests of member states dominate. It is
the prime decision-maker and therefore the most powerful of the Community's organs. In the words of the Directorate-General for Research
of the European Parliament, 'It has now evolved into the actual centre of
political control in the European Union.'[1]

Structure

The council consists of ministers from each of the member states.
Its meetings are also attended by at least one commissioner as well
as by officials of its own secretariat. The council meets in different
formations, depending on the subject matter. Farm ministers meet
to make policy and take decisions on agriculture. Foreign ministers
take charge of external relations, and so on. The foreign ministers'
meeting, held at least once a month except in August, is also known
as the General Affairs Council. As well as discussing foreign policy
matters, foreign ministers exercise general coordination over the work
of the other ministerial councils and tackle particularly complicated
and/or urgent matters which do not readily fall within the scope of
more specialist colleagues. It is also their task to prepare the meetings
of the heads of government, known as the European Council (see
Chapter 7). These are held at least four times a year on a regular basis,
but when special or emergency sessions are added in the frequency
can be much higher.

The instruments of EU decision-taking are set out in Box 6.1. The
actual decision-taking process itself is set out in Figure 8.1 on p. 85.

Box 6.1 Decision-making in the European Union

There are five ways in which the EU institutions are able to change or influence the law in the member states. The Council of Ministers and/ or the commission (in a limited number of instances) are able to issue:

- regulations
- directives
- decisions
- recommendations
- opinions

Legislation, as normally understood, is undertaken through regulations and directives. Both are initiated by the commission and adopted by the Council of Ministers, in most cases nowadays under a co-decision procedure with the European Parliament and, when appropriate, after consulting the Economic and Social Committee and the Committee of the Regions. Regulations are binding in their entirety and directly applicable in all member states. Directives are binding on the member states as regards the result to be achieved, but leave the form and methods of achieving it to the discretion of the national authorities (most often by transposing the terms of the EU directive into national law).

Decisions by the council or the commission, derived from the authority bestowed by the Rome treaty or through regulations or directives already adopted, may be addressed to a government, an enterprise or an individual. They are binding in their entirety on those to whom they are addressed.

Recommendations and opinions are not legally binding. A sixth way in which national laws are affected is by case law resulting from decisions taken by the European Court of Justice, whose role is to interpret the Rome treaty and its secondary legislation for member states, and to adjudicate in disputes between the other institutions or between any of them and one or more member states (see Chapter 10).

The presidency

The council has a rotating chairmanship or presidency, with ministers from each member state taking turns for a six-month period in the chair. The foreign ministry of the country concerned undertakes, with the help of the council secretariat, the organisation of the council's business during the six months. Each semester is therefore known as the French presidency, the Dutch presidency, and so on, according to which nationality is in the chair. Under the Lisbon treaty, a permanent president has been appointed to head the European Council for a renewable term of 2.5 years. He chairs meetings of the European Council, coordinates with the different heads of government, and deals on their behalf with government leaders from outside countries. A second senior appointment under the Lisbon treaty is of a high representative for foreign affairs and security policy, who chairs meetings of the Foreign Affairs Council and acts as a vice-president of the commission. She is responsible for recruiting and running the European External Action Service (EEAS), which provides diplomatic representation throughout the world and manages the many aid projects provided by the EU – by far the world's largest public aid donor. The high representative is appointed for a term of five years. Other than the Foreign Affairs Council, the different specialist meetings of the council continue to be chaired by the country running the six-monthly presidency.

Part of the rotating presidency's duty is to strive to get agreement on as many issues as possible during its time in office. It is therefore expected to produce compromise proposals whenever there is deadlock and to cajole its own national representatives as well as those of other member states to modify their demands. The rota of the presidency was previously determined alphabetically, but from 1996 onwards a new order was agreed, primarily to ensure that the presidencies of the larger states were reasonably well spaced out, rather than being bunched together as they had been. The rota until 2020 is shown in Table 6.1. Holding the presidency

Table 6.1 Countries holding the presidency, 2010–20

	January–June	*July–December*
2010	Spain	Belgium
2011	Hungary	Poland
2012	Denmark	Cyprus
2013	Ireland	Lithuania
2014	Greece	Italy
2015	Latvia	Luxembourg
2016	Netherlands	Slovakia
2017	Malta	United Kingdom
2018	Estonia	Bulgaria
2019	Austria	Romania
2020	Finland	

Source: Council of Ministers.

places a heavy burden, particularly on smaller states with fewer diplomatic resources, but most of them have risen to the occasion. The new arrangements under the Lisbon treaty should somewhat reduce the burden on them, and – in practice – the smaller the member state, the more help it gets from the council's secretariat.

Permanent representatives

Few items reach the agenda of council meetings without having been previously discussed, usually exhaustively, at a lower level. Each member state maintains a large delegation in Brussels, known as its Permanent Representation. These are staffed not only by diplomats but also by officials from each of the domestic ministries that is liable to be affected by EU decisions. They are backed up by other officials in their home capitals who are deputed to liaise with them.

Coreper

The heads of delegations, the permanent representatives, who have the rank of senior ambassadors, meet at least once a week in the Committee of Permanent Representatives, known as 'Coreper', its French acronym. Coreper will work methodically through all the issues awaiting ministerial decision. If, on the basis of the instructions received from their national governments, the permanent representatives find themselves in complete agreement on a draft proposal it goes on the council agenda as an 'A' point. This means that, barring an unforeseen late change of heart by a member state, the council will adopt the item without further debate. More often the permanent representatives find that their viewpoints are still fairly wide apart, and the proposals are referred to lower-level expert groups for more detailed discussion. In most cases, it is only when all but one or two governments are in agreement that an issue is put on the Council of Ministers' agenda in the hope of getting a decision.

Other working groups

Even though the permanent representatives are highly versatile, they cannot possibly be experts on all the highly detailed topics which may appear on their agenda. A substantial range of subjects is entrusted to their deputies, who have a parallel weekly meeting, misleadingly known as Coreper I, while the permanent representatives' own meeting is called Coreper II. Agricultural issues are by tradition invariably dealt with by the Special Committee for Agriculture, consisting of senior officials of national ministries or of the agricultural councillors at the permanent representations. A large number of working groups staffed by less senior officials meet regularly to haggle over the details of virtually every proposal for Union legislation.

Legislative role

Unlike in a nation state, where the parliament enacts legislation, the legislative role in the EU is shared between the Council of Ministers and the European Parliament in the process known as co-decision (see p. 84). In its non-legislative role, the council decides on its own. Union legislation, in the form of directives or regulations (see p. 67), can only be initiated by the commission which submits its draft texts to the council and parliament for adoption. The non-binding opinions of the Economic and Social Committee are frequently required. As the adoption process advances, the draft law in question passes from council to parliament for successive readings. In the light of these, the commission can modify its draft text. If at the end of this process, the council and parliament still do not agree on the final text to be adopted, a conciliation procedure is foreseen.

Meetings

In its various formations, the council meets around 80–90 times a year, usually for one day, sometimes two and occasionally for longer. Often two or three council meetings take place simultaneously, with, for example, transport ministers in one chamber and finance ministers in another.

Making decisions

When a proposal actually reaches a council meeting, except as an 'A' point, it is by no means assured of being adopted. The Treaty of Rome laid down precise rules on decision-making within the council, but these have not always been applied in the manner originally intended. Under Article 148 of the treaty, decisions may be taken by a simple majority, by a qualified majority, or unanimously.

Simple majority decisions are restricted to minor matters, often of a purely procedural nature. Under the Rome treaty it was envisaged that most decisions would be reached by a qualified majority, leaving the unanimity rule for a limited number of issues of major national importance. During an initial transitional period, which was due to end in 1965, unanimity was prescribed for a much wider range of issues, but when the time for the change-over came, President Charles de Gaulle of France blocked it, causing a major crisis with the other five original members of the EEC (see p. 12).

The Luxembourg compromise

As a result of this crisis, the five members reluctantly acquiesced in the so-called 'Luxembourg compromise' to ensure continued French membership of the Community. The key sentence says:

> Where, in the case of decisions which may be taken by a majority vote on a proposal from the commission, very important interests of one or more partners are at stake, the Members of the Council will endeavour, within a reasonable time, to reach solutions which can be adopted by all the Members of the Council while respecting their mutual interests and those of the Community, in accordance with Article 2 of the Treaty.

If member states had subsequently stuck to the terms of the 'compromise', with its specific reference to 'very important interests', it would have had limited impact on the decision-making process. In reality, however, the council chose to interpret the notion very broadly, showing extreme reluctance to bring any issue to a vote, and thereby effectively extending the unanimity rule to a wide range of decisions which could not conceivably involve the 'very important interests' of a member state. Accordingly, the Luxembourg compromise has seldom been formally invoked. One occasion was in May 1982 when the UK government attempted to block a farm price settlement for purely tactical reasons related to a quite different issue (the UK budget dispute). The other members rejected the UK claim and proceeded to approve each of the 20-odd draft regulations involved in the settlement by qualified majority voting.

Amendments under the Single European Act

After that there was a growing feeling, shared by the French government, that qualified majority voting should be used more often. Although the Luxembourg compromise, which had no legal force, still stands, the Single European Act, which came into force in July 1987, amended the Treaty of Rome to reduce the number of issues on which unanimity was required. In particular, qualified majority voting was authorised for most of the 300 or so measures which had to be adopted to complete the 1992 single market programme on time. The Maastricht treaty also extended qualified majority voting to include new sectors like transport and the environment. The list was further extended by the Amsterdam (1999) and Nice (2003) treaties. As a result it became increasingly harder in the areas concerned for proposals to be held up for years because one or two member states objected to them. Under the Lisbon treaty, qualified majority voting has been extended even further so that the unanimity rule now applies only in a limited number of sensitive areas such as foreign and defence policy, taxation and institutional changes.

Decisions are taken

Given the complexities of EU voting procedures, it is hard to see, even with more majority voting, how any decisions are made at all, given the difficulty of persuading 28 nation states to sink their differences. In fact many decisions are taken on a horse-trading basis, with governments giving way on particular points which are not of primary importance to them ('would like' rather than 'must have') in exchange for similar concessions from other member states on often unrelated issues.

Allocation of votes

Under the qualified majority system, the member states were allocated votes roughly in proportion to their size. The share-out has been adapted with each successive enlargement. Prior to the welcome simplification under the Lisbon treaty, the previous allocation gave Germany, France, Italy and the UK 29 votes each, with votes for others on a descending scale down to three votes for Malta (see Table 6.2). Lisbon replaced the complex, ever-changing numbers game with a double-majority formula. To secure a qualified majority a proposal needs the support of at least 55 per cent of the member states, representing at least 65 per cent of the total EU population. This provision took effect in 2014.

Other council responsibilities

Besides adopting EU legislation together, the council has joint responsibility with the European Parliament to adopt the annual EU budget. It also has the power of appointment to the other institutions, such as the Economic and Social Committee and the Court of Auditors. The multifarious nature of its activities has been well summarised by a former British permanent representative, Sir Michael Butler, who wrote:[2]

> In one sense, Coreper and the council together are a forum for a permanent negotiation between member governments on a wide range of issues simultaneously. In another, they are the legislature of the Community. In a third, they are the senior board of directors taking many of the day-to-day decisions on its policies.

Table 6.2 The weighting of votes under the Nice treaty

Members of the Council	Weighted votes	Members of the Council	Weighted votes
France	29	Austria	10
Germany	29	Bulgaria	10
Italy	29	Sweden	10
United Kingdom	29	Denmark	7
Poland	27	Finland	7
Spain	27	Ireland	7
Romania	14	Lithuania	7
Netherlands	13	Slovakia	7
Belgium	12	Cyprus	4
Czech Republic	12	Estonia	4
Greece	12	Latvia	4
Hungary	12	Luxembourg	4
Portugal	12	Slovenia	4
		Malta	3
Total EU-27	**345**		

Note: Acts of the council shall require for their adoption at least 258 votes in favour, cast by a majority of members, where this treaty requires them to be adopted on a proposal from the commission. In other cases, for their adoption acts of the council shall require at least 258 votes in favour cast by at least two thirds of the members. When a decision is to be adopted by the council by a qualified majority, a member of the council may request verification that the member states constituting the qualified majority represent at least 62 per cent of the total population of the Union. If that condition in shown not to have been met, the decision in question shall not be adopted.

Subsidiarity and enhanced cooperation

These are two mechanisms for easing the log-jam of pending EU legislation awaiting adoption, or blocked by differences among member states. They work in different ways.

Subsidiarity acts by removing minor legislation from EU responsibility. It is the principle whereby the EU does not take action (except in the areas where it has exclusive competence), unless its joint action is more effective than action taken at national or local level. The principle of subsidiarity is defined in Article 5 of the Treaty on European Union, and two protocols in the Lisbon treaty.

Enhanced cooperation, on the other hand, allows a group of like-minded EU countries to move ahead of their partners in a specific area, provided the non-participating partners agree to this procedure. The Lisbon treaty sets the minimum threshold for establishing enhanced cooperation at nine member states. Other member states can join the enhanced cooperation group at a later stage. Enhanced cooperation must contribute to enhancing the process of integration within the Union and must not undermine the single market or the Union's economic and social cohesion. The enhanced procedure has been sparingly used. The Council of Ministers adopted a decision on January 22nd 2013, authorising 11 member states to go ahead with their requested enhanced cooperation on the adoption of a financial transactions tax (the so-called Tobin tax). The issue had deeply divided member states within the council, with no prospect of agreement at that level.

Location

The council and its secretariat are located in the Justus Lipsius building in Brussels, a vast, granite-clad mausoleum facing the Berlaymont across the street. It was opened in 1995. During three months of the year (April, June and October), however, it meets in Luxembourg. This is a legacy from the merger of the three Communities in 1965, one of which – the ECSC – had been based in Luxembourg.

Notes

1 Fact Sheet 1/B/2, European Parliament, Directorate-General for Research, 1987.
2 Michael Butler, *Europe: More than a Continent*, Heinemann, London, 1986, Page 30.

7   The European Council

The Treaty of Rome made no provision for meetings of the heads of government of the member states, and during the first ten years of the EEC they met only three times. Yet it gradually became clear that a more regular exchange of views was necessary to give a sense of strategic direction to the Community and to resolve problems to which the Council of Ministers and the European Commission had not been able to find solutions through the EC's normal processes.

Inauguration

In December 1974 a summit meeting in Paris formally decided that the heads of government should meet three times each year under the title of the European Council. Starting in Dublin in March 1975, the European Council duly met on this basis until December 1985, when it was reduced to two meetings a year. However, since 1990, when two additional 'emergency' summits were held, it has been accepted that there may, in fact, be three, four or even more meetings of the European Council each year. These meetings took place in the member state currently holding the presidency of the Council of Ministers, with its prime minister (or, in the case of France, its president) taking the chair. Under the Treaty of Nice, all normal meetings of the European Council have been held in Brussels since 2004.

Status

The Single European Act, adopted in December 1985, gave legal recognition to the European Council without, however, defining its powers. In fact it has the same status as an ordinary meeting of the Council of Ministers, although it has usually avoided giving formal effect to the decisions it has taken, leaving it to a subsequent meeting of foreign ministers to adopt them on a 'rubber stamp' basis. Indeed, a major purpose of the European Council is to remain informal. Their meetings take place without the presence of national officials, the heads of government sitting round the table, accompanied only by their foreign ministers, while the president of the commission is supported only by one vice-president. The more sensitive discussions normally take place in the intervals between the actual sessions (which are spread over two days), particularly during and after dinner on the evening of the first day when most if not all of the heads of government speak in English and simultaneous interpretation is dispensed with.

Increasing influence

The European Council has, to a large extent, replaced the commission as the motor of the Community. This was especially notable during the period 1974–81, when president Valéry Giscard d'Estaing and chancellor Helmut Schmidt cooperated closely to play a leadership role. Their joint departure within a few months heralded the beginning of a period of 2–3 years in which few significant decisions were taken by the European Council. The deadlock was broken at Fontainebleau in June 1984 when, at the initiative of president François Mitterrand, a solution was finally found to the UK budget problem (see pp. 18–20) which had plagued the Community for several years, and the way was cleared for the entry of Spain and Portugal.

Since then the go-ahead for other major new Community initiatives have come from the European Council. These include the launch of the 1992 Single Market programme, the acceptance of a united Germany within the EC, the convening of intergovernmental conferences on economic and monetary union and on political union, and the decision to negotiate membership with the countries of central and eastern Europe. The European Council also agreed the Single European Act at Luxembourg in December 1985, the Treaty on European Union at Maastricht in December 1991, the Treaty of Amsterdam in June 1997, the Treaty of Nice in December 2000, and the Treaty establishing a Constitution for Europe at Thessalonica in June 2004. The Lisbon treaty itself was similarly agreed at a meeting in the Portuguese capital in October 2007. More recently, it met on innumerable occasions on the euro crisis, the refugee influx or over the tensions with Russia. Such major and often difficult issues can only be resolved at a summit, as only the heads of government have the authority and political clout not only to impose unwelcome decisions but also to reconcile them with political forces and pressure groups in their home countries.

Decision-making on minor issues held up

On the debit side, however, is the undoubted fact that the existence of regular summit meetings actually slows down decision-making on many less far-reaching issues which would otherwise be resolved at a lower level. Time and again the heads of government have been called upon to discuss technical matters on which their subordinates have failed to agree because they were unwilling to take the responsibility. The European Council ought not to have to act as a final court of appeal, except on issues of the first importance, but it seems condemned to do so.

Under the Lisbon treaty, the European Council now has a permanent president, elected by its members for a renewable term of two and a half years, to preside over its meetings and coordinate its work. It was implicitly assumed that the candidate would be a current or former prime minister, and the person chosen to be the first occupant of the post, at a special meeting of the European Council on November 19th 2009, was the Belgian prime minister, Herman Van Rompuy. He was replaced in 2014 by Donald Tusk from Poland, another serving premier.

8   The European Parliament

The European Parliament has come a long way. Its initial mission was to bring a measure of democratic control and accountability to the other institutions of the EC. Like parliaments down the ages, it has had to fight for its rights. It is not the sole, or even primary, legislative power in the EU. It shares this function with the more powerful Council of Ministers. But is has other areas of authority, including the right to sack the European Commission through a vote of censure. Although for some critics it still has the reputation of a talking shop, and of a repository for free-loading political has-beens, those seeking evidence of the parliament's legislative clout need only observe the swarms of lobbyists representing business interests from around the world who descend on Strasbourg when parliament is sitting.

The European Parliament is the successor to the Assembly of the ECSC, which was set up in Strasbourg as a purely advisory body in September 1952. It had 78 members, all of them members of national parliaments who had been deputed to attend the Assembly as an ancillary duty to their main functions. It shared the premises of the already-established parliamentary assembly of the Council of Europe. The Assembly was expanded to 142 members in 1958, when its competences were extended to the EEC and Euratom, which merged with the ECSC seven years later. Parliament's membership was increased to 198 in 1973, when Denmark, Ireland and the UK joined, and its powers (particularly in the budgetary field) were modestly increased under treaties signed in Luxembourg in April 1970 and in Brussels in July 1975.

Direct elections since 1979

Much more significant than anything previous were the first direct elections to the parliament in June 1979 when 410 members of an enlarged parliament were elected, during a 4-day period, from 9 member states.

In the second direct elections in June 1984, 434 members were returned from 10 member states: 81 each from France, West Germany, Italy and the UK, 25 from the Netherlands, 24 from Belgium and Greece, 16 from Denmark, 15 from Ireland and 6 from Luxembourg. They were later joined by 60 Spanish and 24 Portuguese members. Yet this much larger parliament of 518 full-time members directly elected by over 100 million voters was given no greater formal power than the previous appointed Assembly of part-timers. Later, membership rose to 626, including 59 members from Austria, Finland and Sweden who joined in 1995. In 2004 the membership rose to 732, with the entry of 10 more countries. It went up again in the 2009 vote after the entry of Romania and Bulgaria 2 years earlier to 754. Following Croatia's entry, the number of seats at the 2014 election was adjusted slightly to 751.

Euro-MPs

Members of the European Parliament (MEPs) are elected for fixed five-year terms. The next election is due in June 2019. Under Article 138 of the Rome treaty, there should be a common electoral system in all member states. The parliament itself proposed one in 1982 and again in 1993. However, the Council of Ministers was unable to agree to this, largely because the then UK government was reluctant to abandon its first-past-the-post system in favour of proportional representation (PR). Thus the first four direct elections were held with different systems applying in the member states, although all except the UK used variations of PR. The Labour government elected in the UK in May 1997 agreed that the UK, too, would adopt PR for the next Euro-elections in June 1999. Thus, although these elections were held under 15 different systems, all MEPs were for the first time chosen by proportional representation, mostly based on the d'Hondt system. This has continued to be the case in subsequent elections.

Salaries

MEPs were previously paid the same salary as MPs in their home countries which meant they varied widely. Since July 2009, however, all MEPs have been eligible to receive the same salary. It is fixed at 38.5 per cent of the salary of a judge at the European Court of Justice. In 2015, this amounted to €8,020 per month before tax and €6,250 after tax. MEPs elected before 2009 have the option of being paid under the previous system, but few have chosen to do so. There are also generous tax-free travel, attendance, research and secretarial allowances which are paid on the same basis to all members.

Political groups

MEPs do not sit in national delegations, nor as representatives of national parties, but in cross-national political groups. After the 2014 election there were seven of these, with 52 members choosing to remain non-affiliated, as shown in Table 8.1. The two largest groups combined can command 55 per cent of MEPs and, when they work together can dominate the proceedings. The European People's Party comprises Christian Democrat and Centre Right parties from all the 28 member states bar the UK. The British Conservatives used to belong to this group, but in a highly controversial move, split off in 2009 to form their own Eurosceptic group, the European Conservatives and Reformists (ECR). The Socialists & Democrats group, comprising Labour, Socialist and Social Democratic parties, is the only group with members from all 28 countries.

Compared with the previous elections in 2009, the ECR (whose biggest components are the UK Conservatives and Poland's Law and Justice Party) and the even more Europhobic group, the Europe of Freedom and Direct Democracy (EFDD), did well in the 2014 vote. The EFDD includes the United Kingdom Independence Party (UKIP) which wants Britain out of the EU altogether. The ECR beat the Alliance of Liberals and Democrats, which includes the British Liberal Democrats, into third place. On the left, the European United Left allied with the Nordic Green Left group made significant progress.

Table 8.1 Political groups in the European Parliament (2014–19 legislature)

Election results	Number of seats	
	2014	(2009)
European People's Party (Christian Democrats) (EPP)	221	(265)
Socialists & Democrats (S&D)	191	(184)
European Conservatives and Reformists (ECR)	70	(54)
Alliance of Liberals and Democrats for Europe (ALDE)	67	(84)
European United Left/Nordic Green Left Group (EUL/NGL)	52	(35)
Greens/European Free Alliance (EFA)	50	(55)
Europe of Freedom and Direct Democracy (EFDD)	48	(32)
Independents (non-affiliated) (NI)	52	(27)
Total	751	(736)

Voter turnout at the 2014 election: 42.61 per cent.

Source: European Parliament.

France's right-wing Front National, which came first in the 2014 European elections in France winning 21 seats, started the new legislature among the non-affiliated MEPs. It could not meet the criteria to create a formal group (a minimum of 25 MEPs from at least seven member states). Then in June 2015, the leader of the Front National, Marine Le Pen, announced that the party had created a new group, the Europe of Nations and Freedom (ENF), with 39 MEPs from eight different countries. Formal group status means members can head parliamentary committees and delegations, while the group as such is entitled to operating subsidies from the parliament's budget. Their departure reduced the number of non-affiliated independent members to 13.

The strong Green representation in the parliament remains split between two groups: the Green/European Free Alliance Group, who are allied with home rule or separatist groups, including the Scottish National Party and Plaid Cymru of Wales, and the Confederal Group of the United European Left/Nordic Green Left, a more avowedly left-wing group. (For a more detailed breakdown of group membership see Appendix 6.) Voting in the European Parliament is less subject to party discipline than in most national parliaments and *ad hoc* coalitions are often formed on issues that cross normal ideological and national barriers. There is, accordingly, often some uncertainty about how the parliament may vote on a particular issue.

Falling voter turn-out

Since 1979 the European Parliament has been elected simultaneously in all the member states. The legislature runs for five years, with no provision for early dissolution. Voter turnout, which started at 61.99 per cent in 1979, has fallen at each successive election although it has stabilised for 2009 (42.97 per cent) and 2014 (42.61 per cent). Eight elections have been held:

1 The 1979 election was held in nine member states on June 7th–10th 1979 for a total of 410 seats. Greece, which joined the Community on January 1st 1981, subsequently elected 24 members on October 18th 1981.
2 The 1984 election was held in ten member states, on June 14th–17th. Spain and Portugal, which joined the EC on January 1st 1986, subsequently elected 60 and 24 members respectively, on June 10th and July 19th 1987.
3 The third election, for a 518-seat chamber, was held on June 15th–18th 1989.

4   The fourth election, for an enlarged house of 567 members, took place on June 9th–12th 1994. Separate elections were held during 1995 and 1996 to elect a further 59 members from the new member states of Austria, Finland and Sweden, bringing total membership to 626.

5   The fifth election, also for a 626-member house, was held in all member states on June 10th–13th 1999.

6   The sixth election, for a house of 732 members, took place on June 10th–13th 2005.

7   The seventh election, this time for 736 members, was held on June 4th–7th 2009. An additional 18 'observers' were elected who were

Table 8.2 European Parliament elections, 2014

Country	Seats	Voting method
Austria	18	PR, national lists
Belgium	21	PR, regional lists
Bulgaria	17	PR, national lists
Croatia	11	PR regional lists
Cyprus	6	PR, national lists
Czech Republic	21	PR, national lists
Denmark	13	PR, national lists
Estonia	6	PR, national lists
Finland	13	PR, national lists
France	74	PR, national lists
Germany	96	PR, regional lists
Greece	21	PR, national lists
Hungary	21	PR, national lists
Ireland	11	PR, single transferable vote
Italy	73	PR, regional lists
Latvia	8	PR, national lists
Lithuania	11	PR, national lists
Luxembourg	6	PR, national lists
Malta	6	PR, national lists
Netherlands	26	PR, national lists
Poland	51	PR, regional lists
Portugal	21	PR, national lists
Romania	32	PR, national lists
Slovakia	13	PR, national lists
Slovenia	8	PR, national lists
Spain	54	PR, regional lists
Sweden	20	PR, national lists
United Kingdom	73	PR, regional lists
(of which: Northern Ireland	3	*PR, single transferable vote)*

Source: European Parliament.

only eligible to take their seats once the Lisbon treaty came into force. Their addition took the total membership of the parliament to 754.

8   The electoral systems used in 2014, and the breakdown of the 751 members by country, are shown in Table 8.2.

Powers of the European Parliament

The European Parliament has supervisory powers over the commission and the council (including the right to censure the commission), the right to participate in the EU legislative process along with the Council of Ministers, and budgetary powers.

Supervisory powers

Defined by the Treaty of Rome, these include the right to put questions to the commission and the Council of Ministers. Parliament debates the Commission's Annual General Report and discharges the annual EU budget. The Parliament can adopt a motion of censure which would lead to the resignation of the commission as a body. Questions to the Council of Ministers are answered by ministers from the country currently holding the rotating presidency, who attend each plenary session of the parliament for this purpose. In addition the prime minister of this country makes a personal report to the parliament after each meeting of the European Council. The commission also submits its annual programme of work in advance to the parliament, as well as its annual report, which can only be used as the basis for retrospective checks.

Parliament's power to dismiss the commission remained for many years a theoretical threat. The motion of censure needed a two-thirds majority of the votes cast, representing a majority of MEPs. It is not possible to censure an individual commissioner – a lesser, but perhaps more effective sanction. In practice MEPs regarded its power of censure as a nuclear deterrent or ultimate threat. Yet in March 1999 they rolled it out. Angered by its inability to secure the dismissal of Edith Cresson, a French commissioner accused of nepotism and other shortcomings, a large majority of its members got ready to vote to dismiss the whole commission. Sensing the inevitable, the entire Santer Commission resigned, prompting a major crisis (see pp. 62–3). One effect was undoubtedly to raise the profile of the Parliament and make the Council of Ministers and the commission more wary of direct confrontation. Similarly, in November 2004, the imminent threat of the parliament's refusal to endorse the Barroso commission forced the replacement of two potential commissioners to whom the parliament objected (see pp. 34–5). The Maastricht treaty authorised the parliament to appoint a European ombudsman to consider complaints of maladministration by the EC institutions (other than the Court of Justice). The ombudsman can receive complaints from any citizen of the Union or any natural person residing in a member state or legal person (that is, a company or organisation) having its registered office there. Initially, he received about 1,000 complaints each year, but only about one-quarter of these were admissible as the others did not fall within the jurisdiction of EU institutions. The number of complaints has since increased by around 10 per cent a year. The present ombudsman is Emily O'Reilly, a former broadcaster and journalist, and previously the Irish national ombudsman. Her five-year mandate began in December 2014.

Legislative role

Under the original Rome treaty, the Council of Ministers adopted EEC legislative acts in all key policy areas. During this process, it had to consult the European Parliament in certain cases. But the council had no need to heed its opinions on draft regulations and directives submitted by the commission to the council for adoption, although it sometimes did incorporate amendments proposed by the parliament where these had the support of the commission. The legislative role of the parliament was significantly strengthened by the Single European Act of 1987 and, especially, by the Maastricht treaty, which took effect in November 1993. Maastricht introduced the principle of co-decision between the council and the parliament, initially on a limited basis, but the scope of policy areas covered by co-decision, where the council and the parliament have an equal role, was extended by the Treaties of Amsterdam (1999) and Lisbon (2009). The Lisbon treaty renames it the 'ordinary legislative procedure'. It covers the full range of EU policies – from agriculture to transport including the environment, internal market, regional support, social and consumer policy, security and justice, and trade. There are a few notable exceptions: Parliament has the right to approve or reject international treaties negotiated by the EU, but it cannot amend them. Its role remains consultative in matters like managing the single currency, taxation and foreign and defence policy.

The flow-chart in Figure 8.1 sets out the procedure under co-decision for parallel readings of draft legislation by the council and parliament, indicating the different points at which the legislation may be adopted. Essentially, it provides for two readings each by parliament and council of a draft law. If the two do not agree at the end of this stage, the conciliation procedure begins.

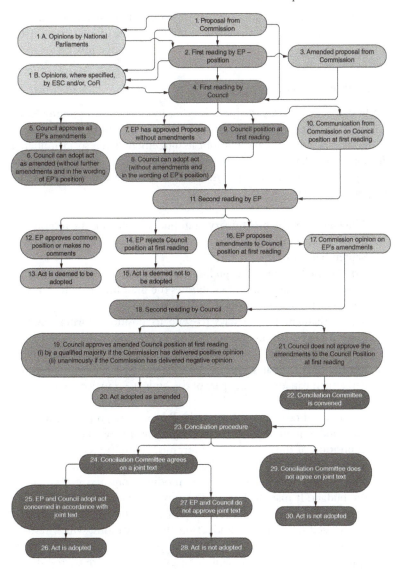

Figure 8.1 The decision-taking process

The Maastricht treaty gave the parliament a new right of initiative, whereby it may, by a majority vote, require the commission to propose action in any area. The parliament may, at the request of a quarter of its members, set up a temporary committee to examine allegations of infringement or bad administration of Community law, unless the matter is *sub judice*. Despite the cumulative impact of the changes described in this section, the parliament still falls somewhat short of being a full partner with the Council of Ministers in the EU legislative process.

Budgetary powers

On budgetary matters, parliament is officially designated as jointly forming the budgetary authority with the Council of Ministers. No annual EU budget may be adopted without its agreement. Even so, its influence, although considerable, is clearly less than that of the council, as a brief description of the process will make clear. There are five stages in the budgetary process:

1   The tabling of the preliminary draft budget, which is the responsibility of the commission. This is laid before the Council of Ministers by September 1st of the previous year.

2   The council amends the preliminary draft, invariably reducing the expenditure proposed, and establishes the draft budget, which is submitted to the parliament by October 5th.

3   The parliament has 45 days to state its position, during which it may propose amendments or modifications. Before the Lisbon treaty it could not amend the so-called compulsory part of the budget, notably agricultural spending. Lisbon removed this restriction and parliament can amend any part of the budget – a major increase in its powers.

4   The council takes a decision on the Parliament's proposed modifications and amendments. If the parliament insists on them against the opposition of the council, a compromise has to be reached between the two institutions by means of the conciliation procedure.

5   The parliament may amend these modifications and it then adopts the budget. It may decline to do so by a two-thirds majority of the votes cast, representing a majority of all members. The parliament has refused to adopt the budget on three occasions, which resulted in the EU entering a new calendar year without a budget being approved. When this happens, total expenditure is restricted during each month to one twelfth of the total budget for the previous year. On each of these occasions the parliament subsequently adopted a revised draft which differed only marginally from the budget it had originally rejected. On the whole, it has enjoyed more success when it has used the established conciliation procedures and has played off one member state against another in the Council of Ministers than when it has gone for outright rejection. Every year, however, there is

a struggle of wills between the council and parliament, with the latter invariably wanting a larger budget and one less heavily committed to agriculture.

Location

The member states have not yet fulfilled their treaty obligation to establish a single seat for the parliament, and its effectiveness is undermined by the geographical fragmentation of its work. The monthly plenary sessions are held in Strasbourg (with additional sittings in Brussels). Most committees meet in Brussels, while a large part of its secretariat is based in Luxembourg. This, plus the fact that it needs to conduct its business in 24 different languages with simultaneous interpretation, and the requirement that documents shall be translated into all languages, greatly increases the cost of running the institution, whose budget for 2015 amounted to €1.79 billion, or just over €3.5 per EU resident. Most MEPs would undoubtedly prefer Brussels as the sole location, but the Luxembourg and French governments vehemently oppose this and have prevented a decision on a permanent seat from being taken. Under the treaties this would need to be unanimous. A protocol to the 1997 Amsterdam treaty confirmed that 12 plenary sessions per year, including the budget session, will continue to be held in Strasbourg, that additional plenary sessions and committee meetings will be in Brussels and that the secretariat will remain in Luxembourg.

Sessions

The parliament normally meets in plenary session for one week in each calendar month except August, with additional part sessions in March and October devoted respectively to farm prices and the annual budget. Much of its work, however, takes place in committees, of which there are currently 22, and a rather larger number of subcommittees. These usually meet during two other weeks each month, leaving at least one week free for MEPs to devote to party or constituency activities.

9 The Economic and Social Committee and the Committee of the Regions

A purely advisory body, the Economic and Social Committee (ESC) must be consulted by the European Commission and the Council of Ministers over a wide range of issues. The Treaty of Rome specifies a number of areas where consultation is mandatory before directives and regulations may be approved, but the council and the commission customarily consult the ESC over many other issues. In general, there is little hindrance to the ESC offering opinions on any subject on which its members may wish to pronounce. Its opinions are non-binding.

Membership

The members of the ESC represent civil society interest groups from all EU countries. The committee provides them with a useful sounding board whenever legislation that concerns them is being prepared. The members are divided into three groups:

- Group I representing employers;
- Group II representing workers;
- Group III representing various interests such as consumers, farmers, the self-employed, academics, and so on.

Members are appointed by the Council of Ministers on the nomination of their governments, which normally consult with the interest groups most concerned (particularly the trade unions and employers' organisations) before choosing their nominees. The current membership is 350, consisting of 24 each from France, Germany, Italy and the UK, 21 each from Spain and Poland, 15 from Romania, 12 each from Austria, Belgium, Bulgaria, the Czech Republic, Greece, Hungary, the Netherlands, Portugal and Sweden, 9 each from Denmark, Finland,

Ireland, Lithuania, Slovakia and Croatia, 7 each from Latvia and Slovenia, 6 from Estonia and 5 each from Cyprus, Luxembourg, and Malta. The members are appointed for a renewable term of five years; the current term of office ends in September 2020. The ESC elects its own chairman, who serves for 2.5 years, and it is customary to rotate the chairmanship between the three groups. Economic and Social Committee members are part-timers, who take time off from their normal jobs.

Location and working practices

The headquarters of the ESC is in Brussels, where it meets every month. Its detailed work is, however, undertaken in specialist sections (currently six), which draft opinions for approval by the ESC meeting in plenary session. The sections are:

- Agriculture, rural development and the environment
- Economic and monetary union and economic and social cohesion
- Employment, social affairs and citizenship
- External relations
- Single market, production and consumption.
- Transport, energy, infrastructure and information society

On issues like the right of workers to be consulted or to participate in management, the ESC normally splits on left–right lines, with the members of Groups I and II on opposing sides. In these circumstances, the members of Group III are left with the casting votes. More often than not they have come down predominantly on the trade union rather than the employers' side. On most questions considered by the ESC, however, divisions occur within each group rather than between them. The influence of the ESC is in any event seldom significant on controversial political matters. Where it can, and does, influence the content of Community legislation is on more technical issues, where the expertise of its members is often brought to bear.

Committee of the Regions

A similar consultative body, the Committee of the Regions was set up under the Maastricht treaty, and met for the first time in March 1994. It provides sub-national authorities (i.e. regions, counties, provinces, municipalities and cities) with a voice within the EU institutional context on the many issues which concern them directly. In particular, it must be consulted on six policy areas:

- Citizenship, governance, institutional and external affairs
- Territorial cohesion policy
- Economic and social policy
- Environment, climate change and energy
- Natural resources and agriculture
- Culture, education and research

Like the ESC, it has 350 members appointed for a five-year renewable term. The national membership quotas are the same as for the ESC. The committee is based in Brussels.

10 The European Court of Justice

The task of ensuring that EU law is applied in all member states in accordance with the provisions of the treaties is entrusted to the European Court of Justice (ECJ),[1] based in Luxembourg. As the scope of EU law has grown and as its case load has expanded, the ECJ has been structured into three courts. The first and senior court is the European Court of Justice itself. The second is the General Court (initially known as the Court of First Instance). This was set up under the 1987 Single European Act to take over more routine cases to ease the ECJ's workload. The third court, the EU Civil Service Tribunal, was set up in 2005 to rule on disputes between EU civil servants and the institutions who employ them. This function was previously the responsibility of the General Court.

Composition

The ECJ itself consists of 28 judges (one from each member state) and 11 advocates-general. The judges are chosen by the Council of Ministers, on the nomination of member states, 'from persons whose independence is beyond doubt and who possess the qualifications required for appointment to the highest judicial offices in their respective countries or who are Juriconsultants of recognised competence' (Article 167 of the Treaty of Rome). They are appointed for a renewable term of six years, half the court being renewed every three years. The advocates-general are appointed on the same basis. The judges select one of their number to be president of the court for a renewable term of three years. For more important cases, and invariably in cases brought by a member state or a Community institution, the court sits as a single body. Other cases are assigned to chambers set up within the court: there are currently six such chambers. At any stage a chamber may refer a case to the full court if it considers that it raises points of law requiring definitive rulings.

Jurisdiction

In general six types of cases come before the ECJ or its chambers:

- disputes between member states;
- disputes between the EU and member states;
- disputes between the institutions;
- disputes between individuals, or corporate bodies, and the EU (including staff cases); these types of case are now handled by the General Court and the Civil Service Tribunal;
- opinions on international agreements;
- preliminary rulings on cases referred by national courts.

The last type of case is of crucial importance for ensuring that EU law is uniformly applied in all member states. It also illustrates an essential difference between the European Court of Justice and the US Supreme Court, with which it is often compared. Both courts are supreme in the sense that there is no appeal against their decisions. But the US court is at the apex of a structure of federal, state and district courts, all of whose rulings may be appealed upwards to it. The Court of Justice is, by contrast, the only EU court, with no hierarchical relationship to the lower courts, all of which form part of one of 28 different legal systems. When a case comes before a national court involving EU law, which takes precedence over national laws, the national court can seek on the issue involved a preliminary ruling from the ECJ, which the judges in the national court must then apply when giving their own judgments. In the application and interpretation of purely national laws, which make up the great bulk of cases in other courts, the European Court of Justice has no jurisdiction whatever.

Court procedure

Proceedings before the court may be initiated by a member state, an EU institution (most often the commission) or by a corporate body or individual (providing he or she has a direct personal interest in the subject of the case). The court procedure involves two separate stages, one written and one oral. In the first stage, on receipt of a written application from a plaintiff, the court establishes that it falls within its jurisdiction and that it has been lodged within the time limitations determined by the treaties. The application is then served on the opposing party, which normally has one month in which to lodge a statement of defence. The applicant has a further month to table a reply, and the defendant one more month for a rejoinder.

Each case is supervised by a judge-rapporteur, who is appointed by the president. On receipt of all the documents the judge-rapporteur presents a preliminary report to the court, which decides whether a preparatory enquiry (involving the appearance of the parties, requests for further documents, oral testimony, and so on) is necessary, and whether the case shall be heard by the full court or be assigned to one of the chambers. The president then sets the date for the public hearing, at which the two sides appear before the judges, present their arguments and call evidence if they so wish. The judges and the advocate-general (whose role is somewhat similar to that of the examining magistrate in French courts) put to the parties any questions they think fit. The advocate-general gives their opinion some weeks later, at a further hearing, analysing the facts and the legal aspects in detail and proposing a solution to the dispute.

The advocate-general's opinion often gives a clear indication of which way the judgment will go, but this is not invariably the case. The judges consider their ruling in private, on the basis of a draft prepared by the judge-rapporteur. If, during their deliberations, they require additional information they may reopen the procedure and ask the parties for further explanation, oral or written, or order further enquiries. The judgments of the court are reached by majority vote. Dissenting opinions are not published. Where the court is equally divided the vote of the most junior judge is disregarded, although in most cases it is arranged that an uneven number of judges will be sitting (the quorum for the full court is seven). The judgment is given at a public hearing, which, on average, occurs some 18 months after the receipt of an application.

Case load

The case load of the court has built up steadily since its foundation in 1952. Judgments had been delivered in more than 10,000 cases by the end of 2014. Table 10.1 gives a detailed breakdown by subject matter of the cases heard in 2014.

For many years, given its importance and complexity, cases involving the common agricultural policy were the most frequent. But following significant reforms and simplification of the CAP these fell dramatically, and issues concerning the environment, taxation, freedom of movement, intellectual property rights and the area of freedom, security and justice now predominate. In earlier years a large number of cases had concerned complaints brought by employees of the different EU institutions on such matters as recruitment, salaries, promotion, disciplinary procedures, and so on, which under national administrations would go

Table 10.1 Court of Justice: 2014 cases analysed by subject matter

	Reference for a preliminary ruling	Direct actions	Appeals	Requests for an opinion	Total	Special forms of procedure
Access to documents			1		1	
External action by the European Union	2				2	
Agriculture	9	1	3		13	
State aid	11	6	15		32	
Citizenship of the Union	7	1	1		9	
Economic, social and territorial cohesion			1		1	
Competition	8		15		23	
Financial provisions (budget, financial framework, own resources, combating fraud and so forth)	4				4	
Law governing the institutions	2	12	11		25	2
Education, vocational training, youth and sport			1		1	
Employment			1		1	
Energy		4			4	
Registration, evaluation, authorisation and restriction of chemicals (REACH regulation)	2				2	
Environment	22	15	4		41	
Area of freedom, security and justice	49	3	1		53	
Taxation	54	3			57	
Freedom of establishment	26				26	
Free movement of capital	5	2			7	
Free movement of goods	10	1			11	
Freedom of movement for persons	6	5			11	
Freedom to provide services	16	1	1	1	19	
Public procurement	20		1		21	
Commercial policy	8		3		11	
Common fisheries policy			2		2	
Economic and monetary policy	2		1		3	
Common foreign and security policy	1	1	5		7	
Industrial policy	8	1			9	

(Continued)

Table 10.1 (Continued)

	Reference for a preliminary ruling	Direct actions	Appeals	Requests for an opinion	Total	Special forms of procedure
Social policy	20	5			25	
Principles of EU law	21	1	1		23	
Intellectual and industrial property	13		34		47	
Consumer protection	34				34	
Approximation of laws	19	2			21	
Research and technological development and space			2		2	
Trans-European networks			1		1	
Public health		1	1		2	
Social security for migrant workers	4	2			6	
Transport	24	5			29	
Customs union and Common Customs Tariff	19		5		24	
TFEU	**426**	**72**	**111**	**1**	**610**	**2**
Privileges and immunities	1	1			2	
Procedure						6
Staff Regulations	1				1	
Others	**2**	**1**			**3**	**6**
Euratom Treaty		**1**			**1**	
OVERALL TOTAL	**428**	**74**	**111**	**1**	**614**	**8**

Source: European Court of Justice.

to employment tribunals. As mentioned above, these are now devolved to the civil service tribunal.

Who brings the cases

Cases involving member states, normally alleging failure to carry out their obligations under the treaties, are often initiated by the commission. Occasionally, one member state is brought to court by another. As Table 10.2 shows, Italy has historically been the major culprit. The Italian parliament is notoriously slow in passing laws, and a large number of these actions have been for failure to apply directives, adopted by the Council of Ministers, within the appointed time. Other countries with a poor record of meeting their obligations include France, Greece and (given its size) Luxembourg. The record of member states which joined in 2004 and 2007 is shorter and probably does not accurately reflect their comparative performance;

Table 10.2 General trend in the work of the Court (1952–2014): new actions for failure of a member state to fulfil its obligations

Country	New actions	Country	New actions
Austria	136	Italy	641
Belgium	382	Latvia	1
Bulgaria	8	Lithuania	3
Croatia	0	Luxembourg	264
Cyprus	12	Malta	15
Czech Republic	28	Netherlands	146
Denmark	40	Poland	71
Estonia	22	Portugal	195
Finland	57	Romania	
France	415	Slovakia	13
Germany	278	Slovenia	13
Greece	396	Spain	241
Hungary	15	Sweden	54
Ireland	205	United Kingdom	137
Total	**3,719**		

Source: European Court of Justice.

but it is notable that Poland, followed at a distance by the Czech Republic, are doing less well than the others. Of the longer-established EU members, Denmark has the best compliance record. The commission heads the lists both of complainants and defendants. It is its duty to take action, against individuals and companies as well as member states, to ensure that the treaties are being applied, notably in competition cases. However, it is also the commission that is the defendant in virtually all actions alleging loss or damage caused by the implementation of EU policies.

Sometimes cases have involved one institution lodging a complaint against another. The Council of Ministers has more than once initiated action against the European Parliament for allegedly exceeding its budgetary powers, while the Parliament took the council to court for failure to implement a common transport policy within the period foreseen by the Rome treaty.

General Court (Court of First Instance)

The 1987 Single European Act (see p. 55) provided for the establishment of a Court of First Instance, which would hear routine cases in certain sectors arising from the application of EU legislation brought by companies and individuals, including actions by EU officials. This court, which also consists of 28 judges, began work in September 1989. Its main function has been to rule on cases in sectors like competition policy, state aids, trade, transport, agriculture and intellectual property rights (essentially trade mark protection). In 2005, the Council of Ministers decided to offload staff disputes to a lower-level Civil Service Tribunal. Staff cases being heard by the tribunal have a right of appeal, on points of law only, to the General Court. But even without this responsibility, the General Court's workload went on rising and the time taken to reach a ruling has lengthened to two years or more. The amount of fines for anticompetitive behaviour that were being contested before the court by international corporations in 2015 exceeded €7 billion. To break the logjam, the Council of Ministers agreed in June 2015 to double the number of judges in the General Court to 56 (two per member state) in stages by 2019, and to fold the civil service tribunal (together with its seven judges) back into the General Court.

Beneficial effect of judgments

The judgments of the European Court of Justice have helped to consolidate the Union, ensuring that its citizens as well as national governments are both protected by, and subject to, the provisions of EU law. Many of its judgments have prevented governments from backsliding on the obligations they (or their predecessors) assumed in signing the treaties. Moreover, although it has few sanctions against member states – being unable, for example, to send erring ministers to prison – its judgments have nearly always been complied with, occasionally after some delay, and sometimes reinforced by a further ruling by the court. The Maastricht treaty gave the court the power to impose fines on member states failing to comply with its judgments within a time-limit set by the commission. One landmark judgment provided vital underpinning for the basic principle behind the free movement of goods across EU internal borders and the mutual recognition of national standards. It concerned a bid by the German authorities in Hessen to ban the import from France of *Cassis de Dijon* (a fortified wine) on the ground that it was understrength for that category of drink in Germany. In 1979 the court ruled that where a product (in this case an alcoholic drink, but it has subsequently been applied to other foodstuffs) is legally retailed in one member state, its sale cannot be prohibited in another member state except on grounds of public health. This principle that member states could not ban each other's products on arbitrary or spurious grounds was to become a key tool in putting the single European market in place.

Note

1 Not to be confused with the European Court of Human Rights, based in Strasbourg, which was set up by the Council of Europe, under the European Convention of Human Rights, signed in 1950. All EU member states recognise the jurisdiction of this court in human rights cases.

11 The Court of Auditors

The least known of the EU's institutions is the Court of Auditors, based in Luxembourg. It was established in 1977, when it replaced an earlier Audit Board which had less sweeping authority.

Membership

There are 28 members, one from each member state, who are chosen from persons who belong or have belonged to external audit departments in their own countries, or who are otherwise specially qualified. They are appointed for a renewable six-year term by the Council of Ministers, and appoint their own chairman from among their number for a renewable term of three years.

Responsibilities

The court's task is to examine all accounts of revenue and expenditure of EU institutions – especially the EU's annual budget – and of any other bodies set up by the Union, to ensure that all revenue has been received and all expenditure incurred in a legal manner. It also has the responsibility of ensuring that the financial management has been sound. Its function is similar to that of bodies like the Comptroller and Auditor General's department in the UK.

An influential role

The court produces an annual report, as well as periodic specific reports undertaken at the request of any of the Union's other institutions or on its own initiative. It has frequently thrown up evidence of wasteful expenditure, especially on support to agriculture, and occasionally of financial misconduct. Its role is highly influential, and its reports regularly lead to a considerable tightening up of EU procedures. In December 2014, the court fixed procedures for cooperation with the commission's anti-fraud office (OLAF) where suspicions had arisen in the course of its audit work of fraud, corruption or other illegal activity involving EU funds (see also Chapter 15, p. 121).

12 The European Investment Bank

The European Investment Bank (EIB) is both an EU institution and a Bank. Established in 1958, under Article 130 of the Rome treaty, it is the EU's public bank for financing capital investment promoting the balanced development of the Union. The Luxembourg-based EIB raises the bulk of its financial resources on capital markets (where it has a AAA rating), and on-lends the proceeds, on a non-profit basis, for capital investments which meet priority EU objectives. Much of its lending activity is focused on the Union's less prosperous regions. But EIB loans underwritten by member states were crucial to secure funding from other investors for big cross-border infrastructure projects like the Channel tunnel and the Oeresund combined rail and road bridge linking Denmark and Sweden. It also contributes to EU development aid programmes, notably under the EU's cooperation or association agreements with 12 countries in the Mediterranean region and with 79 African, Caribbean and Pacific countries under the Cotonou agreement (see Chapter 36). It has also lent considerable amounts to the former Soviet republics, as well as to countries in Asia and Latin America.

Members and financial resources

The shareholders of the EIB are the 28 member states of the EU. They have collectively subscribed the bank's capital of €164 billion (of which €7.5 billion is paid up). During 2014, it borrowed €62.6 billion and lent €59.4 billion. It is now, by a wide margin, the largest multinational borrower and lender on international financial markets.

Activities in the EU

Since 2008, the EIB Group has provided almost €500 billion for projects across Europe. In this way, the EIB responded to the sovereign debt crisis

Table 12.1 Geographic breakdown of finance contracts signed

€ million	2014	2010–14
Austria	1,496	8,454
Belgium	1,916	7,577
Bulgaria	610	1,334
Croatia	535	2,294
Cyprus	265	1,553
Czech Republic	1,198	5,584
Denmark	875	2,291
Estonia	252	781
Finland	1,039	4,906
France	8,213	30,176
Germany	7,726	33,512
Greece	1,556	7,734
Hungary	756	6,141
Ireland	932	2,848
Italy	10,888	45,192
Latvia	108	379
Lithuania	80	419
Luxembourg	50	595
Malta	0	140
Netherlands	2,194	7,148
Poland	5,496	26,481
Portugal	1,319	8,642
Romania	590	2,795
Slovakia	556	3,229
Slovenia	111	2,279
Spain	11,898	49,077
Sweden	1,411	7,430
United Kingdom	7,013	26,213
European Union	**69,081**	**295,203**

Note: Totals may not add up due to rounding.

Source: European Investment Bank.

with a sharp increase in activity, doubling its support for those countries which were hit the hardest. The EIB lends to all member states. Table 12.1 shows the amount which each received in 2014, and over the five-year period from 2010. During this time Spain was the biggest beneficiary of EIB loans, followed by Italy. Germany was the third largest borrower. It increased the amount of loans from the EIB significantly after reunification, principally to fund investments in eastern Germany. The top three were followed by France, Britain and Poland, which is by

Table 12.2 Loan contracts signed with non-EU countries in 2014

Region	billion
EFTA and pre-accession countries	2.5
Southern neighbours (Mediterranean)	1.7
Eastern neighbours	1.2
Africa Caribbean & Pacific group (plus South Africa)	1.2
Asia and Latin America	1.4
Total (non-EU)	**7.9**

Source: European Investment Bank.

far the biggest taker of EIB loans among EU countries in central and eastern Europe.

In 2014, the EIB signed loan agreements worth a total of €76.6 billion, divided among four main categories.

1   The biggest amount (€22.2 billion) went on supporting small and medium-sized enterprises (SMEs) – 285,000 of which received EIB funding in 2014.
2   The second category was strategic infrastructure (€20.6 billion), essentially transport or energy projects or those concerning urban infrastructure like social housing or hospitals.
3   The third concerned climate action and the environment (€19.1 billion), including the move towards a low-carbon economy,
4   Innovation (€14.7 billion) with a focus on research, education and training plus innovation-enabling infrastructures.

About 10 per cent of EIB lending is beyond the EU's borders. The geographical distribution of loan agreements signed in 2014 is given in Table 12.2. The biggest single beneficiary group are the EFTA members and countries which are actual or potential candidates to join the EU.

EIB structure

The EIB Board of Governors consists of the finance ministers of the EU member states who meet once a year. It also has a part-time Board of Directors (28 members nominated by the member states and one nominated by the European Commission), and a full-time Management Committee, made up of the bank's president and seven vice-presidents. They are appointed by the Board of Governors for a renewable six-year term.

European Bank for Reconstruction and Development

Since 1990 the EIB has been lending money to countries in eastern
Europe to help towards their transition to market economies. It also contributed to the establishment in April 1991 of the European Bank for
Reconstruction and Development (EBRD), which has its headquarters
in London, and whose specific function is to lend money for this purpose,
including to all the successor states of the Soviet Union. Although 40
countries participated in its establishment, more than half of the EBRD's
capital of US$10 billion was contributed by the EU and its member
states. The EIB's share in the bank's capital is 3 per cent.

13 Other EU bodies

Besides its main institutions described on the preceding pages, the EU has a number of specialised agencies, foundations and centres set up by a decision of the European Commission or the European Council. Most were established in 1994 or 1995, following decisions made at the Brussels summit in December 1993, although two were established 20 years earlier. In a different category was the European Monetary Institute, set up under the Maastricht treaty as a forerunner to the European Central Bank, which replaced it in June 1998. The bank is based in Frankfurt, and its functions are described in Chapter 19.

European Agency for the Evaluation of Medicinal Products (EMEA)

Located in London, the EMEA became operational in January 1995. Its purpose is to ensure that in the European single market pharmaceutical products are marketed with identical conditions of usage based on an independent scientific evaluation to protect both the consumer and the industry.

European Environment Agency (EEA)

The EEA was set up in Copenhagen in 1994 to deliver high-quality environmental information to member states and to the general public. The agency's main aims are to describe the present and foreseeable state of the environment and to provide relevant information as input for EU environment policy.

European Training Foundation

The European Training Foundation started work in Turin in January 1995. It coordinates and supports all EU activities in the field of post-compulsory education.

European Centre for the Development of Vocational Training (CEDEFOP)

Established in Berlin in 1975, CEDEFOP moved to Thessaloniki 20 years later. The centre contributes to the development of vocational training in Europe through its academic and technical activities.

European Monitoring Centre for Drugs and Drug Addiction (EMCDDA)

The EMCDDA was set up in Lisbon in 1994. The centre's aim is to provide 'objective, reliable and comparable information at European level concerning drugs, drug addiction and their consequences'. Given the complexity of the drugs phenomenon, the centre's task is to provide an overall statistical, documentary and technical picture of the drugs problem to member states and EU institutions as they prepare counter-measures.

European Foundation for the Improvement of Living and Working Conditions

Established in Dublin in 1975, the foundation's aim is 'to contribute to the planning and establishment of better working and living conditions through action designed to increase and disseminate knowledge likely to assist this development'. Effectively an advisory body, its main task is to supply the commission and other EU institutions with scientific information and technical data.

Office for Harmonisation in the Internal Market (OHIM)

The OHIM (Trade Marks and Designs) began work in September 1994 in Alicante. The office is responsible for the registration and protection of EU trade marks and designs, which apply throughout the Union. The aim of the OHIM is to contribute to harmonisation in the internal market in the domain of intellectual property, in particular trademarks and designs.

Community Plant Variety Rights Office

This office became operational in April 1995, and is based in Angers, France. It is exclusively responsible for the implementation of the new regime of plant variety rights, like patents and copyrights. Plant breeders may ask for protection throughout the EU by a single application to the Community Plant Variety Rights Office.

European Agency for Safety and Health at Work

Located in Bilbao, the agency began work in October 1995. Its first priority was to create a network linking national information networks and to facilitate the provision of information in the field of safety and health at work.

Translation Centre for Bodies in the European Union

The Translation Centre for Bodies in the European Union was set up in 1994 in Luxembourg. It carries out translations for most of the bodies and agencies mentioned here.

Other agencies

Since 2001 a number of other agencies have been created, most of which came into operation much later than intended because of a repeated failure by the European Council to agree on their location. Two of the more important of these, the European Food Safety Authority (EFSA) and Eurojust (the European judicial cooperation unit), had to start work in temporary locations but are now firmly established respectively in Parma and The Hague (see Appendix 5).

14 The bureaucracy

Facts, figures and costs

Number of employees

Despite frequent criticisms that the EU runs a vast bureaucracy, its pay-roll is modest compared with the national civil services of the member states. The European Commission has fewer than 25,000 employees, including about 5,000 in scientific research institutes or other specialised agencies. The remaining EU institutions together employ about half that number. The breakdown across the institutions in 2015 is shown in Table 14.1.

Recruitment

Recruitment to the commission and the other institutions, apart from a limited number of senior posts to which national governments make nominations, are filled by open competitions, which are advertised in the EU Official Journal, and in leading newspapers in the member states. Normally there is no upper age limit for new recruits, although most Eurocrats join early in their careers, in their 20s or early 30s. Appoint-

Table 14.1 EU employees 2015

	Permanent	*Temporary*
Commission	23,970	458
Council of Ministers	3,036	36
European Parliament	5,591	1,148
Court of Justice	1,547	451
Court of Auditors	733	139
ESC and Committee of the Regions	1,156	84
External action service	1,644	1
Total	**37,677**	**2,317**

Source: European Commission.

ments are made without regard to race, creed or sex and, in principle, no posts are reserved for nationals of any specific state. In practice, there are unofficial national quotas designed to ensure that each EU country gets a reasonable share of posts at each level of the administration. Otherwise the general qualifications are as set out in Article 28 of the EU's Staff Regulations. An official may be appointed provided that he/she passes an entrance exam, is the citizen of an EU member state, and has a working knowledge of a second EU language in addition to their own. Candidates for posts as interpreters or translators must have a good knowledge of two official EU languages other than their own.

Training

In addition to its permanent staff, the commission offers in-service training via its traineeship office for up to 1,400 university graduates a year. The traineeships generally last for five months. There are two intakes a year. Places are keenly sought after and are awarded on a competitive basis. There is, of course, no guarantee of future employment in EU institutions, but the internships provide excellent experience for those interested in future careers at a European level, whether within the institutions or outside.

Salaries

The salary scales for employees of the commission and the other European institutions are based on 16 career grades, as defined in the Staff Regulations. The highest grade (16) applies to directors-general and a small number of other very senior officials. The lowest grade (1) includes junior filing clerks and attendants. The remuneration of members of the commission is linked to the maximum of the 16th grade. The president of the commission receives 138 per cent of this (€306,653 a year), vice-presidents 125 per cent (€277,767) and commissioners 112.5 per cent (€249,990). They all also qualify for the various allowances paid to employees, notably the expatriation allowance, which adds 15 per cent to the above figures for all except the Belgian commissioner.

EU employees pay income tax to the EU (currently at a standard rate of 25 per cent) rather than to the country where they work. The rates of pay are set rather higher than for national civil servants in order to compensate for living and working in a different country. In addition to basic salaries, they also receive tax-free expatriation and head of family and children's allowances, and a number of other perks, such as generous health-care coverage and free education for children at one of the

Table 14.2 Basic monthly salaries by grade 2012 (€)

Grade	Intra-grade salary levels				
	1	2	3	4	5
16	17,054.40	17,771.08	18,517.81	—	—
15	15,073.24	15,706.64	16,366.65	16,822.00	17,054.40
14	13,322.22	13,882.04	14,465.38	14,867.83	15,073.24
13	11,774.62	12,269.40	12,784.98	13,140.68	13,322.22
12	10,406.80	10,844.10	11,299.79	11,614.16	11,774.62
11	9,197.87	9,584.37	9,987.12	10,264.98	10,406.80
10	8,129.38	8,470.99	8,826.95	9,072.53	9,197.87
9	7,185.01	7,486.94	7,801.55	8,018.60	8,129.38
8	6,350.35	6,617.20	6,895.26	7,087.10	7,185.01
7	5,612.65	5,848.50	6,094.26	6,263.81	6,350.15
6	4,960.64	5,169.10	5,386.31	5,536.16	5,612.65
5	4,384.38	4,568.62	4,769.60	4,893.04	4,960.64
4	3,875.06	4,037.89	4,207.57	4,335.63	4,384.38
3	3,424.90	3,566.82	3,718.79	3,822.25	3,875.06
2	3,027.04	3,154.24	3,206.79	3,378.23	3,424.90
1	2,675.40	2,787.82	2,904.97	2,985.79	3,027.04

Note: On January 3rd 2016, one euro was worth £0.7481 and US$1.0898.

Source: Official Journal of the European Union.

European schools maintained by the commission. The salary scales are published from time to time in the EU Official Journal, where they are expressed monthly in euro. The most recent scales, which came into force on July 1st 2012, are shown in Table 14.2. Apart from the top grade, which has three incremental steps, there are five salary levels in each grade.

Part III

The competences

The EU is still a long way from becoming the political union to which its founders aspired. As for its eventual role as a European government-in-waiting, progress has been markedly lopsided. The creation of a customs union with internal free trade and a common external tariff and the development of a common agricultural policy remained the most concrete achievements of the Union in the early years. But there are now many other areas of economic activity where it has a competence, which is often shared, to varying degrees, with the member states. The Maastricht treaty enshrined the principle of 'subsidiarity' by asserting that decisions should be 'taken as closely as possible to the citizens', but nevertheless extended the responsibilities of the EU institutions in several directions. So did the subsequent Amsterdam, Nice and Lisbon treaties, The European single market, the single currency and the Schengen passport-free area of personal mobility are the most significant of these. Part 3 goes through the principal fields of action of the European Union without claiming to provide a comprehensive account of all its activities.

15 Financing the Union

The EU's budget is modest compared with those of the member states: no more than 2.5 per cent of the sum of the national budgets, and about one sixteenth the size of the US federal budget. In 2015 each EU citizen would have paid an average of €278 to the Union, a fraction of what he or she pays in national taxes. Despite its relatively small size, the EU's budget has been a source of big disputes between the member states and between them, the commission and the European Parliament.

Revenue

Sources

The EU's revenue sources have changed over the years. The ECSC, which had its own operational budget, was financed by a production levy on coal and steel firms. The general Community budget was originally financed by a system of national contributions based mainly on the GDP of the member states. In 1970 it was decided progressively to replace these contributions by the Community's 'own resources'. These are sources of revenue which, although collected mainly in the member states, belong to the EU as a right. These too have regularly been revised and updated. At present they consist of four separate elements (see Table 15.1):

1   Contributions from member states based on national income (74 per cent of the total in 2015). A simple multiplier is applied to the calculated gross national income (GNI) for each country. This is the variable and final component in the budget-setting process. Within a given ceiling, the actual figure is adjusted to obtain the budget total

Table 15.1 Budget revenue, 2015–16 (€m)

Revenue sources	2016 (draft)	2015 (actual)	% change
Customs duties & sugar levies	18,590.00	16,825.90	10.48
VAT-based resource	18,812.78	18,264.48	3.00
GNI-based resource	104,538.81	103,180.11	1.32
Other revenue	1,599.84	3,010.06	−46.85
Total	**143,541.43**	**141,280.55**	

Source: European Commission.

required. Budget revenue is currently capped at 1.23 per cent of GNI for the EU as a whole.

2   Traditional 'own resources' such as customs duties, agricultural duties and sugar levies (12 per cent of the 2015 total).

3   A proportion of value-added tax. VAT rates and exemptions vary in different countries, so a formula is used to create a 'harmonised tax base' upon which the EU charge is levied (13 per cent of the budget in 2015).

4   Other revenue, such as unspent amounts from the previous year and fines paid by companies for breaking ant-trust rules (1 per cent).

Expenditure

Table 15.2 shows the expenditure included in the EU's 2015 budget, and compares it with 1973, the year the UK became a member. The annual EU budget first exceeded €100 billion in 2004, the year ten new member states joined.

The principal elements in the budget are as follows. See Table 15.3 for a detailed breakdown of the spending estimates.

Table 15.2 EU budget comparison 1973 and 2015 (€ at current prices)

1973		2015	
Total budget: 4.5 billion	% of total	Total budget: 145 billion	% of total
Agriculture & fisheries	80.6	Sustainable growth	47.8
Structural funds	5.5	Natural resources	39.4
Administration	5.5	Administration	5.7
Miscellaneous	5.4	EU as a global player	5.5
Research, energy, Industry & transport	1.6	Citizenship, security & justice	1.6
Overseas development	1.4		

Source: European Commission.

Table 15.3 EU budget 2015: expenditure by policy sector

	Budget 2015 (€ million)	% change on 2014
SMART AND INCLUSIVE GROWTH	**66,782**	**4.37**
Competitiveness for growth and jobs	**17,552**	**6.48**
Large infrastructure projects	2,509	3.80
Horizon 2020 & Euratom Research	9,912	6.46
Competitiveness of companies and SMEs	295	16.21
Education training & sport	1,608	3.17
Jobs and social innovation	125	1.52
Connecting Europe Facility (CEF)	2,225	12.59
Other actions & programmes	878	3.88
Economic, social & territorial cohesion	**48,230**	**3.64**
Investment for growth & jobs	45,147	3.75
Cohesion fund contribution to CEF	1,217	23.80
European territorial cooperation	738	46.01
Youth employment initiative	1,407	−22.00
European aid to most deprived	525	4.75
Other actions & programmes	196	pm
SUSTAINABLE GROWTH: NATURAL RESOURCES	**58,809**	**−0.6**
European agricultural guarantee fund	43,456	−0.7
European agricultural fund for rural development	13,824	−1.2
European maritime and fisheries fund	1,035	10.00
Environment and climate action	435	7.5
Other actions & programmes	59	−23
SECURITY AND CITIZENSHIP	**2,147**	**−1.2**
Asylum. Migration and integration fund	417	3.3
Internal security fund	395	−2.1
Justice, citizens' rights, consumers, health	245	pm
Food and feed	259	2.0
Creative Europe	178	−1.6
Other actions and programmes	655	−5.6
GLOBAL EUROPE	**8,408**	**1.0**
Instrument for pre-accession support	1,572	−0.4
European neighbourhood instrument	2,036	−7.1
Development cooperation instrument	2,446	4.5
Partnership instrument: third country cooperation	119	−0.3
European instrument for democracy & human rights	182	−1.3
Instrument for stability and peace	320	0.6
Humanitarian aid	929	0.9
Common foreign and security policy (CFSP)	321	2.0
Other actions and programmes	485	35.6
ADMINISTRATION	**8,661**	**3.0**
Pensions and European schools	1,719	6.6
Administrative spending of EU institutions	6,941	2.2
– of which European Commission	*3,270*	*0.4*
– of which other institutions	*3,654*	*3.8*
OTHER SPECIAL INSTRUMENTS	**515**	**−11.6**
TOTAL 2015 BUDGET COMMITMENTS	**145,322**	**1.8**

Source: European Commission.

Agriculture and fisheries

In the 2015 budget, farming and fisheries are included under the heading 'Sustainable growth: natural resources'. They represented some 41 per cent of estimated expenditure in 2015, of which fisheries represented a small part. Agricultural spending has fallen as a share of the EU budget in recent years. The main reason it remains high is that it is the one big economic sector where a substantial amount of public funding passes through the EU's budget. This is not the case in other policy areas. Farm spending tends to squeeze other programmes like research and innovation, where the Union ought to be making a larger contribution. Steps have been taken to hold down agricultural spending, and at least to ensure that it rises at a slower rate than EU expenditure as a whole (see pp. 171–3).

Regional policy

Spending to develop poorer regions accounts for the biggest outlay under the 2015 budget heading 'Economic, social and territorial cohesion' which makes up 33.8 per cent of the total. This is spread over three so-called structural funds: the European Regional Development Fund – ERDF (the largest), the European Social Fund (ESF) and the Cohesion Fund. The ERDF was established in 1975, following the accession in 1973 of the UK, Denmark and Ireland. It helps to finance development programmes, infrastructure investment and industrial and service projects in poorer regions and areas particularly hit by recession. The fund normally operates on the basis of matching contributions from the member state concerned. Under the Maastricht treaty, a Cohesion Fund was established to provide assistance for infrastructure investment in the poorest member states. This covers member states with a GNI of less than 90 per cent of the EU average. It therefore currently applies to the countries who joined in 2004 and 2007 plus Greece and Portugal. Most social spending goes through the European Social Fund, which co-finances training and retraining schemes and aid for recruitment.

Innovation, energy, industry and transport

These sectors come under the budget heading entitled 'Competitiveness for growth and jobs' which made up 12.1 per cent of EU spending in 2015. Most of this, nearly €10 billion, was earmarked for the EU's Horizon 2020 funding programme for research and innovation. However, the EU and its member states still lag behind Japan and the United States in the amount spent on R&D. According to the latest available figures, Japan spent the equivalent of 3.38 per cent of GDP, with the US on 2.81 per cent and the EU on 2.01 per cent – just ahead of China on 1.98 per cent.

External activities

The EU is the world's largest aid donor, if you include donations by individual member states. Financial and technical assistance, which accounted for about 5.5 per cent of the 2015 budget, is split geographically, starting with the EU's neighbours in eastern Europe and the Mediterranean. Part of this money funds cross-border projects to foster good relations with neighbouring countries, which may also receive direct funds for other projects. Money also goes to candidate countries, such as Turkey, Macedonia, Montenegro, Serbia and Albania. Development aid goes to reduce poverty and boost economic development in Latin America, Asia, Central Asia and the Middle East. The Cotonou (formerly Lomé) agreement provides financial and technical aid to African, Caribbean and Pacific countries, which are mostly former colonies of EU member states. However, support for ACP countries traditionally comes via the European Development Fund (EDF) which member states finance separately, and not from the EU budget.

Administration

Administration costs, around 5.7 per cent of the total EU budget, covers staff salaries, pensions, buildings and equipment. As much of the EU's work takes place in Belgium and Luxembourg, this is where almost three-quarters of the spending goes. The European Commission accounts for about half of the total spending on EU administration, employing just under 25,000 people in 2015.

Crime and border control

Listed under 'Security and citizenship', this item represents only 1.4 per cent of the budget. In 2014, the EU received more than 625,000 asylum applications, an increase of 160 per cent over five years, while many thousands of economic migrants were smuggled illegally across the EU's land and sea borders. Most EU spending on asylum and immigration goes on developing a coordinated approach to border management, through the European external borders agency (Frontex), and assisting refugees and asylum seekers.

Appropriations and expenditure

The 2015 budget will amount to €145.3 billion in commitment appropriations, a slight increase of 1.8 per cent compared with 2014. Appropriations for payments in 2015 were €141.3 billion. This corresponds to 1.00 per cent of EU gross national income. Alert readers will note that the budget figures for a given year, notably the most recent, tend to vary in the tables presented in this chapter (and elsewhere in this book). This depends *inter alia* on whether the figures relate to appropriations for commitments or for expected (and actual) payments. As dynamic management tools, the annual budgets are also subject to several revisions.

Financial frameworks

Like any government institution, the EU operates on an annual basis. But in 1988, after a succession of budget crises, the institutions put in place a medium-term financial framework, setting binding budget guidelines for a seven-year period. This lays down maximum amounts ('ceilings') by broad category of expenditure ('headings') for each year. The current framework covers the period 2014–20. The financial framework figures are enshrined in an Inter-institutional Agreement between the European Parliament, the Council of Ministers and the European Commission which also sets out rules and procedures for managing the framework on a year-to-year basis (procedures for revision, technical adjustment, and so on). The 2014–20 budget guidelines place limits on spending in all EU policy areas for each of the seven years (see Table 15.4) – but a detailed annual budget still has to be agreed every year.

Under the 2014–20 agreement, the annual average ceiling on payment appropriations for the financial framework amounts to 1.03 per cent of EU-28 GNI. The total expenditure commitment for the seven-year period is €974.8 billion, or an average of €139.3 billion a year.

Winners and losers

For many years the EU published no precise information as to who were the net contributors and net beneficiaries of the EU budget. Everybody knew that Germany was, by far, the biggest contributor, that the UK's contribution was substantially reduced by the annual rebates it had received since 1984 and that Ireland – in relation to its size – was the biggest beneficiary. When the UK secured the rebate in 1984 it was one of the poorest countries in the EU. It was also widely recognised that it

Table 15.4 EU multiannual budget guidelines 2014–20: commitments and payments (€ million – 2011 prices)

	2014	2015	2016	2017	2018	2019	2020	Total
Smart & inclusive growth	**49,713**	**72,047**	**62,771**	**64,277**	**65,528**	**67,214**	**69,004**	**450,544**
– competitiveness	*15,605*	*16,321*	*16,726*	*17,693*	*18,490*	*19,700*	*24,079*	*125,614*
– economic, social & territorial cohesion	*34,108*	*55,726*	*46,045*	*46,584*	*47,038*	*47,514*	*47,925*	*324,940*
Sustainable growth: natural resources	**46,981**	**59,765**	**58,204**	**53,448**	**52,466**	**51,503**	**50,558**	**372,925**
– farm spending	*41,254*	*40,938*	*40,418*	*39,834*	*39,076*	*38,332*	*37,602*	*277,454*
Security & citizenship	**1,637**	**2,269**	**2,306**	**2,289**	**2,312**	**2,391**	**2,469**	**15,673**
Global Europe	**7,854**	**8,083**	**8,281**	**8,375**	**8,553**	**8,764**	**8,794**	**58,704**
Administration	**8,245**	**8,385**	**8,589**	**8,807**	**9,007**	**9,206**	**9,417**	**61,629**
Total commitment appropriations	**114,430**	**150,549**	**140,151**	**137,196**	**137,866**	**139,078**	**140,242**	**959,512**
(% of GNI)	0.88	1.13	1.03	1.00	0.99	0.98	0.98	1.00
Total payment appropriations	**128,030**	**131,095**	**131,046**	**126,777**	**129,778**	**130,893**	**130,781**	**908,400**
(% of GNI)	0.98	0.98	0.97	0.92	0.93	0.93	0.91	0.95
Margin available (% of GNI)	0.25	0.25	0.26	0.31	0.30	0.30	0.32	0.28
Own resources ceiling (% of GNI)	1.23	1.23	1.23	1.23	1.23	1.23	1.23	1.23

Source: European Commission.

Table 15.5 Contributions by member states to EU budget 2015: net contribution under 'own resources' per cent of total (€ millions)

	Amount	%		Amount	%
Austria	2,995	2.44	Italy	15,013	12.22
Belgium	3,817	3.11	Latvia	243	0.20
Bulgaria	398	0.32	Lithuania	347	0.28
Croatia	415	0.34	Luxembourg	321	0.26
Cyprus	153	1.08	Malta	71	0.06
Czech Republic	1,330	0.12	Netherlands	5,703	4.64
Denmark	2,548	2.07	Poland	3,883	3.16
Estonia	190	0.15	Portugal	1,610	1.31
Finland	1,944	1.58	Romania	1,422	1.16
France	20,940	17.05	Slovakia	688	0.56
Germany	26,691	21.73	Slovenia	345	0.28
Greece	1,718	1.40	Spain	10,044	8.18
Hungary	931	0.76	Sweden	4,006	3.26
Ireland	1,413	1.15	United Kingdom	13,633	11.10
Total	**122,813**				

Source: European Commission.

derived little benefit from the 80 per cent of the EU budget devoted to agriculture because of the small size of its farming sector. All other member states contributed to the UK rebate. However, by 2005, thanks in a large part to North Sea oil and gas, the UK had become relatively rich and was under fierce pressure to give up the rebate. At the same time, the amount of the budget spent on agriculture had declined from 70 to 40 per cent. The other EU members, rich and poor alike, felt the situation was unfair. So at a summit in December 2005, the UK sacrificed part of its rebate, mainly so as to pay a fair share of the costs of EU enlargement. The subsequent UK rebate in the 2007 budget was around €5.2 billion. It was little changed at €5.4 billion in 2015.

Under the complex rebate formula, the UK receives back from the budget 66 per cent of the difference between what it pays to the budget and what it receives from it. The calculation is based on the UK's GNI and its value-added tax receipts. In the meantime, the other big net payers, Germany, the Netherlands, Sweden and Austria, have secured a deal to pay less towards the UK rebate. They also pay lower VAT-based contributions to the budget. The difference is borne by the other 23 member states.

In absolute terms, Poland is now (2013 figures) the biggest recipient of EU budget funding followed by France, Spain, Germany and Italy. The latest figures for the contributions of each member state are shown in Table 15.5.

Fraud

It is estimated that fraud perpetrated against the EU budget runs to around €700 million each year, covering issues ranging from unpaid VAT and tax evasion to elaborate mafia scams. The European Anti-Fraud Office (OLAF) was set up in 1999 to investigate fraud that harms the EU budget. It is an independent investigative body, but it has no judicial or disciplinary powers and it cannot oblige national prosecutors to act. Currently, OLAF has 400 staff, of which 160 are investigators. Of the investigations concluded in 2014, 44 per cent of the 156 cases involved just 4 member states in central and eastern Europe: Romania, Hungary, Bulgaria and the Czech Republic. Another 40 cases involved EU staff and officials. A total of 474 cases were ongoing at the start of 2015. According to OLAF, €206 million of fraud money was paid back to the European Commission in 2014, compared with €117 million in 2013 and €95 million in 2012.

The European Court of Auditors has regularly refused to sign off the EU's financial accounts. The ECA'S annual report usually criticises many areas of budget spending for irregularities, non-respect of EU procedures and 'errors'. For example, the ECA found that the error rate in 2013 was 4.7 per cent overall (4.8 per cent in 2012), against a 'standard' error rate of 2 per cent, but it rose to 6.9 per cent in areas like regional policy, energy and transport and 6.7 per cent for rural development, the environment and health. The European Commission blames member states, which handle the bulk of EU budget payments, for most audit failings. The ECA is more sweeping in its criticism; the 2014 annual reports says the 'lack of focus on performance is a fundamental flaw in the design of much of the EU budget'.

16 Trade

The goals of the European Union's trade policy are threefold. They are set out in the Rome treaty: create growth and jobs in Europe, promote development around the world, and strengthen ties with important trading partners. The initial task was to create a customs union (or 'common market') whereby member states removed tariffs on goods moving between them and applied the same external tariff to goods imported from outside. Thus French, German or Italian cars could be sold duty-free across the EU. By the same token, a Japanese car, imported through Antwerp where duty was paid, could then be sold anywhere in the EU without additional duty being charged.

Removal of tariff barriers

The Treaty of Rome provided for the removal of all tariff barriers inside the Community within 12 years. In fact the original six member states completed the process 18 months early, in 1968. The consequence was an enormous and sustained growth in intra-EU trade, incorporating later entrants in stages: the UK, Ireland and Denmark by 1977; and Greece by 1986. Spain and Portugal, which joined in 1986, removed all their tariffs against other members by the end of 1992. Austria, Finland and Sweden (as EFTA countries) had already removed theirs long before joining the EU in 1995. As they removed internal tariffs, the original Six aligned their external tariff on goods from outside countries. Originally set at an average of around 10 per cent in the late 1960s, this was gradually reduced, following successive rounds of multilateral trade negotiations in the General Agreement on Tariffs and Trade (GATT).

By the time of the GATT Uruguay round agreement December 1993, this weighted average had fallen to around 3 per cent, and was set for further cuts under negotiations within the World Trade Organisation (WTO) which replaced the GATT in 1995. After a false start in Seattle in 1999, where the WTO conference was effectively hijacked by anti-globalisation protestors, negotiations for a new trade-liberalising round began in Doha, Qatar, in November 2001. But the negotiations came up against the vexed issue of agriculture protectionism and a new series of non-tariff barriers on issues like copyright, technical standards, test procedures and others. These were not to the liking of many developing and emerging countries. Doha was due to end in 2005. It was still uncompleted ten years later. In fact, the failure of Doha meant that many leading trading nations turned away from multilateral global trade deals to bilateral or regional pacts with like-minded partners. By this time also, the motor of expanding global trade had moved from western industrialised nations to Asia.

Member states represented by EU

The Rome treaty stipulated that the commission should represent EU countries on external trade issues, and the member states formally transferred some of their sovereign powers to the Community. As a result some 165 countries established diplomatic relations with the EC. The EU, normally represented by the commission, speaks for the member states in the WTO and the North Atlantic Fisheries Organisation. The EU has signed agreements with most countries in the world as well as some 30 multilateral agreements. Most of them concern EU trade, and their effect has been to modify its pattern profoundly. The EU's trading arrangements concern four main categories of countries: European Economic Area; other developed countries; former communist countries; developing countries.

EFTA

EU's largest trading partner

In 1973 the EC formed an industrial free-trade area with the then seven countries of the European Free Trade Association (EFTA): Austria, Finland, Iceland, Liechtenstein, Norway, Sweden and Switzerland. Customs duties and restrictions on trade in manufactured goods were abolished, and some reciprocal concessions were made for agricultural produce. This effectively extended the size of the common market for manufactured goods to 370 million people. EFTA was the EU's largest trading partner.

European Economic Area (EEA)

Following the launch of the EC's single market programme in the mid-1980s, the EFTA countries sought closer association with the Community. Negotiations began in December 1989 to establish a European Economic Area in which the EFTA states would assume many of the obligations and disciplines of EC membership, including the acceptance of the free movement of capital, persons and services, in return for sharing most of the expected benefits of the single market. The EEA should have started on January 1st 1993, but the founding agreement was rejected by a referendum in Switzerland in December 1992. Following further negotiations with the remaining countries it only came into effect in January 1994, with Switzerland left out and Liechtenstein's membership deferred until 1995. For three of the countries concerned, however, the EEA acted as no more than a staging post on the way to full EU membership. Austria, Finland and Sweden joined the EU in January 1995. Norway also negotiated full membership, but its voters rejected the move (for the second time) in a referendum in December 1994; so it remains in the EEA, along with Iceland and Liechtenstein. The Swiss government negotiated a series of bilateral agreements with the EU which incorporate much of the substance of the EEA. But its membership application, submitted at the time the EEA was signed, was indefinitely suspended (see also p. 281). Switzerland is the EU's fourth largest trading partner, after the United States, China and Russia.

Other developed countries

North America

Traditionally, trade relations with the US are governed by multilateral agreements in the GATT and the WTO and the structures created by these organisations, particularly for dispute-settlement. Both sides profess free-trade principles, but each often accuses the other of protectionist tendencies and/or of giving unfair advantages to its own exporters through state subsidies. Disputes concerning agriculture and steel, in particular, became increasingly frequent during the 1980s, leading on occasion to the introduction of counter-measures which were usually withdrawn when the other side belatedly offered concessions. Similar disputes concerning EU restrictions on the importation of hormone-treated meat and discrimination against banana imports by US companies in Latin America have more recently been resolved using the disputes procedure of the WTO, whose judgments on both these issues favoured the US position.

Perhaps the most damaging dispute in recent years erupted in October 2004, when the United States challenged the EU's subsidies for the manufacture of large Airbus passenger aircraft at the WTO. The EU retorted with a counterclaim against US federal subsidies for plane-maker Boeing in Seattle. World Trade Organisation panels in 2011 separately upheld both the US and EU claims that the other's actions had caused 'serious prejudice' (for Boeing) and 'loss of sales' (in the case of Airbus). But the panels refused to order compensation in either case. The dispute, the longest in the history of GATT or the WTO, is still ongoing. In December 2014, the EU submitted a new challenge targeting alleged local state subsidies for Boeing to persuade the company to maintain new aircraft production in Seattle.

The context of EU relations with Canada is similar to that with the United States, although in 1976 an EU–Canada framework agreement was concluded which established mechanisms for commercial and economic cooperation. In November 1990 a transatlantic declaration was signed between the EC, the United States and Canada, providing for closer cooperation in areas of common interest and a more permanent dialogue to resolve or contain the trade disputes that would inevitably continue to occur.

Japan

The EU's trading relations with Japan have been difficult at times, largely owing to the substantial trade deficit the EU had with Japan in the 1980s and 1990s. Japan imported half as much from the Union as it exported to it. This imbalance was particularly painful because Japanese exports focused on a fairly small number of sectors – cars, electronics, audio-visual equipment, computers and telecommunications – where European firms had been struggling to maintain or achieve a viable share in the world market. Although Japanese tariffs are, on average, lower than the EU's, the Union repeatedly criticised Japan's non-tariff and administrative barriers for blocking high-tech imports from Europe. The EU imposed quotas on car imports, via so-called voluntary agreements on the part of Japan, and restrictions on electronic goods. High-level meetings with Japanese ministers and officials took place regularly. The pressure applied at these meetings eventually resulted in Japanese initiatives to encourage importers and to ease or remove impediments in their domestic market. The EU's trade deficit with Japan has shrunk dramatically in recent years. By 2015, it had fallen to €1.3 billion – with EU exports to Japan at €53.3 billion and imports at €54.6 billion.

China

In the ten years from 2005 to 2014, the volume of trade between the EU and China more than doubled from €213 billion to €467 billion. China is now the EU's biggest trading partner after the US. It is the EU's number-one outside supplier, leaving the EU with a deficit in its bilateral trade with China of €137 billion in 2014. Its main exports to the EU are computers and office equipment, telecommunications material, electrical and non-electrical machinery.

Former communist countries

Trade with the countries of central and eastern Europe before the collapse of communist rule in 1989–90 was hampered by the lack of normal relations and by the inherent inefficiencies of command economies. After the collapse of the Soviet Union in 1991, trade and cooperation agreements were signed with Poland, Hungary, Czechoslovakia, Bulgaria and Romania. Most subsequently became EU members. The partnership and cooperation agreement of 1997 forms the basis for the trade relationship between the EU and Russia. Russia is the EU's third largest trading partner. Its main exports to the EU are oil and gas. Following the annexation by Russia of Crimea in March 2015, the EU placed an embargo on the export to Russia of material for the transport, telecoms and energy-related sectors (see p. 270).

Association agreements

Negotiations began in 1990–91 on far-reaching association agreements (known as Europe Agreements) with the new democracies of central and eastern Europe. These would provide tariff-free access for most of their manufacturing goods while maintaining restrictions on their exports of textiles and agricultural products. The first three agreements were concluded with Czechoslovakia, Hungary and Poland in December 1991. It was the first step towards EU membership. Less comprehensive agreements were signed with other former communist countries, from the Balkans to the Caucasus and even Central Asia. The countries of the western Balkans were offered Stabilisation and Association Agreements (SAAs) with one-way trade preferences in their favour, and the possibility of eventual EU membership. Armenia, Azerbaijan and Georgia have seen trade with the EU intensify since their inclusion in the European Neighbourhood Policy in 2004, and the Eastern Partnership initiative in May 2009. Partnership and Cooperation Agreements (PCAs) have been signed with Central Asian countries, but these are non-preferential.

Developing countries

The Mediterranean

The EU has signed association agreements with all Mediterranean countries except Syria. These give duty-free access to all, or most, of their industrial products, specific concessions for some of their agricultural produce and a certain amount of financial aid and technical assistance. A similar agreement has been concluded with the countries belonging to the Gulf Cooperation Council.

In 1987 Turkey applied for full membership (see p. 284), and entered into a customs union with the EU on December 31st 1995. An earlier two-stage agreement for a customs union, including agricultural produce, came fully into force during 1997. Membership negotiations with Turkey began in 2005.

The ACP

EU relations with the 79 African, Caribbean and Pacific countries are governed by the 20-year Partnership Agreement, signed in Cotonou, Benin, on June 23rd 2000 (see p. 26 and Appendix 7). This replaced a series of trade and aid conventions (the so-called Lomé conventions), first signed in the Togolese capital in February 1975. All the ACP countries, except Cuba, are signatories to the Cotonou agreement: 48 African countries, covering all sub-Saharan Africa, 16 countries in the Caribbean and 15 states in the Pacific. Of the 50 least developed countries covered by the EU's pledge to import 'Everything but Arms', 40 are ACP. South Africa is a signatory of the Cotonou agreement but its membership of the ACP group is qualified. The trade regime under the Cotonou agreement proposed by the EU represented a new departure, which unsettled many ACP partners. To promote sustainable development, eradicate poverty and to comply with WTO rules, the ACP group and the EU agreed to conclude regional Economic Partnership Agreements (EPAs) that will progressively remove barriers to trade between them and enhance cooperation in all areas relevant to trade. Negotiations on EPAs have been difficult and slow. The majority of ACP countries are either in the process of implementing an EPA or have concluded EPA negotiations with the EU but not ratified the outcome. A milestone was passed in February 2014, when 16 west African countries, representing between them 38 per cent of EU–ACP trade, concluded their EPA. It was open for signature in 2015. (For more details on EPAs, see Chapter 36.)

In 2014, the EU sold goods worth €85.6 billion to ACP countries and imported goods worth €91.2 billion from them. Trade with ACP countries accounts for 5.2 per cent of the EU's global trade.

Asia

Besides China and Japan, India and South Korea are also among the EU's top ten trading partners (see Table 16.1). A free trade agreement between the EU and South Korea became operational in 2011. The EU has separate economic and cooperation agreements with India and Pakistan, and a cooperation agreement with the ten-nation Association of South-East Asian Nations (ASEAN). The first Asia–Europe (ASEM) summit meeting, in March 1996, which included Japan, China, South Korea and the ASEAN countries, established a framework for consultation at heads of government level every two years. The ASEM now includes meetings of economic ministers, finance ministers and the Asia–Europe Business Forum. The ASEM leaders have also agreed a Trade Facilitation Action Plan to reduce and remove non-tariff barriers to trade between the two regions, and an Investment Promotion Action Plan to promoting two-way investment flows.

Latin America

Two-yearly summits are also a feature of the EU's relations with Latin America and the Caribbean. The EU has economic and trade cooperation agreements with most of the principal countries, including the Mercosur association, the five members of the Andean Pact and the six countries of the

Table 16.1 The EU's top ten trading partners 2014 (€ billion)

Exports		Imports	
United States	310.9	China	302.5
China	164.7	United States	205.2
Switzerland	140.3	Russia	181.8
Russia	103.3	Switzerland	96.6
Turkey	74.6	Norway	84.0
Japan	53.3	Japan	54.6
Norway	50.2	Turkey	54.2
South Korea	43.1	South Korea	39.0
UAE	42.8	India	37.1
Brazil	36.9	Brazil	31.1

Source: Eurostat.

Central American isthmus. All Latin American countries benefit from the EU's system of generalised trade preferences. The EU is Latin America's third most important trading partner after the US and China. EU trade with the countries of the region grew steadily in the ten years to 2012 when it reached €223 billion, but it had dropped back to €202 billion in 2014.

Trade policy

Industrial products

The external trading policy of the EU is based on the principle of free trade, so far as industrial products are concerned. But it resorted to trade restriction in the face of surging imports of automobiles and electronic equipment from Japan in the 1980s. It has also at certain points restricted imports in the shipbuilding, steel and, particularly, textile sectors. Textile imports into the EU were regulated by the Multi-Fibre Arrangement (MFA), a deal agreed in 1973 to open up markets to developing country suppliers while the ailing textile industries of the industrialised world were slowly run down. Under the Uruguay round agreement, the MFA was gradually dismantled over a period of ten years until 2005 and the EU market progressively opened up to textile imports.

In the mid-1990s, the EU also began negotiating Mutual Recognition Agreements (MRAs) with its main trading partners. These were designed to cut red tape in safety and testing standards by setting single certification procedures for various products. For example, with the United States, it meant companies were able to test their products in the EU according to American rules of certification to gain access to the American market, and vice versa. The EU has MRAs with the United States in sectors like chemicals, medical devices, foodstuffs, pharmaceuticals, automobiles and tyres, and cosmetics. The EU has similar agreements with Australia, Canada, Japan and New Zealand.

Agriculture

The EU applies a protectionist trade policy to agriculture (as do most industrialised countries) Virtually no temperate products are imported into the EU since import levies (see Chapter 21) effectively make them uncompetitive. On the export side, the EU was blamed in the 1980s and 1990s for dumping its farm surpluses on export markets, often undercutting third world farmers. Export subsidies have been significantly reduced since then, most recently in the 2013 CAP reform. At the same time, the

EU remains the world's largest food importer. It has worked to open up its market in the last 20 years, and more than two thirds of its imports of farm produce come from developing countries – more than the US, Japan, Australia, Canada and New Zealand combined. Bilateral agreements with many countries fix low tariffs on farm imports, and the world's 50 poorest nations can export unlimited quantities to the EU duty-free.

Trade defence

Within the multilateral WTO framework, the EU can apply a number of instruments to defend itself against what it might see as unfair trade, most importantly anti-dumping and anti-subsidy measures. The WTO rules allow for anti-dumping measures to be used against predatory pricing, when a manufacturer in one country exports a product at a price which is either below the price it charges in its home market or is below its costs of production. Countervailing measures are used when government subsidies are determined as the factor behind the dumping. They are applied only after a commission investigation – using complex calculations – into whether dumping is taking place and whether the dumped imports are causing material injury to EU producers, importers, users and consumers. Countries hit by EU anti-dumping or countervailing measures can appeal against them through the WTO.

The world's leading trader

EU trade practices are important *inter alia* because it is the world's biggest trading power (see Table 16.2). It has to export finished goods to pay for the imports of energy products and raw materials it needs,

Table 16.2 The world's biggest traders: percentage share of global trade 2004 and 2014

	2004		2014
European Union	19.5	European Union	16.4
United States	17.5	United States	13.7
China	7.6	China	12.9
Japan	7.4	Japan	4.9
Canada	4.2	South Korea	3.5
South Korea	3.4	Canada	3.0
Mexico	2.5	India	2.9
Russia	2.0	Russia	2.6
India	1.5	Mexico	2.3
Total share of world trade	**65.6**		**62.2**

Source: Eurostat.

given the rarity of local sources. Nearly 45 per cent of the EU's energy needs are met by imports, as well as three quarters of other vital raw materials. Although trade between member states has expanded enormously since the establishment of the Community, its share of world trade has declined in recent years in the face of much stronger competition, particularly from Asian countries – but not Japan, whose share of world trade has declined proportionally more than that of the EU or the US.

17 The single market

The four freedoms

The Treaty of Rome was meant to create an economic space where goods, services, capital and people are able to move as freely as within a single country. These were the so-called four freedoms. But it was a long time coming. The first step – a 'common market' without internal tariffs and where member states applied the same tariff to their imports from outside – failed to deliver expected benefits for citizens and businesses. By the 1980s, tariffs were long gone. But it had become clear that many unforeseen obstacles were preventing companies and individuals enjoying the full benefits of trade liberalisation – lower prices, higher quality products and wider choice thanks to economies of scale and increased competition, as well as the higher growth, job creation and welfare gains associated with market integration. Complex frontier formalities, different national regulations, standards and testing procedures plus divergent excise duties and VAT rates and other so-called non-tariff barriers hampered cross-border trade and the free movement of workers and other citizens.

- Frontier formalities delayed and added to the cost of transporting goods from one member state to another.
- It was still impossible for many EC citizens to work in other member states because they did not recognise each other's professional qualifications, despite the provisions of the Rome treaty concerning free movement.
- Divergent national regulatory provisions prevented service industries like insurance from operating on a Community-wide basis.
- Differential indirect tax rates distorted intra-Community trade.
- Public procurement contracts (representing nearly 19 per cent of EU GDP) were effectively reserved for national suppliers in each member state rather than being put out to open tender.

The single market takes form: enter Delors and Cockfield

After the doldrums of the early 1980s which ended at the Fontainebleau summit in June 1984 (see p. 20), the plan to revitalise the EC by completing the single market was the brainchild of former French Socialist finance minister Jacques Delors who became president of the European Commission in 1985. Along with his vice-president Arthur Cockfield, a British Conservative peer who was in charge of the EC internal market, he put his proposal to the European Council in June 1985. EU leaders duly instructed the commission to draw up a detailed programme with a specific timetable for completing the single market by 1992. At the same time, the Community's leaders summoned an intergovernmental conference to speed the process by amending the Rome treaty to apply qualified majority voting to most of the internal market issues which had previously required unanimity; this eventually led to the Single European Act, which took effect on July 1st 1987 (see pp. 20–1).

White paper on single market

Cockfield produced a document listing some 300 actions which would need to be taken if the single market was to materialise. These were divided into three categories:

Physical barriers The white paper set as its target the total abolition, not simply the alleviation, of frontier controls on goods by 1992.

Technical barriers These were barriers created by different national regulations and standards. The commission proposed that its laborious programme to harmonise national standards for thousands of different manufacturing processes should be replaced by a system of mutual recognition of national standards, pending the adoption of European standards. Other proposals included:

- the liberalisation of public procurement;
- the establishment of a common market for services such as transport, banking, insurance and information and communications;
- the free movement of capital throughout the Community;
- the removal of legal restraints on the formation of EC-wide companies;
- the adoption of a Community trademark system.

Fiscal barriers These mainly concerned the approximation of VAT and excise-duty rates. The commission did not consider that total harmonisation was necessary and was content to see actual VAT levels vary by up to 2.5 per cent on either side of whatever reference rate was chosen.

The 300 measures were later consolidated into 282 proposed directives or regulations. By the target date of December 31st 1992 no fewer than 258 of these (over 90 per cent) had been adopted by the Council of Ministers, with 79 per cent already being implemented by the member states.

The Schengen Agreement

The EU's passport-free Schengen areas is one of the EU's most tangible achievements along with the single market and the single currency. The removal of frontier controls for goods within the single market highlighted the persistence of border checks and systematic passport controls for persons crossing internal EC frontiers. Member governments had already been discussing for several years ways of allowing passport-free movement. They could not agree: should, for instance, free movement apply only to EC citizens? Some governments, notably the UK, argued that removing border checks would cause problems for the control of terrorism, illegal immigrants, drug-trafficking, and the containment of animal-borne diseases. Faced with this impasse, five member states – France, Germany, Belgium, Luxembourg and the Netherlands – signed an intergovernmental agreement in June 1985 in the Luxembourg town of Schengen to set up gradually a territory without internal borders. Their agreement took the form of a convention in 1990, creating the 'Schengen area'. The principle was to remove all internal frontier controls and to reinforce passport, visa, immigration and police checks at the EC's external frontiers. The first practical action to remove internal border checks began in 1995 when the five initial Schengen participants were joined by Spain and Portugal. Following the signing of the Treaty of Amsterdam in 1997, this intergovernmental cooperation was incorporated into the EU framework. To offset the removal of internal passport controls, the Schengen agreement imposed two types of measures.

External borders

The free movement of people is guaranteed under the agreement, which removes checks at most of the EU's internal frontiers and strengthens controls at the EU's external borders. There are no border controls when travelling by land between the Schengen members. But more rigorous passport, visa and immigration requirements are applied at the external Schengen borders for nationals of non-EU countries. These reinforced controls are carried out in accordance with a single set of rules and procedures.

•   Common rules applying to people crossing the EU external borders, including the types of visa needed and how checks at external borders have to be carried out.

• Harmonisation of the conditions of entry for visitors, immigrants, refugees and asylum-seekers and of the rules on issuing visas for short stays (up to three months).
• Enhanced police cooperation (including rights of cross-border surveillance and hot pursuit).
• Establishment and development of the Schengen Information System (SIS) for exchanging data and intelligence.

Visitors from outside the EU seeking to visit one or more Schengen area countries must apply for a visa in their home country from the consular services of the EU member state they want to visit first. Once this visa is checked on arrival by border police in the country which issued it, the holder is free to travel on without further checks to other 'Schengen' countries just like local EU residents.

The Schengen borders code allows member states temporarily to reintroduce internal border controls if a serious threat to public policy or internal security has been established. The reintroduction of controls at internal borders must remain an exception and must respect the principle of proportionality. The scope and duration of such a temporary reintroduction of border control at the internal borders is limited in time (generally 30 days, but can be up to 6 months) and should be kept to the bare minimum needed to respond to the threat in question. The reintroduction of border control is a prerogative of the member states. In addition, the Council of Ministers set up Frontex in 2004 to reinforce and streamline cooperation between national border authorities. Based in Warsaw, Frontex (the European Agency for the Management of Operational Cooperation at the External Borders of the Member States of the European Union) applies the concept of integrated border management to assist member states in working together. Frontex has several operational areas including planning and implementing joint operations, providing a rapid response capability, training, risk analysis and information sharing.

Judicial matters

To prevent criminals of all sorts using Schengen to their advantage, the EU created a system of frontier-free police and criminal justice cooperation. Europol, the European police force, is part of that response. So is the Schengen Information System. On the one hand, the SIS allows border authorities to check for illegal immigrants, especially those refused entry by one country and trying to enter another, and cooperate in searches for missing persons. But the SIS is widely used by national police to exchange information on wanted or suspected wrongdoers. Under the Eurojust system, member states second senior prosecutors, policemen and lawyers to a central team working to fight organised crime. Schengen has also reinforced judicial cooperation through a faster extradition system and the transfer of enforcement of criminal judgments. This makes it possible, *inter alia*, for people convicted in one country to serve their sentences in another.

By 2015, 22 of the 28 member states were part of Schengen together with non-EU neighbours Switzerland, Liechtenstein, Norway and Iceland. Four EU members were preparing to join: Bulgaria, Croatia, Cyprus and Romania. The only member state intent on keeping its border controls is the UK; but Ireland also stayed out of Schengen in order to maintain existing arrangements for passport-free travel between Ireland and the UK. The six EU countries which do not belong to Schengen also use the Schengen Information System, but only for law-enforcement cooperation and not for border management.

The single market since 1992

The 1992 programme was launched for the benefits it would bring to member states, their businesses and their citizens. According to the European Commission, internal trade among EU member states rose in the first 20 years of the single market from €800 billion a year to €2,800 billion, an increase from 12 per cent of the combined EU GDP to 22 per cent. But these overall figures mask a less positive reality, with member states sometimes backsliding on their obligations.

The Lisbon strategy

By 2000, it was clear that the supposed completion of the single market had left much unfinished business, with the European Commission launching a staggering 1,500 lawsuits against EU governments for failing to respect single-market rules. At the Lisbon summit in March 2000, EU leaders agreed an agenda to tackle financial barriers, streamline labour markets and make the EU the world's most competitive region by 2010. The leaders agreed to create at least 20 million jobs in a decade, matching America's job-creation and technology-harnessing record with practical steps. They even identified the action areas:

- Creating a legal framework to support the expansion of e-commerce.
- Easing telecoms regulations for fixed and mobile services and access to the internet, especially for schools.
- Liberalising other utilities in the gas, electricity, postal and transport sectors.

- Building a European research area.
- Reducing red tape for SMEs and innovative start-ups.
- Liberalising financial services.

Heads of government also agreed a European Social Policy Agenda, which aimed to liberalise labour markets and provide crucial guarantees for workers. Lisbon also launched the idea of a regular spring summit on economic and social affairs. A key decision at Lisbon was to endorse the Financial Services Action Plan (FSAP). This included some 42 measures, from binding regulations to voluntary codes of conduct, covering the entire financial services field from securities and banking to insurance, and from financial institutions to retail customers. The results include the Money Laundering Directive, an agreement on cross-border payments regulation, and adoption of the European Company Statute.

However, despite its heady language, it was soon clear that the Lisbon strategy would not meet its 2010 target. In 2005, the strategy was recalibrated on actions that promote growth and jobs in a context of sustainable development rather than global competitiveness. At the same time, the commission focused efforts to get the single market back on track, particularly in the services sector.

There were two reasons for this: firstly, services accounted for about two thirds of the EU economy, and secondly, in the post-industrial digital world, services and products were often bundled together in a single package. It submitted a draft directive to liberalise the services sector early in 2004.

Services Directive

The Council of Ministers and the European Parliament adopted the Services Directive under the co-decision procedures (see p. 84) in 2006. It took effect in December 2009. The objective of the directive, widely seen as one of the most important for a decade, is to remove legal and administrative barriers to trade in services. The simplification brought in by the directive seeks to increase transparency and make it easier for businesses and consumers to provide or use services in the single market. Opening their frontiers to service providers of all sorts unsettled some EU member states, afraid of being undercut by countries with lower labour costs. However, they and MEPS eventually backed the directive, but excluded a range of services. The directive will not affect local labour laws or collective agreements in member states, and does not include health care, social services, public transport, financial services and some other areas. MEPS also removed the controversial 'country of origin' principle, which would have allowed businesses to operate in another member state under the rules of their home country. The conditions under which service providers based in one country can operate in another and the terms under which they can 'post' workers to jobs elsewhere in the EU have been among the most difficult issues concerning the principle of free movement within the single market. It is sometimes accused of provoking a race to the bottom – something it expressly set out to avoid.

The single market and the economic crisis

Although its introduction in 2009 coincided with the full impact of the global economic crisis, the Services Directive achieved some early results in terms of reducing national barriers. But a commission study in 2014 found the pace of national reforms had since slowed considerably. Reform efforts in 2012–14 were uneven across member states, according to the commission.

When the financial and economic crisis hit in 2008, the single market faced contradictory pressures from member states seeking either to retrench or reinforce the single market in response to the crisis. The protectionist tendency led by the then French president Nicolas Sarkozy lost out. However, the single marketeers also faced criticism: some said the liberalisation of various financial service rules had made the crisis worse, allowing rapacious speculators to indulge in unlimited and unsecured financing gambling. The upshot of the crisis was, however, that progress on the single market took a back seat. Efforts continued to create integrated markets for the production, distribution and delivery of electricity and gas, including the construction of more cross-border interconnectors between national grid systems. But new initiatives, outside the financial sector and the creation of a banking union in response to the euro crisis, have been rare. For its part, the commission has been keen to launch and consolidate the digital single market as its next target.

18 Competition policy

Adam Smith, the father of liberal economic thought, warned in his *Wealth of Nations* in 1776 that 'People of the same trade seldom meet together, even for merriment and diversion, but the conversation ends in a conspiracy against the public, or in some contrivance to raise prices.' As attitudes had changed little in 200 years, the authors of the Treaty of Rome built in safeguards for their nascent customs union by outlawing price-fixing and other anticompetitive behaviour. Thus Articles 85 and 86 (Articles 101 and 102 TFEU) were inserted to uphold free competition between firms and other entities from different member states. The first article outlaws deals between companies to fix prices, share out markets, limit production, technical development and investment, and other restrictive practices. The second bans 'abuses of dominant position' by firms or groups of firms. Furthermore, Articles 92–94 of the Rome treaty (107 and 108 TFEU) forbid government subsidies ('state aids') to companies which distort or threaten to distort competition.

A global reference

In their wisdom, the treaty authors vested the power to apply competition rules in the European Commission. This kept decisions out of the hands of member states and the Council of Ministers who are sometimes tempted to put political considerations or support for their big companies ('national champions') before the common good. The result has been to create a gold-standard anti-trust system in Europe on a par with that of the United States. The name of the European Commissioner in charge of applying competition policy in Brussels is a familiar one in boardrooms around the world. Global companies investigated for alleged anticompetitive offences include Microsoft, Intel and the Russian energy giant Gazprom. The commission's trust-busting powers combine the role of investigator and judge, although companies and governments involved can appeal against the commission's rulings to the European Court of Justice. Many do. The court has also reaffirmed its key role in the EU system by reminding the commission of the risk of arrogance, excess centralisation and complacency that comes with the exercise of important powers.

The commission launches a case either on its own initiative or following complaints by member states, companies or individuals. Several hundred cases are dealt with each year. The commission was given the power to investigate possible anticompetitive behaviour in 1962, and jurisdiction over large mergers in 1990. In principle, the commission enforces the EU competition rules together with the national competition authorities of the EU countries. All EU countries have these authorities with the power to deal with local cases where violations of competition rules happen within just one country.

In many instances cases are resolved by voluntary policy changes by the countries or companies being investigated. A famous early case involved IBM, accused in 1980 of abusing a dominant position in the computer market by withholding information on new products and 'bundling' its products (that is, selling several of them together in a package, so that customers must either take all of them or none). After spending a small fortune in lawyers' fees, IBM eventually backed down in 1984 and came to a voluntary agreement with the commission to modify its trading practices.

Financial penalties

Where the commission investigation finds no evidence or presumption of wrong-doing, it drops the case. Where breaches of free-competition rules are confirmed, the commission orders changes in commercial practices and policies of the parties concerned, or fines them, or does both. Fines run to millions of euro, or even billions where a group of companies are found to have run a big illegal cartel. Fines levied by the commission cannot exceed 10 per cent of turnover of the corporation concerned. The biggest fine for a single company for one offence was the €1.06 billion imposed on US chipmaker Intel in 2009. But it was another American IT giant, Microsoft, which was involved in two separate anti-trust problems in 15 years that has paid the largest fines. In March 2004 after a five-year investigation, the commission ruled that Microsoft had abused its dominant position on the software market. It ordered Microsoft to sell a version of its main Windows software without the movie and music playing Windows Media Player, and to disclose more information to rivals about how its server software works. The commission also set a then-record fine of €497.2 million, to which it later added €1.18 billion for not complying with the ruling. In a second case, involving a commitment by Microsoft to offer clients a choice of web browser to install with Microsoft Windows, the commission fined Microsoft €561 million in March 2013. The total amount of fines imposed by the commission for cartel or anti-trust offences regularly exceed €1 billion a year. Like previous years, the €2.2 billion levied in 2014 went to the EU budget where member states' contributions are reduced by the equivalent amount. In 2014 for the first time, the commission investigated possible unlawful tax reductions for selective companies which might hinder free competition and harm taxpayers' interests. These concerned tax rulings by Ireland in favour of Apple, by Luxembourg (Amazon, Fiat and McDonald), and the Netherlands (Starbucks).

The right of appeal

The commission's powers of investigation include 'dawn raids': its staff can visit companies without warning to demand access to documents and records, and to take away copies of documents, computer files and emails as evidence. It then holds hearings with the companies concerned to discuss the case before giving its verdict. Convicted firms may appeal to the Court of Justice against both the conviction and the size of the fine, which has sometimes been reduced on appeal. The court has built up a large body of case law. EU competition law takes precedence over national law and is directly applicable in member states. Businesses and individuals believing themselves to be victims of infringements of EU competition rules can bring direct actions before national courts.

Down the years, the commission has acted against the following types of cartel agreements:

- *Market-sharing agreements.* These have included the quinine cartel, which led the commission to impose its first fines (1969); the car glass producers' cartel, where Asahi, Pilkington, Saint-Gobain and Soliver were fined over €1.3 billion for illegal market sharing (2008); and the deal between German energy group E.ON and Gaz de France (GDF) Suez to carve up gas markets between them, which cost them €553 million in fines (2009).
- *Price-fixing agreements.* In 1998 British Sugar and three other firms, controlling 90 per cent of the UK market, were fined €50.2 million for concluding price-fixing agreements for white sugar. And in 2007, the Otis, ICONE, Schindler and ThyssenKrupp groups were fined over €990 million for a lifts and escalators cartel.
- *Exclusive purchase agreements.* These have been banned for a wide variety of products ranging from gramophone records to heating

equipment. Computer chipmaker Intel was fined a record €1.06 billion in 2009 for squeezing out competition by paying PC-makers and retailers not to use rival chips.

- *Agreements on industrial and intellectual property rights.* In a 1982 case, involving maize seed, the Court of Justice ruled against the total territorial protection granted by a patent licensing contract.
- *Exclusive or selective distribution agreements.* These have been misused in the automobile and other sectors to restrict parallel imports. Among companies which have been heavily fined, or otherwise penalised, for applying such agreements have been Ford, AEG-Telefunken and the Moet-Hennessy French drinks group. In 1998 Volkswagen was fined €102 million for prohibiting its Italian dealers selling cars to foreign buyers.

The commission has used its power to give bloc exemptions or individual waivers, where it judged that the threat to competition was small or non-existent and was outweighed by the likely public benefits. It has been particularly concerned not to hamper cooperation between small and medium-sized enterprises, and it has identified a number of types of agreement which it felt should escape the general ban.

EU jurisdiction over mergers runs wide

Until 1990 the commission had no specific power to vet corporate mergers, although it intervened on several occasions, using the general authority given to it under Articles 85 and 86 of the Rome treaty, when they posed a threat to effective competition in the Community. A dormant proposal for a merger regulation was revived in 1987 and took effect in September 1990. It gave the commission jurisdiction over larger-scale company mergers and takeovers affecting more than one member state and exceeding certain thresholds. The main thresholds concerned were:

- €5 billion for the worldwide turnover of the companies concerned;
- €250 million for the individual turnover within the EU of at least two of the companies concerned, while no more than two thirds of this turnover should be concentrated within a single member state.

Projected mergers which met these criteria had to be reported in advance to the commission, which decided within one month whether they might restrict free competition. If not, the merger could go ahead; otherwise an investigation would be launched to be completed within a further four months.

With the merger regulation, the number of notifications of mergers substantially increased. In 1997 172 notifications were submitted and 135 final decisions were adopted. One concerned Boeing's acquisition of McDonnell Douglas, which came under the commission's jurisdiction because of the extensive European operations of the two aircraft companies. The merger was eventually approved, but only after Boeing had significantly modified its original proposal and had given commitments concerning several specific elements.

More controversy with the Americans

By 2001, the commission had received 335 notifications and adopted 322 final decisions. The most controversial decision of the year again involved two American companies in the avionics sector: General Electric's (GE) planned takeover of Honeywell. The case also contrasted the EU's competition policy with its focus on preventing *ex-ante* abuses of dominant positions and the more laissez-faire American anti-trust rules. The €47 billion merger was cleared easily enough in the United States, and Jack Welch, GE's ebullient chairman, assumed the EU decision would be a mere formality. But the commission found the bid would create an unhealthily dominant aerospace giant, giving it leverage to eliminate competition. It was the first time the commission had killed off a merger between two American companies that had already been approved in the United States.

The merger between music groups Sony and Bertelsmann in 2004 created different problems. It would reduce the music sector's five 'majors' to four, and – according to critics from among independent labels – would further cement an effective cartel. The commission's own statement of objections on the deal said it would strengthen a collective dominant position in the market for recorded music and in the wholesale market for licences for online music. Yet, its final verdict was that there was no 'smoking gun' to prove such a cartel existed, and the deal was cleared.

The commission twice, in 2006 and again in 2013, blocked attempts by low-cost carrier Ryanair to acquire a majority state in Irish airline Aer Lingus due to serious concerns that it would hurt competition by creating or strengthening Ryanair's dominant position on a number of routes, but Ryanair maintained the minority shareholding of 29.4 per cent it had acquired in Aer Lingus. In 2014, the commission cleared the acquisition by Etihad, the Abu Dhabi-based airline, of joint control of Alitalia, subject to minor divestments to maintain competition on some routes in Europe. In recent years the number of mergers vetted by the commission but involving only companies based outside the EU has risen from just over 10 per cent of total cases in 2006 to 18 per cent in 2013.

Government subsidies

Government subsidies to either publicly-owned or private firms are normally banned if they distort or threaten to distort competition. Some types of aid are exempt from control, including: special help at times of natural disasters; aid to depressed regions; and aid to promote new economic activities and/or technologies.

Member states are supposed to notify the commission of all aid planned, and it decides whether the aid can be exempted from the treaty rules. It has the power to order the repayment of unauthorised aid and may impose fines on member states that break the rules. In 2014, the commission took 866 decisions concerning state aid and recovered €301 million in state aid that had been illegally paid by EU governments. State funding in favour of companies can be considered compatible with EU rules when it is made on terms that a private sector investor would accept under market conditions (the market-economy investor principle).

Two landmark state aid cases occurred during 1988, when Sir Leon Brittan, the competition commissioner, required both the French and UK governments to secure repayment of illegal state aids that they had provided. The French government reluctantly agreed to reclaim FFr6 billion (more than €900 million) paid to Renault, which then failed to fulfil the conditions the commission had attached to the project. The UK government was also forced to seek repayment of secret 'sweeteners', worth £44 million that it had paid to British Aerospace as an inducement to buy the Rover car company.

A necessary shake-up

In 2002, the commission's anti-trust procedures and actions came under serious attack from the European Court of Justice, when it overturned three of its anti-merger rulings. The court echoed criticism from many practitioners that the commission's anti-trust approach and structures, little changed in 40 years, required a serious overhaul. In effect, the system had become too centralised, rigid and unwieldy, with the commission too overburdened to carry out its vital investigative analyses with the depth and rigour required, and with many companies hard put to supply prior information and documents demanded by the commission. In one of the three cases, involving French electrical groups Schneider and Legrand, the court slapped down the commission's economic reasoning, saying it contained 'several obvious errors, omissions and contradictions'.

The criticism prompted radical reforms to competition policy and law, which came into force on May 1st 2004. The new structure rebalanced power between the commission and the national competition authorities of the member states. Only major cases would be dealt with by the commission. In addition, investigation deadlines were made more flexible. As a result, the commission would be able to carry out the in-depth analyses and assessments as required. The new rules did away with any automatic requirement to notify the commission in advance of planned or upcoming mergers. It was left to the players involved to decide whether their agreement risked breaching EU competition rules or not. Thus, EU policy moved to a system of *ex-post* surveillance and control. The reforms made the merger control mechanism more like that in the United States, with more market oversight, economic and consumer assessments, and clearer deadlines and where the onus is on businesses to decide if they are acting within the law. New investigation deadlines were set. The first-phase investigation takes 25 working days, and a second-phase in-depth probe takes 90 working days, but both timetables can be extended.

19 Economic and monetary policy

Although the Rome treaty is silent on the topic of economic and monetary union as such, it did provide for closer cooperation among member states on their economic and monetary and financial policies. Article 103 requires them to treat short-term economic policy as a matter of common concern and to consult each other on relevant measures. The subsequent articles enjoin EC countries to apply economic policies which maintain a balance in their external payments, while assuring stable exchange rates and low inflation. Competitive devaluations are outlawed and capital liberalisation encouraged. Article 105 sets up a Monetary Committee, tasked *inter alia* with permanently monitoring the monetary and financial situation of member states. The committee was to play an essential role in the EC's subsequent quest for currency stability. For although EMU was not included as a formal EU objective until the Maastricht treaty of 1992, currency stability and economic and monetary union were never far from the EC agenda.

It was the Hague summit in December 1969 that gave the then Luxembourg premier and finance minister Pierre Werner the job to draw up a blueprint for monetary union. Werner, who submitted his plan to governments in October 1970, set 1980 as the target date for irrevocably locking national exchange rates against each other – or even creating a single currency. There were differences of approach to EMU among member states at the time, but broad agreement on the aim. The biggest arguments were between the 'economists' who argued economic and fiscal union should precede and thereby facilitate monetary union and the 'monetarists' who thought the opposite: create monetary union and a single currency first, and governments will be forced to apply the appropriate economic and fiscal policies to make the system work. The monetarists won the intellectual argument. But alas nobody seemed bothered that the enforcing economic disciplines were to lag far behind.

The snake in the tunnel

With hindsight, the Werner plan was hopelessly ambitious. But it was blown off course at the time primarily by outside events: the collapse of the Bretton Woods system of fixed exchange rates when the US cut the link between the dollar and gold in the summer of 1971; the Yom Kippur war of 1973; plus the oil embargo and the general economic and currency instability that ensued. Post Bretton Woods, an attempt was made as part of the so-called Smithsonian agreement in December 1971 to reset parities between the dollar and European currencies. This would have meant wider fluctuation margins between EC currencies than were compatible with the aims of the internal market, the common agricultural policy and economic convergence. The EC countries therefore created a system within a system – the 'snake in the tunnel' – whereby their currencies moved against each other within narrow margins (the snake) while fluctuating collectively within wider limits against the dollar (the tunnel). The tunnel disappeared when the US freely floated the dollar in 1973. The EC currency snake, increasingly bruised and battered, continued on its own. The new EC countries, the UK, Ireland and Denmark withdrew their currencies from the snake within weeks of joining, after massive speculative attacks. The French and Italian currencies each left and re-joined the snake twice. By 1977, only the German, Benelux and Danish currencies remained. The core of the EC currency snake survived and was incorporated into its successor, the European Monetary System (EMS) which was launched in March 1979. It was an update, which learned from the experience of the snake, with more flexibility, a less mechanical procedure, and more room for coordinated exchange rate adjustments.

The European Monetary System

The EMS was based on a concept of fixed but adjustable exchange rates. Originally proposed by Roy Jenkins in October 1977 (see p. 16), the EMS owes its implementation to support from the then French president Valery Giscard d'Estaing and chancellor Helmut Schmidt of Germany. The EMS included an exchange rate mechanism (ERM), bolstered by various financial solidarity mechanisms and a common reference currency, the European Currency Unit (ecu).

Under the ERM, each participating currency had a central rate against the ecu. Only eight currencies participated initially, the UK 'temporarily' staying out when the system was inaugurated in March 1979. The three later entrants to the EC – Greece, Spain and Portugal – felt that they were not yet ready to join. Spain eventually joined in June 1989 and the

UK finally followed suit in October 1990. Portugal joined in April 1992, leaving Greece as the odd man out. The central rate for each currency could be 'realigned' if necessary by mutual agreement of the participating countries. From the ecu central rate, bilateral central rates were calculated for every currency against each of the other participants. Each currency was allowed to fluctuate by +/−2.25 per cent around these central rates, or by +/−6 per cent in the case of the UK pound and the Spanish peseta.

The EMS helped to bring about a greater convergence in the economies of the member states, and the disciplines built into the system were credited with playing a part in the marked reduction in inflation in the early 1980s in all the participating states. On average, inflation fell from 12 per cent in 1980 to 5 per cent in 1985, and the average divergence between countries went down from 6.2 to 2.8 per cent. Other countries outside the EC recognised the value of the ERM in providing tighter guidelines for their own economic policies. Three Nordic countries – Finland, Norway and Sweden – each tied their own currencies to the ecu in 1990 or early 1991.

In 1992 the ERM came under great strain, partly because of the recession and partly because the removal of capital controls meant that vast amounts of currency changed hands each day, opening the system to manipulation by speculators. Things were made worse by the fact that the pound had entered the ERM at an unrealistically high exchange rate and the UK government stubbornly resisted pressure for an orderly devaluation. Consequently, in September 1992 massive speculative movements led to the forced devaluation of several currencies, and the pound and the lira were withdrawn from the ERM altogether and allowed to float. A similar speculative attack in July 1993 was fended off by a decision to widen temporarily the fluctuation margin within the ERM to 15 per cent either side of the bilateral central rates. In practice, the currencies did not fluctuate much beyond the previous more narrow limits, which suggests that, unlike the previous year, none of the currencies was seriously over- or under-valued. The mechanism remained in operation, but without the participation of the UK, Italy and Greece. Italy re-joined the ERM in November 1996, and Greece in March 1998, leaving the UK and Sweden outside. The ERM lost much of its significance on December 31st 1998, when the exchange rates of the 11 national currencies joining the euro were irrevocably fixed (see p. 153), leaving only the Greek drachma and the Danish krone to fluctuate within agreed bands.

Economic and monetary union

The relative success of the EMS and the clear commitment of member states to complete their single market by 1992 relaunched the initiative for economic and monetary union. Given the disruptive effect on cross-border trade within the community of frequent competitive devaluations and the transaction costs estimated at about 3–4 per cent of buying and selling goods in different currencies, the move made sense to the great majority of EC countries. In addition some members, especially France, felt that the EMS was being dominated by Germany and the mighty Deutschmark, over which it had no control; far better a single currency run by common rules and joint institutions where everybody has a say. So, it was not surprising that a European Council in Hanover in 1988 appointed a committee headed by the then commission president Jacques Delors to set the process in motion once again. The Delors committee, mainly consisting of central bankers from the member states, produced a proposal in 1989 for a three-stage approach towards EMU, but without attaching any timetable:

- *Stage one.* Cooperation and coordination in the economic and monetary fields were to be improved. This would lead to a strengthening of the EMS, the role of the ecu and the terms of reference of the Committee of Central Bank Governors. The introduction of a multilateral surveillance procedure would pave the way for more effective coordination and for closer convergence of national economic policies and performances.
- *Stage two.* This could not begin until a new treaty (or amendments to the Rome treaty) had been agreed, laying down the basic institutional and operational rules necessary for the realisation of EMU. Stage two included the creation of a federal-type European System of Central Banks (ESCB or EuroFed) which would become increasingly independent as regards monetary policies and intervention on foreign-exchange markets. However, the national central banks would still retain ultimate responsibility for decision-making.
- *Stage three.* Starting with irrevocably locked exchange rates and the transfer of responsibilities provided for in the new treaty, this stage would see the adoption of a single currency.

The Delors committee's approach was acceptable to 11 of the then 12 member states, but the UK reacted coolly to the concept of a single currency. Although it agreed to stage one beginning on July 1st 1990, it emphatically reserved its position regarding stages two and three. Despite British objections, the EC heads of government decided at the Strasbourg summit in December 1989 that the requisite majority existed to convene an inter-governmental conference to decide the treaty changes which stages two and three would require. It was subsequently agreed that two IGCs, one on EMU and one on political union, should be held, both convening in Rome in December 1990 and completing their work in time to report to the Maastricht summit, scheduled for December 1991.

An earlier Rome summit in October 1990 agreed that stage two of EMU, with the creation of the European System of Central Banks, would begin on January 1st 1994. At the IGC on EMU, the UK put forward a plan for a thirteenth currency, or 'hard ecu', instead of the single currency advocated by the Delors report. Although the UK proposal was listened to politely by other member states, the prevailing view was that a single currency was necessary if the main benefits of EMU were to be secured. This is effectively what was decided at the Maastricht summit in December 1991, when the Treaty on European Union was agreed.

Maastricht bans bailouts

The treaty included four chapters on EMU: on economic policy, monetary policy, institutions and trans-national provisions. The chapter on economic policy required member states to conduct their economic policy so as to achieve the objectives of EMU and 'in accordance with the principle of an open market economy with free competition'. Member states were to regard their economic policies as a matter of common concern and to coordinate them through the Ecofin[1] Council. The broad guidelines of economic policy were to be defined by the European Council and then adopted by the Ecofin Council by qualified majority vote.

A multilateral surveillance procedure was already in place under which, to ensure closer coordination and sustained convergence in economic performance, the Ecofin Council, on the basis of reports from the commission, monitors economic developments in each member state. Where it considers that economic policies are not consistent with the broad guidelines agreed, the council is entitled, by qualified majority vote, to make policy recommendations to a member state which it may choose to make public. If, in the future, a member state persists in applying policies inconsistent with the guidelines, and in particular if it persists in incurring excessive budget deficits, it may lay itself open to a range of sanctions culminating in a freeze on lending from EU institutions, a requirement to make non-interest bearing deposits and, ultimately, the imposition of 'fines of an appropriate size'. The treaty makes clear that there is no question of the EU bailing out a member state that gets into financial difficulties, although financial assistance may be available in the event of 'natural disasters' or other problems not caused by the improvidence of the member state concerned.

On monetary policy, it laid down that the primary objective 'shall be to maintain price stability', that is, a minimal level of inflation. For this purpose the European System of Central Banks (ESCB) would be set up, and a new European Central Bank (ECB) would be established at the beginning of the third stage of EMU.

The treaty confirmed that the second stage of EMU would commence on January 1st 1994, by which date all member states were expected to have taken steps to ensure the free movement of capital, and to have adopted multi-annual programmes to ensure lasting convergence necessary for EMU, in particular with regard to price stability and sound public finances. At the beginning of stage two, the European Monetary Institute (EMI) was set up as forerunner of the ECB. Its members were the various national banks, and it replaced the Committee of Governors and the European Monetary Cooperation Fund (created as a follow-up to the Werner plan). Its task was to prepare for stage three.

The Maastricht criteria

The EMI, together with the commission, reported to the Ecofin Council on progress by member states to bring their national legislation in line with EMU. The council was then to assess which of them fulfilled the four conditions for adoption of a single currency, as defined in the treaty:

- Its inflation should, over the previous year, not have exceeded by more than 1.5 per cent the average of the three best performing states.
- Its currency had been within the narrow band of the ERM for at least the preceding two years and had not been devalued during that period.
- Its long-term interest rates had not exceeded by more than 2 per cent over the preceding year the average of the three best performing states.
- It respected the limits for annual budget deficits (less than 3 per cent of GDP) and for long-term government debt (less than 60 per cent of GDP).

However, the deficit and debt criteria were to be applied with some flexibility. An excessive deficit was defined in the protocol as one exceeding 3 per cent of GDP in the annual budget but with exceptions for countries which had 'reached a level that comes close' to 3 per cent or if the excess was a result of 'only exceptional and temporary' factors. By the same token, the long-term debt ceiling, which for several member states, notably Belgium and Italy, was far above 60 per cent, the treaty referred only to the need for debt levels to be 'sufficiently diminishing and approaching the reference value at a satisfactory pace'. The inference was that countries whose economies were generally in a good shape and were meeting the other criteria would not be excluded from EMU if they failed to meet the deficit or debt targets exactly.

A special protocol to the treaty gave the UK the right to opt out, even if it fulfilled these conditions. It stipulated that the UK should not be obliged to enter the third stage without a separate decision to do so by its government and parliament. A similar dispensation was subsequently granted to Denmark.

The Madrid summit in December 1995 decided that the new mone-tary unit should be called the euro rather than the ecu which it replaced at parity, one-for-one. The name euro would in English be lower case and invariable (with no 's' in the plural). The change of name was a sop to the German government which felt the ecu had acquired a negative image among its citizens. So was the printing of a €500 note. No other EU country had high-denomination notes of this value except Germany with a DM1,000 note. In the early days of the single currency, the €500 notes were a god-send to trans-Alpine criminals, and money-launderers from every corner of Europe and beyond. They have been withdrawn from normal circulation in a number of member states. The euro would be subdivided into 100 cents. A competition took place in 1996 for the design of euro banknotes. There would be notes for 5, 10, 20, 50, 100, 200 and 500 euro, and coins for 1, 2, 5, 10, 20 and 50 cents and for 1 and 2 euro. Many banking transactions and official payment operations would begin in euro in 1999 but notes and coins would be introduced three years later. Part of the reason was the scale of the operation to pro-duce enough notes and coins to replace the outgoing national currencies. There would be a period of up to two months during which the old and new currencies would circulate in parallel with products in shops labelled with double pricing, before the old currency ceased to be legal tender.

Box 19.1 A lesson in currency stability

Those seeking to track the single European currency from the start need to go back beyond the 1969 Hague summit to 1962. This was when the original Six created a unit of account (UA) as a reference currency to manage an array of common agriculture prices across several local currencies, each subject to fairly frequent upward and downward adjustments. They chose a value for the UA of 0.88867088 grams of fine gold. Those bothered to make the calculation will see that this is the metric equivalent of the Bretton Woods gold exchange standard of US$35 per ounce. In other words, at its creation, one UA equalled one dollar. Over the years, the UA became the European Unit of Account (EUA) with an expanded function for managing EC budget resources in 1974, then the ecu in 1979 and the euro in 1999, each currency replacing its predecessor at parity. It is worth noting therefore that 64 years on, at the beginning of 2016, and despite big see-saws in between, the UA's successor and the dollar were back within 10 per cent of their original one-to-one relationship.

The stability and growth pact

In 1997, largely in response to German concerns about whether sloppy fiscal and budget policies among eurozone countries could destabilise the currency, the Stability and Growth Pact was agreed. It not only required members of the eurozone to keep their annual budgetary deficits below 3 per cent of GDP, but also set up measures to fine countries which breached the limits. In spring 1998 the commission and the EMI examined the record of the 15 member states and reported that 11 met the Maastricht criteria and were thus eligible to join stage three of EMU on the due date of January 1st 1999. They were Austria, Belgium, Finland, France, Germany, Ireland, Italy, Luxembourg, the Netherlands, Portugal and Spain. Two other states – the UK and Denmark – met the criteria, but were exercising their right to opt out, at least at the outset of stage three. Sweden had met the economic criteria but had not taken steps to ensure the independence of its central bank, which was also a requirement for EMU membership. Despite progress, Greece had failed to meet the criteria. These recommendations were endorsed by the European Council in Brussels on May 1st and 2nd 1998.

EMU and the euro launched

So 11 countries adopted a common currency on January 1st 1999. Greece was able to join two years later. The UK government remained reticent, reiterating that in principle it favoured joining, but that it was unlikely to hold the referendum to which it was committed until after the next general election, which took place in May 2001. By May 2005, when a further election was held, there was still no sign of the promised referendum taking place. The May 1998 summit also appointed the first president, and five vice-presidents, of the ECB. The president was Wim Duisenberg, a former Dutch finance minister and central bank governor, who had headed the EMI since 1996. On December 31st 1998 the Ecofin Council met and agreed the irrevocably fixed rates of the participating currencies against the euro (see Table 19.1).

The three years between EMU launch and the issue of physical notes and coins were largely uneventful. The value of the new currency, fixed at its launch at €1 for US$1.17, initially weakened against the dollar, falling below parity in 2000 but recovering to previous levels two years later. Until the coming of notes and coins, the euro was used in company accounts as well as for commercial and official payments and settlements. It featured as a borrowing currency in international bond and other financial markets and was traded on foreign exchanges.

Table 19.1 Conversion rates for the euro

	Rate	Currency
€1 =	13.7603	Austrian schillings
	40.3399	Belgian francs
	40.3399	Luxembourg francs
	1.95583	German marks
	166.386	Spanish pesetas
	5.94573	Finnish markkaa
	6.55957	French francs
	0.787564	Irish pounds
	1,936.27	Italian lire
	2.20371	Dutch guilders
	200.482	Portuguese escudos

Source: European Central Bank.

There were regular calls on Duisenberg to cut interest rates on the new currency to revive the EU economy, but he usually ignored them. The finance ministers of the eurozone met regularly as the Eurogroup, one day before the Ecofin Council. Jean-Claude Juncker, Luxembourg's prime minister, became the first chairman of the Eurogroup finance ministers in 2005. He served until January 2013 when he was replaced by Dutch finance minister Jeroen Dijsselbloem for a term ending in July 2016. The Eurogroup chairman speaks for the euro nations at sessions of the IMF and the World Bank and attends ECB governing council meetings.

Notes and coins by the billion

The introduction of notes and coins – an unprecedented logistical and administrative task – was meticulously planned. On December 15th 2001, banks and post offices across the eurozone were given 'starter packs' of euro coins of every denomination to sell to the curious public. On December 31st, most banks had replaced national notes with euro in their cash machines. Around 56 billion coins and 13 billion notes had been produced. By January 4th, 99 per cent of cash machines had been switched over to euro. Doomsday scenarios of robberies, a flood of counterfeit notes and chaos as shops and customers struggled to adapt to the new currency failed to materialise, as a range of information campaigns stirred retailers and the general public into awareness. By January 15th, more than 90 per cent of cash payments were being made in euro. During the two-month transition period with the euro and the national currency as legal tender and dual pricing in shops, change was always given in euro. This period varied in length, with the Netherlands, Ireland and France having earlier cut-off points, but by March 1st 2002 all national currencies had ceased to be legal tender in the eurozone. The notes were the same throughout the eurozone, but the eight different coins had national emblems on one side. As well as the 12 eurozone countries, the mini-states of Andorra, Monaco, San Marino and the Vatican used the euro and had 'national' coins. Initially encouraged by the EU for political reasons (to help them break with Serbia) Montenegro and Kosovo, although outside the Union, unilaterally adopted the euro without any formalities. The situation is now a legal embarrassment for the EU. France's former African colonies also peg their common regional currency to Europe's. That means around 500 million people rely on the euro or euro-pegged currencies. But the euro still comes a poor second to the dollar as a reserve currency. Its share of global reserves fell to 22 per cent at the end of 2014 (down 5 per cent in 5 years), while the dollar's share rose slightly during this period to 63 per cent.

Germany and France set a bad example

Early in the euro's life, the Stability and Growth Pact came under strain. When Portugal overstepped the deficit mark in 2002 it was warned, and the government immediately moved to bring the budget into line. But then France and Germany, the two biggest euro economies, repeatedly failed to stay below the ceiling, blaming the difficult economic climate for excessive budget deficits. The commission recommended action against both countries – including orders forcing the French and German governments to cut spending and raise taxes by specific amounts – but economic and finance ministers voted not to take the process any further. And in November 2003, the Council of Ministers decided to suspend excessive deficit measures against France and Germany, effectively putting the stability pact on ice indefinitely. The commission took the whole council to the Court of Justice for violating the pact. In July 2004 the court ruled that ministers were wrong to suspend the pact, but added that eurozone governments were not obliged to follow the commission's recommendations on limiting their deficits. At the same time, the commission also proposed loosening Stability Pact conditions by including sustained economic slowdown as an 'exceptional circumstance' as a reason to ease the rules. The Council of ministers adopted these changes in June 2005.

Lambs to the slaughter

But no amount of tinkering with the Stability and Growth Pact could have prepared the EU for what was to follow. The worst economic and financial crisis since the great depression of the 1930s, which was

Table 19.2 Eurozone rescues 2010–15

Date	Country	Amount/billion	Status
May 2010	Greece	€110	
November 2010	Ireland	€85	ended December 2013
March 2011	Greece	€130	
May 2011	Portugal	€78	ended June 2014
March 2012	Spain	€100	ended January 2014
March 2013	Cyprus	€10	ends March 2016
August 2015	Greece	€120	runs to 2018

Source: European Commission.

triggered by the collapse of Lehmann Brothers in 2008, shook the EU to its foundations. The inadequate degree of economic cooperation among its members, its weak banking supervision and the flimsy structure supporting the euro nearly brought the house down. The single currency survived, essentially because of the unremitting political commitment to the euro on the part of core members, led by Germany and France. For them the single currency had come to symbolise the very process of European integration. Even the ultraorthodox anti-interventionists in the German finance ministry acknowledged that the end of the euro would, in all probability, mean the end of the EU. The market-makers and pundits, located mainly outside the eurozone and ready to kill off the euro at a week's or even a day's notice at the height of the crisis in 2011 and 2012, failed to grasp this reality. Some investors lost money as a result. The message only finally sank in after the landmark speech by ECB governor Mario Draghi in London in July 2012 when he declared the bank would 'do whatever it takes' to save the euro. The piecemeal, haphazard and exasperatingly slow response from the EU leadership throughout the crisis in meeting the immense challenge it faced did not bolster confidence.

By the time the crisis eased following the third Greek rescue in 2015, banks from the UK to Cyprus, and Germany to Spain had been bailed out or nationalised or both. Giving priority to austerity inevitably stifled growth prospects. The EU had suffered a double-dip recession. In 2009, GDP fell by 4 per cent and industrial output by 20 per cent. After two years of growth, the EU re-entered recession in 2012. Unemployment had soared, especially among young people and real wages had fallen. Financial support, alongside austerity and reform programmes, was drawn up to rescue governments in Ireland, Portugal, Spain and Cyprus (once each) and Greece (three times) (see Table 19.2). Romania, a non-euro

Table 19.3 The euro's pulling power

Year of eurozone membership	Number	Countries joining
1999	11	Belgium, Finland, France, Germany, Ireland, Italy, Luxembourg, Netherlands, Portugal, Spain
2001	12	Greece
2006	13	Slovenia
2008	15	Cyprus and Malta
2009	16	Slovakia
2011	17	Estonia
2014	18	Latvia
2015	19	Lithuania

Source: European Central Bank.

country received €4 billion balance of payments support from the EU and the IMF in September 2013. The IMF participated in each of the eurozone rescue operations, forming a so-called Troika with the commission and the ECB much-loathed by Greece and its long-suffering citizens. Commitments by core EU countries to the euro notwithstanding, Greece came within a hair's breadth of being ejected from the eurozone in 2014 – a move of unforeseeable consequences for the EU, if not for global financial stability.

In many ways the crisis crystallised around Greece and the EU's repeated rescue efforts. Nerves between Greece and its lenders, already taut under governments headed by traditional parties, reached breaking point under the government of premier Alexis Tsipras and his left-wing Syriza party which was elected by austerity-weary Greek voters in January 2015. The Greek bailouts contained no debt-relief, for which there were no eurozone provisions, although private sector investors took a 50 per cent haircut on their Greek assets as part of the second rescue operation in 2011. The political narrative of the Greek drama is set out in Chapter 3.

Paradoxically, as many in Germany, the Netherlands, Finland and elsewhere were shoving Greece toward the euro exit, other member states were still clambering to join the single currency. Between 2001 and 2015 membership rose from 12 to 19 (see Table 19.3). The three most recent newcomers were the Baltic states. Besides the expected economic benefits, Estonia, Latvia and Lithuania also see the euro as a codicil to their insurance policy of EU and NATO membership against any ill intentions on the part of their eastern neighbour. As a deterrent to Russian skulduggery, joining the euro is largely symbolic. But adopting the euro further betokens the Baltics' commitment to the EU, its style of parliamentary democracy and rule of law.

Two home truths

Besides bailouts for member governments in distress, the EU has put in place some of the missing building blocks of economic and monetary union whose absence had ensured that the crisis, when it came, was deep and lasting. In the process, two underlying givens have become clear. One is the pre-eminence of Germany as the biggest member state with far and away the most powerful economy. The pace and scope of European integration will still require a shared commitment from Germany and France but the former is the senior partner. The second given to be confirmed is the inability of the EU and its member states to act decisively and swiftly. Throughout the crisis, it acted at the last possible minute, applied delaying tactics, agreeing piecemeal only to the minimum steps necessary for short-term survival. This became known as 'kicking the can down the street'. In the eyes of many Brussels observers and analysts, the traditional dithering of EU leaders and their inability to take timely decisions, played out this time before a global audience, only made the crisis worse.

Some modest results

However, the slow-motion EU response did amount – during a period of five years from 2010 – to the makings of a more credible structure for the EMU. It covered items related to economic governance and coordination of national budgetary policies. It also addressed the biggest shortcomings of the euro system: no lender of last resort, no mechanism for joint bailouts and no in-built structure to transfer fiscal resources from surplus to deficit members, as exists with federal currencies like the dollar, beyond the meagre resources of the EU budget.

For its part, the ECB (in addition to Draghi's do-what-it-takes commitment) started a programme of outright monetary transactions (OMTs) in September 2012 to buy up government bonds of EU governments at risk. It followed with more asset purchases in 2014. The ECB then launched a massive programme of quantitative easing in March 2015 – several years after the US Federal Reserve and the Bank of England had put in place similar programmes. Under the ECB quantitative easing programme, the

Eurosystem will buy sovereign bonds from eurozone governments and securities from European institutions and national agencies. The purchases started on March 9th 2015 and will last at least until March 2017. The original end-date of September 2016 was extended for six months in December 2015. The ECB Governing Council made it clear that the programme is open-ended and that purchases will be conducted until the ECB sees a significant trend towards its inflation target level for the EU of just under 2 per cent.

Tightening the rules

EU legislation to consolidate the eurozone included a system of coordinating national budgets via the European Commission during the first half of each year, known as the European Semester, which began in 2010. A package of measures, the 'six pack', was introduced in December 2011 to reinforce the Stability and Growth Pact. Following a European Council agreement of March 2011, eurozone finance ministers signed a treaty establishing the European Stability Mechanism (ESM) on July 11th. Its actual application was predicated on the adoption by member states of a proposed three-line addition to Article 136 of the TFEU under the simplified revision processes introduced by the Lisbon treaty. This avoided the drawn-out national ratification procedures for minor treaty changes. This treaty amendment was finally adopted in April 2013. It firmly embeds the ESM in the EU legislative structure, as the Germans had urged. The additional text read:

> The Member States whose currency is the euro may establish a stability mechanism to be activated if indispensable to safeguard the stability of the euro area as a whole. The granting of any required financial assistance under the mechanism will be made subject to strict conditionality.

The ESM acts as a permanent source of financial assistance for member states in financial difficulty, with a maximum lending capacity of €500 billion. The ESM, formally launched in October 2012, replaced two earlier temporary EU funding programmes: the European Financial Stability Facility (EFSF), and the European Financial Stabilisation Mechanism (EFSM). All new bailouts of eurozone member states are covered by the ESM. Although signed by the eurozone countries, the ESM is also open to non-euro area EU countries for *ad hoc* participation in financial assistance operations. The ESM treaty also provides for twice-yearly summits of heads of government of euro-zone countries.

The fiscal compact

The ESM treaty was followed by another, the so-called fiscal compact. Vetoed from becoming an EU text by UK premier David Cameron at a European Council in December 2011 the 'Treaty on stability, coordination and governance in the economic and monetary union' was adopted by the other EU states as an intergovernmental treaty and signed on March 2nd 2012. Domiciled in Luxembourg, it took effect on January 1st 2013. Although in 2014, the Czech government reversed earlier hostility to the fiscal compact, it was slow to submit it to parliamentary ratification. The compact tightens further the existing mechanisms to prevent future debt-related crises. It imposes rigid and automatic procedures for avoiding and cutting budget deficits.

- Budgets should be balanced (a structural deficit of no more than 0.5 per cent of GDP).
- Public debt less than 60 per cent of gross domestic product and obligations of those with higher debt levels to reduce them by 1/20th each year.
- Automatic penalties for non-compliant states and supervision by the European Commission.

A banking union

In parallel, legislation has been introduced to build an EU banking union, creating stronger banking structures, notably through higher solvency ratios, other prudential requirements and closer supervision and controls. Two of the three basic pillars of a eurozone banking union are in place.

1   *Single supervision mechanism (SSM)*: The Council of Ministers adopted an SSM regulation in October 2013 which took effect on November 4th 2014. It charges the European Central Bank with the direct supervision and control of the 120 biggest eurozone banks, representing 82 per cent of total eurozone banking assets. National supervisors will continue to monitor the remaining 3,500 smaller banks, but in close cooperation with the ECB.
2   *Single resolution mechanism (SRM)*: The SRM regulation was adopted in April 2014, and took effect on January 1st 2016. It provides a resolution mechanism for banks within the SSM which get into serious

difficulties. The mechanism includes a fund, financed by contributions from banks, which will reach its target size of €55 billion after seven years.

3   *European deposit insurance guarantee scheme*: The third pillar has taken more time to organise. This largely reflects German concerns that funds set aside to protect German savers would be used to rescue savers in other eurozone countries via debt mutualisation. Proposals for a single deposit insurance scheme presented by the Commission in late 2015 foresaw a measured step-by-step approach over a period of years.

Note

1   The accepted abbreviation for the Economic and Financial Affairs Council.

20 Taxation

Direct taxation – the taxes paid on personal income, corporate profits and investment capital – is a sovereign responsibility of each member state. The Union only intervenes where the incidence of this taxation could breach EU free competition rules or cause discrimination among EU nationals. Accordingly, EU tax legislation has almost exclusively concerned indirect taxation: customs duties on the one hand, and VAT and excise duties on the other. Even within the EU context, almost every decision on taxation requires unanimous agreement in the Council of Ministers. This requirement was not relaxed in the Single European Act, which substantially increased the number of policy areas where unanimity was replaced by qualified majority vote. The level of taxation varies enormously within the Union, with Sweden and Denmark being the highest taxed countries and Romania and Slovakia the lowest (see Table 20.1).

General application of VAT

The EU's biggest fiscal innovation was to apply VAT as the principal consumption tax. Value-added tax – a French invention – replaced a variety of different indirect taxes in the member states. Two directives adopted in 1967 provided for those countries not already applying VAT to introduce it within a specific timetable. VAT commended itself to the Community because of its economic neutrality. At each stage in the making or marketing of a product, the tax paid at the preceding stage is deducted from that paid by the vendor. In this way the tax remains proportionate to the value of the goods and services, no matter how many transactions they have been through. The member states reached agreement in 1977 on a common basis for assessing VAT, although it was subject to many exceptions. It was, however, harmonised enough to enable the EC to use it to provide part of its budgetary 'own resources', up to a maximum rate of 1%, raised in 1986 to 1.4%. The member states were unable to agree on precise levels for VAT, the number of different rates or the goods and services that were excluded or subject to a zero rate.

Table 20.1 Tax revenue and implicit tax rates by type of economic activity (2002–12)

	Tax revenue % of GDP			Labour			Implicit tax rate* on Consumption			Capital		
	2002	2011	2012	2002	2011	2012	2002	2011	2012	2002	2011	2012
EU-28	**38.8**	**38.8**	**39.4**	**50.8**	**50.9**	**51.0**	**28.8**	**28.9**	**28.5**	**20.7**	**20.4**	**20.8**
Euro area	**39.5**	**39.5**	**40.4**	**53.0**	**53.3**	**53.3**	**27.4**	**27.3**	**26.8**	**19.8**	**19.8**	**20.2**
Austria	43.6	42.2	43.1	55.2	56.7	57.4	28.5	27.9	27.6	16.5	15.6	15.2
Belgium	45.2	44.2	45.4	54.9	54.6	53.9	24.2	24.1	23.7	20.6	20.8	22.0
Bulgaria	28.5	27.3	27.9	41.8	33.8	32.9	41.6	51.9	53.3	16.6	14.3	13.8
Croatia	37.9	35.3	35.7	38.9	41.4	40.7	50.5	47.3	49.1	10.7	11.3	10.3
Cyprus	30.9	35.3	35.3	32.5	35.7	37.1	38.5	36.2	36.8	29.0	28.1	26.1
Czech Republic	34.6	34.6	35.0	52.9	51.9	51.7	27.9	32.9	33.4	19.3	15.2	14.9
Denmark	47.9	47.7	48.1	54.5	51.3	51.0	33.0	31.5	31.0	12.8	17.6	18.4
Estonia	31.0	32.3	32.5	54.5	52.1	51.0	38.4	41.3	41.9	7.1	6.6	7.1
Finland	44.7	43.7	44.1	52.2	52.3	53.2	29.9	32.3	32.4	17.9	15.4	14.3
France	43.3	43.7	45.0	51.5	52.3	52.3	26.2	25.2	24.7	22.9	23.2	23.6
Germany	38.9	38.5	39.1	60.7	56.0	56.6	26.8	28.2	27.6	12.5	15.8	15.9
Greece	33.7	32.4	33.7	38.3	36.5	41.9	36.7	38.6	36.3	25.0	25.0	21.8
Hungary	38.0	37.3	39.2	50.3	47.3	46.4	37.0	39.1	40.0	12.6	13.6	13.5
Ireland	28.3	28.2	28.7	35.3	43.0	42.7	38.8	34.8	34.8	26.0	22.2	22.5
Italy	40.5	42.4	44.0	49.9	52.0	51.1	26.1	25.3	24.7	23.9	22.7	24.2
Latvia	28.6	27.6	27.9	51.7	50.0	49.0	36.7	38.3	38.4	11.6	11.7	12.6
Lithuania	29.1	27.4	27.2	50.8	46.4	46.5	40.1	41.1	39.8	9.7	12.7	13.9
Luxembourg	39.3	38.2	39.3	38.5	44.2	44.3	27.3	27.8	28.1	34.2	28.0	27.5
Malta	30.0	33.0	33.6	36.9	33.5	34.6	39.3	40.2	38.8	23.8	26.3	26.6
Netherlands	37.7	38.6	39.0	49.7	56.3	57.5	30.2	28.8	28.3	20.1	14.9	14.2
Poland	32.7	32.3	32.5	41.1	38.4	40.4	36.3	39.1	36.3	23.7	22.9	23.7
Portugal	31.4	33.2	32.4	37.7	41.7	41.4	38.1	36.6	37.4	24.2	21.6	21.1
Romania	28.1	28.4	28.3	43.9	39.3	40.0	38.9	44.2	45.1	17.2	16.4	15.0
Slovakia	33.0	28.6	28.3	45.8	44.1	45.4	32.7	36.2	33.4	21.4	19.7	21.2
Slovenia	37.8	37.2	37.6	54.3	52.2	52.5	36.1	37.3	37.9	9.7	10.6	9.8
Spain	34.1	31.8	32.5	48.1	55.0	53.0	27.7	26.8	26.5	25.7	20.9	22.9
Sweden	47.5	44.4	44.2	62.5	57.5	58.6	26.7	28.9	28.4	10.8	13.7	13.0
United Kingdom	34.8	35.8	35.4	38.6	39.1	38.9	33.0	33.2	33.8	28.4	27.7	27.4

* Implicit tax rates (ITR) express aggregate tax revenues as a percentage of the potential tax base for each field.

Source: Eurostat.

Duty-free goes on internal travel

The other form of indirect taxation which member states have continued to levy is excise duty on certain specific products, such as alcoholic drinks, manufactured tobacco and fuels. Despite numerous proposals by the commission, the only common regulations adopted before July 1991 related to the structure of duty on cigarettes. Acting on complaints from the commission, however, the Court of Justice has delivered judgments aimed at preventing member states favouring home produced beers, wines or spirits to the detriment of imported products, which have led to several of them modifying their range of duties. The commission also established a common basis for duty-free allowances for travellers between member states. In principle, duty-free allowances should have been abolished from January 1st 1993 when the EU's internal market was completed. It was decided, however, that until June 30th 1999 duty-free sales could continue at airports, on planes and on ferries travelling from one member state to another. Despite intense lobbying by the duty-free industry, largely financed by tobacco and alcoholic drinks manufacturers, the Council of Ministers refused to reverse this decision in June 1999, and duty-free sales for travellers within the EU ended on the due date.

Harmonisation of indirect tax rates

A strong impetus to harmonise indirect tax rates came in 1985 with the adoption of a specific target date (end-1992) for completing the single market. The commission argued strongly that these rates would have to be 'approximated' if the objective of removing all internal frontier controls was to be achieved. Approximation meant bringing national VAT rates close enough together to avoid any significant distortion of cross-border trade resulting from rate differentials between neighbouring countries. The model was the US where the difference in sales taxes levied by neighbouring states is not large enough to give rise to much bargain-shopping across state-lines. In July 1987 the commission produced its proposals, which it said should be implemented by member states no later than December 31st 1992.

VAT and excise duties

Two rate bands were proposed for VAT: a standard rate within the range of 14–20 per cent, and a reduced rate 'for items of basic necessity' of between 4 and 9 per cent. The items suggested for the reduced rate were food, energy for heating and lighting, water, pharmaceuticals, books, newspapers and periodicals, and passenger transport. Member states were free to fix their national rates at any point within each range. For excise duties, the commission proposed a complete harmonisation, and specified a precise amount of duty for all products attracting excise duty.

No quick fix

It took four years, and a great deal of horse-trading, for member states to come to any sort of agreement on the VAT proposals. In June 1991 a political agreement was reached, although on a greatly amended and watered-down draft text. The amended proposals stipulated that, from

Table 20.2 VAT rates in member states, 2015

Country	Standard rate %	Reduced rate %	Country	Standard rate %	Reduced rate %
Austria	20	10	Italy	22	10
Belgium	21	6/12	Latvia	21	12
Bulgaria	20	9	Lithuania	21	5/9
Croatia	25	5/13	Luxembourg	17	8/14
Cyprus	19	5/9	Malta	18	5/7
Czech Republic	21	10/15	Netherlands	21	6
Denmark	25	none	Poland	23	5/8
Estonia	20	9	Portugal	23	6/13
Finland	24	10/14	Romania	24	5/9
France	20	5.5/10	Slovakia	20	10
Germany	19	7	Slovenia	22	9.5
Greece	23	6.5/13	Spain	21	10
Hungary	27	5/18	Sweden	25	6/12
Ireland	23	9/13.5	United Kingdom	20	5

Source: Eurostat.

January 1st 1993, the standard rate of VAT should be set at a minimum of 15 per cent in all member states; no maximum rate was suggested. In addition, for a list of 20 or so goods and services, regarded as essential and not extensively traded across national borders (including food, domestic heating and lighting, passenger transport, and books and newspapers), one or more reduced rates of at least 5 per cent could be applied. In a major concession to the UK, it was agreed that zero and other rates below 5 per cent could continue if they were already in effect on January 1st 1991.

The amended proposals were finally approved in July 1992, in a directive which stipulated a minimum standard VAT rate of 15 per cent for a four-year period. All the arrangements were linked to a transitional period, to end no later than January 1st 1997, during which VAT on goods exported within the EU would be taxed in the country of destination rather than of origin. After that date all goods should be taxed on the same basis, irrespective of where they were sold. The commission was asked to propose a permanent system, which would make this possible by the end of 1994. Although the commission met this deadline, the member states could not agree on a permanent system of collection. Nonetheless, there was a considerable convergence of VAT rates between 1987 and 1997, partly owing to market forces but also as a consequence of the adoption of the 1992 directive. By the time that ten new member states joined the Union in May 2004, the convergence had increased. The VAT rates in all member states in 2015 are shown in Table 20.2.

Cross-border complexity

Procedures for paying VAT on cross-border transactions within the EU were set out in the VAT directive, adopted by the Council of Ministers in November 2006. It distinguishes between goods and services. The rules are, to say the least, complicated. When selling a product to a business in another EU country, the seller charges no VAT if the buyer is VAT-registered in his country of residence. The latter pays VAT at their end. When selling to private customers in another EU country, the seller must register in that country and charge VAT there at local rates. Small sales volumes are exempted from this rule.

Value added tax on services between traders was now to be levied in the country where services were provided as a matter of principle. The buyer, if registered for VAT, pays in their country of residence at the local rate. When selling to a private customer in another EU country, the seller must normally charge VAT at the **rate that applies in their country, except for telecommunications, broadcasting and electronic services**. New 'place of supply' rules for businesses dealing in cross-border telecommunications, broadcasting and e-services came into effect on January 1st 2015. This means that such services are taxed in the member state of the customer buying the service to ensure that the taxation of e-services reflect where consumption takes place. In this way, VAT goes to the treasury of the country where the buyer is based.

Excise duty proposals virtually abandoned

If the approximation proposals on VAT were radically modified, those on excise duties were virtually abandoned. In place of the complete harmonisation proposed, the Council of Ministers agreed in June 1991 that minimum duties, for the most part well below those actually paid in most member states, should apply. The lack of agreement reflected differences between northern member states, with high duties on alcohol and tobacco, and the Mediterranean countries, large producers of wine and tobacco, which traditionally applied zero or low duties. A 2008 council directive established general arrangements for products subject to excise duty, so as to guarantee the free movement of goods and the proper functioning of the single market.

Tax evasion and tax avoidance

In 1990, the Council of Ministers adopted three directives for a common system of taxation applicable to mergers, and to subsidiary or associated companies when these were based in different member states. In 1998, the commission proposed a minimum withholding tax of 20 per cent on interest earned by EU residents on their investments in another member state. After long delays, the tax was eventually agreed as part of the EU savings directive, which came into effect on July 1st 2005. The aim of the tax is to ensure that citizens of one member state do not evade tax by depositing undeclared funds outside their jurisdiction of residence. The tax is withheld at source and passed on to the EU country of residence.

Since then, tax authorities in the EU have agreed to cooperate much more closely to combat tax fraud and tax evasion. The essential piece of legislation is a council directive of February 2011 defining administrative cooperation in the field of taxation. It established the necessary procedures for better cooperation between national tax administrations – such as exchanges of information on request; spontaneous exchanges; automatic exchanges; participation in administrative enquiries; simultaneous controls; and notifications to each other of tax decisions. It also provided for the necessary practical tools, such as a secure electronic system for the information exchange. This directive was later amended by requiring the automatic mandatory exchange of financial account information.

On December 8th 2015, the council adopted a directive aimed at preventing tax avoidance by multinational corporations located in EU member states. The directive, to apply from January 1st 2017, will impose transparency on special tax deals struck between big corporations and national EU governments via so-called advance rulings and advance pricing arrangements which minimise tax payments. It will require member states to exchange information automatically on advance cross-border tax rulings, as well as advance pricing arrangements. Member states receiving the information can request more details where appropriate.

21 Agriculture

The common agricultural policy: Europe's first common policy

All advanced economies protect their agriculture sector. The EU is no exception. The common agricultural policy (CAP) was, together with the customs union, the economic activity spelled out in the greatest detail in the Treaty of Rome. It was, indeed, for a long time virtually the only common policy that the Community was able to implement. Most European farmers have benefited from the CAP. Food shortages in the post-war period quickly became a thing of the past. But this relative success came at a price. By dominating the EU budget from the very beginning, the CAP stifled the development of other common policies. At the same time, its basic principle of guaranteed prices for farmers generated huge food surpluses. These were exported at subsidised prices, distorting world markets, bringing the EU into conflict with the United States and other food exporters, as well as with developing countries whose farmers could not compete with cheap imports from Europe. The EU has spent the past 30 years reducing the CAP's worst excesses, balancing its benefits more fairly among stakeholders and consumers and supporting new production methods and technologies. European farming now sits more comfortably in the EU economic and physical landscape. Apart from Luxembourg, the UK has the smallest relative farming sector of any member state (see Table 21.1).

Effect on EU agriculture

The aims of the CAP, as set out in Article 39 of the treaty, are essentially threefold:

- guarantee consumers a reliable and secure supply of quality food at affordable prices;

- ensure a decent income level for farmers;
- make farming more efficient through higher productivity and technical innovation.

The CAP has transformed the structure of the Union's agriculture. Generous price support has combined with technology to raise production and productivity. The EU is virtually self-sufficient in all but tropical foods and a number of vegetable proteins and starches for animal feed. A rural exodus has reduced the farming population by two thirds since 1958 while the average standard of living of those remaining has risen. But the impact of the CAP has been skewed. It has helped big farmers much more than small ones. EU citizens have paid higher than market prices in exchange for food security and food safety. Through the EU budget, taxpayers have paid twice for the CAP: once in funding high guaranteed prices for agricultural products, and a second time by funding export subsidies to get rid of the resulting surpluses on world markets. In fairness to the CAP, the problem of its domination of EU spending is partly an optical one. It is the only policy area funded almost entirely via the EU budget. Other policies are financed mainly by member states or are, like R&D policy (see pp. 160–5), jointly funded with the EU.

The CAP is based on three main principles:

- a single market for farm goods (common prices and free movement);
- Community preference (a common tariff against imports from outside the EU);
- shared financial responsibility (costs are paid from a common fund – the EU budget – to which all member states contribute).

How it works

The CAP had an integrated system of measures which maintained commodity price levels within the EU by subsidising (and in some cases limiting) production. There are a number of mechanisms.

Price support

Guaranteed prices to farmers have been the major tool of the CAP down the years – and the cause of its biggest problems. The level of price support has fallen with each successive tranche of CAP reform, starting from 1992. For years, prices for cereals (barley, bread wheat and maize), oilseeds, dairy products, beef and veal, and sugar depended on the intervention price as a guaranteed floor price. When prices fell to the intervention level, the EU bought and stored (at EU cost) any amount of the product in question offered on the market. But price support has been largely replaced by direct income payments to farmers. Market support now represents less than 10 per cent of CAP spending on 'farm support'.

Direct payments to farmers

These were originally intended to encourage farmers to boost home-grown food supplies. A form of direct payment was introduced as 'set-aside' premiums in 1988 for farmers who left part of their land fallow and non-productive. They are now paid to farmers directly as income support and as assistance for complying with sustainable agricultural practices as well as for looking after the surrounding countryside for the benefit of the rural population and visitors alike.

Import levies and import quotas

Levies were set at a level to raise the world market price up to the EU target price. This is defined as the most suitable price for those goods within the EU.

Table 21.1 Agriculture's share of GDP, 2014

	%		%
Austria	1.5	Italy	2.2
Belgium	0.8	Latvia	4.4
Bulgaria	5.3	Lithuania	3.5
Croatia	4.1	Luxembourg	0.3
Cyprus	2.4	Malta	1.6
Czech Republic	2.4	Netherlands	1.6
Denmark	1.3	Poland	3.3
Estonia	3.7	Portugal	2.3
Finland	2.1	Romania	5.4
France	1.7	Slovakia	3.7
Germany	0.8	Slovenia	2.2
Greece	3.8	Spain	2.5
Hungary	4.3	Sweden	1.5
Ireland	1.6	United Kingdom	0.6

Source: Eurostat.

Production quotas

These were introduced in an effort to prevent overproduction of some goods (for example, milk, grain, sugar and wine) that attracted subsidies well in excess of market prices. The need to store and dispose of excess produce wasted resources and brought the CAP into disrepute. A secondary market evolved, especially in the sale of milk quotas.

Five successive reforms

The high costs of the CAP were already alarming European leaders as early as 1967. With self-sufficiency, attained in the 1980s, came almost permanent surpluses of basic items – the notorious butter and beef mountains and milk and wine lakes. More and more CAP resources went on export and storage subsidies. Various reforms since 1992 have sought to remedy the surplus problem and target the environmental sustainability of European agriculture. The aim has been to break the link between subsidies and production, to diversify the rural economy and to respond to consumer demands for safe food, high standards of animal welfare and the conservation of the rural environment.

1   The first reform, adopted in 1992 – and named after the then agriculture commissioner Ray MacSharry – aimed to dismantle the price support mechanisms, reduce guaranteed prices and compensate farmers with a 'direct payment' less closely related to current production levels and based on historic yields. MacSharry introduced new supply control measures. His reforms affected the grain, oilseed, protein crop (field peas and beans), beef and sheep meat markets.
2   The second major reform was adopted in March 1999 as part of the Agenda 2000 package to prepare for the big EU enlargement in 2004. Like the first reform, Agenda 2000 used direct payments to compensate farmers for half of the loss from new cuts in price support. It divided the CAP into two 'pillars': production support and rural development. Agenda 2000 reforms focused on the grain, oilseed, dairy and beef markets. Shortly after, in 2002, EU member states agreed to freeze farm spending (though not rural development) in real terms between 2006 and 2013, despite enlargement.
3   The third reform, in 2003, introduced the Single Payment Scheme (SPS) to break the link between farm support and actual production, attacking overproduction and waste. The SPS linked subsidies to land size rather than production volume, and laid down environmental,

food safety and animal welfare standards as a precondition for receiving payments. The reform also featured a shift in funding from the first to the second pillar; land not farmed must be maintained in good agricultural condition and the rural environment protected. This marked a significant shift in political priorities from production to sustainability.

4   In 2008, the fourth policy review, dubbed the CAP Health Check, funnelled more spending to rural development. The reforms, covering the period 2009–13, made farmers spend 10 per cent of their EU receipts – double the previous amount – on projects to improve the countryside. Milk quotas were to be scrapped in 2015. Instead of paying farmers to produce more, the EU now made payments conditional on farmers meeting environmental and animal welfare standards and keeping their land in good condition.

5   The latest reform package in 2013 tightened the process further. It set out to reduce the imbalance in CAP support payments away from richer farmers and landowners and in favour of small farms, including those in difficult regions. The reform package also narrowed the gap between the higher support payments received by farmers in western Europe and the lower payments received by farmers in central and eastern European member states. It confirmed the ending of milk and wine quotas agreed earlier, and ruled that sugar quotas would disappear in 2017. The level of the CAP budget was effectively frozen until 2020. Its main features were:

- *Income support for farmers and assistance for complying with sustainable agricultural practices*: farmers receive direct payments, provided they apply strict standards on food safety, environmental protection and animal health and welfare. These payments are fully financed by the EU, and account for 70 per cent of the CAP budget. Part of the direct payments are linked to farmers' compliance with sustainable agricultural practices beneficial to soil quality, biodiversity and the environment generally, such as crop diversification, the maintenance of permanent grassland or the preservation of ecological areas on farms. Payments will be based on surface area rather than output levels, encouraging a move away from intensive farming.
- *Market-support measures*: these will continue in well-defined situations (as well as in emergencies) to maintain market stability. Such payments account for less than 10 per cent of the CAP budget.
- *Rural development measures*: these are intended to help farmers modernise their holdings, while protecting the environment

Table 21.2 Agriculture expenditure EU budget 2015

	Commitments (€m)	Payments (€m)
Administrative expenditure on agriculture and rural development	131	131
Interventions in agricultural markets	2,401	2,401
Direct aids	40,909	40,909
Rural development	13,819	11,162
Pre-accession measures in the field of agriculture and rural development	94	177
International aspects of agriculture and rural development	5	4
Audit of agricultural expenditure	87	87
Policy strategy and coordination of agriculture and rural development	56	51
Horizon 2020; research & innovation	101	19
Total	**57,603**	**54,942**

Note: Totals may not add up due to rounding.

Source: European Commission.

(including climate action), contributing to the diversification of farming and non-farming activities, like fostering rural tourism, and the vitality of rural communities. These payments are part-financed by member countries, and generally extend over a number of years. They make up 20 per cent of the CAP budget.

• Agriculture would feature in the EU's Horizon 2020 programme for co-funding research and innovation.

Costs and benefits

The total cost of the CAP of €57.6 billion in 2015 represented 39 per cent of the total EU budget compared with a peak of 72 per cent in 1984. In 2015 (see Table 21.2), nearly two thirds of market support payments of €2.4 billion went to the fruit and vegetables and wine sectors. Only 5 per cent of EU citizens work in agriculture, and the sector generates just 1.6 per cent of EU GDP. Whether European consumers pay too much for their food as a result of the CAP is a moot question. Higher prices in Europe than on world markets now partly reflect high EU food safety and quality standards. An average EU family spends about 15 per cent of its income on food nowadays compared with 30 per cent in 1960. The expansion of the CAP to cover rural development has put farming into a broader context, contributing to the survival of the countryside as a place to live, work, visit and enjoy. Farmers thus receive part of their direct payments for their work as stewards of the countryside, providing a public good the market is unable – or unwilling – to pay for.

Biggest trader in farm goods

The European Union is the world's biggest trader in agricultural products (see Table 21.3). Its exports in 2014 totalled €121.9 billion with imports at €104.1 billion. It is also the biggest importer of farm goods from developing countries. It buys four times more agricultural products from the world's 48 least advanced countries than the US, Japan, Australia, Canada and New Zealand combined. The EU's biggest suppliers of agricultural products in 2014 were Brazil, the US, Argentina, China and Indonesia. Its principal export markets were the US, Russia, China, Japan and Turkey.

The importance of farming to national economies varies across the EU. In Poland, 18 per cent of the population works in agriculture, compared with fewer than 2 per cent in the UK and Belgium. The number of people working on farms roughly halved in the 15 older EU member states between 1980 and 2003. About 2 per cent of farmers leave the industry every year across the EU. Nationally France benefits most, with about 16 per cent of CAP payments in 2014, followed by Spain (12 per cent), then Germany (11 per cent), Italy (10 per cent), Poland (9 per cent) and the UK (7 per cent). France is the biggest agricultural producer, accounting for some 18 per cent of EU farm output. Germany comes second, with about 13.4 per cent. Of the six, four (Germany, the UK, France and Italy) are net contributors to the CAP budget while Poland and Spain are net beneficiaries. Poland in fact makes the biggest profit from the CAP with net receipts in excess of €3.2 billion in 2014.

Table 21.3 EU farm trade by product 2014 (in %)

Exports		Imports	
Wine and spirits	16	Tropical fruits	10
Pasta, pastry, infant food		Oilcakes (for animal feed)	8
& other foodstuffs	13	Coffee and tea	7
Wheat	5	Palm oil	5
Chocolate & confectionery	4	Soya beans	5
Porkmeat	3	Non-tropical fruit	5
Cheese	3	Vegetables	4
Fruit & vegetable preparations	3	Cocoa beans	3
Others	51	Others	53

Source: European Commission.

Food safety

After food-related scares such as BSE and foot-and-mouth disease in cattle and dioxin-contaminated chicken, EU farm ministers set up a European Food Safety Authority (EFSA) in 2002. Based in Parma, Italy, the EFSA provides independent scientific advice on all matters linked to food and feed safety – including animal health and welfare and plant protection — and offers scientific advice on nutrition in relation to EU legislation. The watchdog not only sets food safety standards across the EU but is also responsible for ensuring that they are implemented in the field. Strict traceability of farm products along the food-chain 'from stable to table' has also been established.

Genetically modified foods

By the 1990s, demands for high food-safety levels had already turned public sentiment against genetically modified organisms (GMOs), which were mainly being produced in the US. Many GM crops had received regulatory approval in the United States, but by 1998, the approval process had stalled in the EU. Despite threatening to ignite a trade war with the United States, the EU stood by its effective ban on GM crops. In July 2001, the commission issued two regulations proposing new rules on the traceability of GMOs throughout the food chain, and providing consumers with information by labelling all GM food. The main directive setting the legal framework for growing GMOs in the EU was agreed in 2001 and amended by a second directive adopted in April 2015. It allows member states to restrict or prohibit the cultivation of GMOs in their territory.

22 Fisheries

A provocation

The EU's common fisheries policy (CFP) got off to a bad start – from which it has never really recovered. The original six EEC countries rushed a first version through the Council of Ministers in October 1970 just as four candidates – the UK, Ireland, Denmark and Norway – began their membership negotiations. This robbed the four, all big fishing nations with an 80 per cent share of western Europe's coastal waters, of any say in framing a policy where their legitimate interests far outweighed those of the Six. The basic principle of the CFP – that fishing vessels of all member states could fish in each others' coastal waters 'up to the beaches' – would have been rejected by the four had they been in on the negotiations. As it was, they were presented with a *fait accompli*: take it or leave it. In the end, Norway did not. The bad faith displayed by the Six and the clearly negative impact the CFP would have on its fishing industry was one of the main reasons why the Norwegian people rejected EEC membership in a referendum in September 1972. The UK accepted, reluctantly, the CFP. When it tried later unilaterally to create a reserved coastal zone, it was condemned by the European Court of Justice in July 1991 in a case brought against it by the European Commission and France two years earlier.

The primary goal of the CFP, essentially by setting quotas ('total allowable catches'), has been to redress the effect of long-standing over-fishing and stock depletion, thereby ensuring sustainable fisheries and guarantee incomes and stable jobs for fishermen. It has been revised and updated several times over the years. Overall, the CFP has had only limited success in achieving its objectives. In 2013 the council and parliament reached agreement on a new CFP, covering the long-term environmental, economic and social sustainability of fishing and aquaculture activities.

A full-scale CFP, overhauling and expanding the 1970 text, was introduced in 1983. It still maintained the principle of open access for all EC fishermen. Its main provisions were:

• *Fishing zones*. In principle, the Union's waters are open to all EU fishermen within a 200-mile limit from the Atlantic and North Sea coasts, but within narrower limits in the Mediterranean and Baltic seas. Member states are, however, allowed to retain limits up to 12 miles from their shores, within which fishing is reserved for their own fleets and for boats from other member states with traditional rights. In addition, fishing in an area beyond 12 miles around the Orkney and Shetland islands, for potentially endangered species, is subject to a system of Union licences.

• *Fish stocks*. These are conserved and managed by fixing total allowable catches which are agreed annually by the Council of Ministers for all species threatened by overfishing. They are divided into quotas for each member state.

• *Conservation*. Based on scientific advice, conservation measures consist mainly of limits on fishing in certain zones, minimum mesh sizes for nets and, in certain cases, minimum sizes for fish landed. With the agreement of the commission, member states may apply extra conservation measures of their own, but these must not discriminate against other EU countries.

• *Surveillance*. Measures such as obligatory logbooks, port inspections, aerial controls, and so on, are applied by the member states, under the supervision of the commission, which has a team of inspectors for this purpose.

• *Marketing*. Standards as regards quality, size, weight, presentation and packing are applied throughout the Union, largely through the agency of producer organisations, but subject to inspection by the commission. Guide prices are set by the Council of Ministers with 'withdrawal' prices set at 70–90 per cent, the Union compensating fishermen for catches withdrawn from the market. Export refunds are available when, as is usually the case, the guide and withdrawal prices are higher than world prices. If European supplies prove insufficient, customs duties on imports can be suspended, as has happened with tuna and cod.

• *International relations*. Reciprocal agreements, permitting limited access to each other's waters and markets have been made with several other countries, such as Norway, the Faeroes, Canada and the United States. Other agreements with developing countries in Africa and the Indian Ocean permit EU vessels to fish in their waters in exchange for financial and technical assistance.

The EU is the world's fourth largest producer

The accession of Spain and Portugal in 1986 doubled the number of fishermen in the Community (to about 300,000, although by 2007 it was down to 190,000), and increased the tonnage of the fishing fleet by about 65 per cent and total catches by 30 per cent. Spain and Portugal were required to adapt their fishing policies to the CFP.

At the same time the EU stepped up its financial aid for restructuring fishing fleets – with grants available for scrapping surplus capacity, the construction and modernisation of boats, the development of aquaculture, and improvements in processing and marketing. In 1998 the EU adopted a regulation banning the use of driftnets by all vessels in EU waters except the Baltic. It came into effect on January 1st 2002, and was accompanied by social measures and compensation for the fishermen concerned. The CFP is based to a large extent on the model of the CAP, but costs far less. The total cost for 2007–13 was around €3.8 billion, or around 0.4 per cent of the entire budget. In the 1990s, all sides – fishermen, fish processors, environmentalists, consumers – agreed that the CFP was wasteful and encouraged cheating. Indeed, from the middle of the 1990s, the commission began pushing for more conservation measures, as stocks would soon be exhausted. The sensitivity of the issue was evident during the 'Greenland halibut war' between Spanish fishermen and Canadian authorities off the coast of the Grand Banks, where Canadian fishermen had been forced to stop fishing for cod because of a dramatic collapse in stocks. Within the EU, fleet-cutting programmes were adopted – so-called multi-annual guidance programmes – which included sanctions on member states who failed to meet their targets.

A radical reform of the CFP was agreed by fisheries ministers in December 2002. The reformed CFP came into force on January 1st, 2003. It still struggled with the same unsolved problems, confirming its ineffectiveness. This time it focused more on the sustainable exploitation of fish resources based on sound scientific advice and on the precautionary approach to fishing, as well as on sustainable aquaculture. It took a more long-term approach to fisheries management by setting multi-annual recovery plans for stocks. The commission can take emergency measures where there is a serious threat to the conservation of resources, and member states can adopt conservation and management measures applicable to all fishing vessels within their 12-mile zones. The reformed CFP strengthened control and enforcement via closer cooperation between member states so that each state can control vessels flying its flag throughout EU waters, except in the 12-mile zone of another member state. Fisheries ministers also established an emergency fund to encourage the decommissioning of vessels (the so-called 'Scrapping Fund').

In April 2009, a commission green paper on CFP performance recited a catalogue of failures. Scientists warned that nearly 90 per cent of stocks were overexploited. Many species – cod and hake, for example – were depleted in certain EU waters after years of chronic overfishing, exacerbated by poor controls and modest fines that were not high enough to deter law-breakers and quota-busters. The commission called for radical changes. The result was another reformed CFP which took effect on January 1st 2014. It seeks to make fishing fleets more selective in what they catch, and to phase out the practice of discarding unwanted fish. The reform also changes the way in which the CFP is managed, giving EU countries greater control at national and regional level. The updated CFP has four main policy areas:

- Fisheries management
- International policy
- Market and trade policy
- Funding of the policy

The CFP is funded from the European Maritime and Fisheries Fund. It is one of the EU's five structural and investment funds (see pp. 186–8). Its resources during the EU's 2014–20 financing period is €6.4 billion. Of this, €4.34 billion goes on making fishing more sustainable and more profitable, including measures for market support, local development and marketing and processing. Another €580 million is earmarked for better control and enforcement.

23 Research and innovation

At the outset, EU industrial policy had two main prongs: to help older, declining industries such as textiles, shipbuilding and steel restructure themselves in such a way as to minimise the inevitable pain and disruption; and to assist in the development and spread of new technologies which provide the foundation for future economic growth.

The EC's research programmes date from the 1980s

Although the Community had for many years been involved in fundamental and applied research in nuclear energy, its involvement in industrial research began only in the early 1980s with the growing realisation that the EC was falling seriously behind the United States and Japan, and was also in danger of being outstripped by thrusting new economies like South Korea, Singapore and Taiwan. European cooperation bore fruit in a number of areas where a large capital investment and the capture of a significant slice of the world market were necessary conditions for success. Examples of a joined-up industrial policy included Airbus and Ariane in the aerospace sector, which received loans from the EIB, and JET (Joint European Torus) in the nuclear fusion sector, a powerful experimental research institution built and operated by the EU (see pp. 204–5). The EC also contributed to the development of the highly successful GSM global standard for mobile communications, which became the *de-facto* common world standard for most regions outside North America and Japan. It is available in more than 200 countries.

Looking beyond industrial policy, the commission worried about the wasteful duplication of research expenditure, which, collectively in the EU, compared favourably with both the United States and Japan, but which was too fragmented among the member states to produce comparable results.

The commission's objective was to stimulate cooperation between businesses, laboratories and universities from different member states, with support from the EC budget, to develop new technologies and products fulfilling existing or potential market needs. What needed to be stimulated, in its view, was not just fundamental research but also cross-border joint action in the pre-competitive stage of technological development. Once a new technology had been developed, it would be up to business to take over at the production and marketing stage, where they would also benefit from the more competitive and dynamic commercial environment created by the future internal market.

Multi-annual framework research programmes

Despite these efforts, the European Commission remained unhappy at the degree of commitment of the member states to the coordination of their research programmes. In 1986 the then commission president, Jacques Delors, proposed that the research share of the Community budget (including the amount spent on nuclear research, should be more than doubled, from 3 to 8 per cent of the total. As a first step the commission proposed a new framework programme (FP) for 1987–91, with a total budget of 7.7 billion ecus, although this was whittled down to 5.4 billion ecus by the member states. In 1989, the concept of rolling five-year programmes was accepted, and a simplified framework was approved for 1990–94, with total EC funding of 5.7 billion ecus. There were in all seven framework programmes between 1984 and 2013 (see Table 23.1).

The duration of the seventh framework programme (FP7), was extended to seven years, covering the 2007–13 period with a budget of €50.5 billion. It represented a significant jump in investment over previous programmes. The core of FP7, representing two-thirds of the overall budget, was the 'cooperation' strand, which fostered collaborative research

Table 23.1 EU research and innovation framework programmes

Programme	Period	Amount *b*
FP1	1984–87	3.3
FP2	1987–90	5.4
FP3	1991–94	5.7
FP4	1994–98	13.1
FP5	1998–2002	15.0
FP6	2002–06	17.5
FP7	2007–13	50.5

Source: European Commission.

across Europe and other partner countries through projects by cross-border groups and consortia of industry and academia. Research was focused on ten themes ranging from health and food to information and communications technology, nanosciences, new materials, energy, transport and the environment.

The other elements of FP7 were 'ideas', which established the European Research Council, provider of funding for frontier science; 'people', covering human resources and scholarships for young researchers, fellowships for lifelong training and career development, partnerships between industry and academia and awards for excellence; and 'capacities', which involved upgrades for research infrastructures, development of knowledge and science clusters

New horizons for innovation

The successor to FP7, which runs for the seven-year budget period from 2014 to 2020 has broken with previous linear identification and is called Horizon 2020 (see Table 23.2). The programme structure has been changed, but it covers many of the sectors where FP7 was already active. It is worth nearly €80 billion over seven years – an increase of nearly 30 per cent in real terms compared with the seventh framework programme. The scope of Horizon 2020 has been expanded to encompass the European Institute of Innovation and Technology (EIT) and parts of the former Competitiveness and Innovation Framework Programme (CIP).

Horizon 2020 is built around three main pillars.

- Support for 'Excellent Science' – including grants for individual researchers from the European Research Council and Marie

Table 23.2 Horizon 2020 budget 2014–20 (€ billion)

	Budget share b
Excellent science	24.4
Industrial leadership	17.0
Societal challenges	29.7
EIT	2.7
Euratom	1.6
Other	3.2
Total	**78.6**

Source: European Commission.

Skłodowska-Curie fellowships (formerly known as Marie Curie fellowships).

- Support for 'Industrial Leadership' – including grants for small and medium-sized enterprises and indirect finance for companies through the European Investment Bank and other financial intermediaries.
- Support for research to tackle 'societal challenges'. Seven have been identified:

  1 health, demographic change and wellbeing
  2 food security, sustainable agriculture and forestry, marine, maritime and inland water research, and the bio-economy
  3 secure, clean and efficient energy
  4 smart, green and integrated transport
  5 climate action, environment, resource efficiency and raw materials
  6 inclusive, innovative and reflective societies
  7 secure & innovative societies.

In addition, the Horizon 2020 programme includes funding for the European Institute of Innovation and Technology, research activities carried out under the Euratom treaty and non-nuclear research carried out by the Joint Research Centre, the European Commission's in-house science service. Horizon 2020 has two funding rates for eligible projects: 70 per cent (with co-funding from participants) or 100 per cent. Competition among bidders is fierce with a success rate of about 20 per cent.

Less red tape

Learning from the past, Horizon 2020 has reduced red tape for cross-border groups bidding for and implementing projects. In some circumstances, single entities can now apply. Simplification is the watchword.

- A simpler programme structure which makes it easier for participants to identify funding opportunities.
- A single set of participation rules with simpler forms to complete on eligibility, evaluation, intellectual property rights, etc.
- Electronic submissions.
- A shorter time from submission to contract signature (a maximum of eight months).
- Simpler funding rules with flat rates for administrative costs, and fewer financial controls and audits.

Bridging the valley of death

Despite often matching efforts, the EU is less successful than other countries in turning the devices, applications, products and services developed by researchers into items ready to sell on the market. In the past, experts have argued that EU research was more scattered and less focused than elsewhere, or that its insistence on supporting 'pre-competitive' research meant that it neglected the vital commercialisation phase of innovation. This is no longer the case. Horizon 2020 applies a single set of rules to projects along the whole innovation chain, from frontier research and technological development to 'close to market' applications. The last are specifically aimed to bridge the valley of death, where innovation may be trapped with no route to market, and to shorten the time to market for valid research achievements.

European Research Area

The Lisbon European Council in March 2000 identified research and development as essential to make the EU 'the most competitive and dynamic knowledge-based economy in the world'. As part of this agenda, the leaders endorsed the commission's project to create a European Research Area (ERA), where think-tanks and university departments from member states work together regularly and effectively, maximising the EU's potential for innovation. It was to be 'a unified area open to the world, in which scientific knowledge, technology and researchers circulate freely'.

The information society

When new multimedia technologies took off in the 1990s, the European Commission quickly realised that it was essential to foster the entrepreneurial spirit needed to let them thrive in Europe. It produced an Information Society Action Plan which covered a wide range of issues, including telecommunications deregulation, the development of trans-European networks in mobile communications and access to internet broadband services. It addressed standardisation, interconnection, interoperability, intellectual property, privacy and security on the web, and data protection. In recent decades, the EU has introduced legislation, leading to greater consumer choice, falling costs, and higher standards of service, through:

- a sound regulatory framework for electronic communications, promoting competition and consumer rights;

- promoting investment in broadband networks supporting high-speed Internet;
- supporting wireless technologies, through the radio spectrum policy programme;
- protecting mobile users from high roaming charges when travelling in the EU or internationally;
- taking a leading role in international discussions on Internet development and governance.

Community patent

Registering a patent in the EU is slow and expensive: it costs an average €49,900 compared with €10,330 in the United States and €16,450 in Japan. Translation accounts for about 40 per cent of the cost in Europe. For 30 years, the EU and stakeholders – governments, industry, labour organisations – have striven to produce a single and less costly EU patenting system that would help underpin and strengthen innovation. At present an innovation has to be patented in each member state either directly by the innovator, or by using the European patents office (EPO) in Munich. Draft legislation on a unitary system whereby a patent granted by the EPO would automatically be valid in all EU member states has long been blocked over language and translation issues. In 2011, to get round this problem, the Council of Ministers authorised 25 member states seeking to adopt the EPO unitary patent system to use the so-called enhanced cooperation procedures to go ahead without the other two (Italy and Spain). Croatia, which joined the EU in 2013, is not part of the enhanced cooperation agreement. Ratification of this agreement is expected in 2016.

24 Regional policy

Unlike social policy and the European Social Fund (ESF), regional development was not included as a core policy in the Rome treaty. It came later. However, the preamble to the treaty acknowledged the importance for the balanced development of the community of reducing 'the differences between the various regions and the backwardness of the less favoured regions'. It was under pressure from the countries who joined in 1973, especially the UK and Ireland, that the European Regional Development Fund (ERDF) with a modest budget of 1.4 billion units of account (UA) was set up two years later. At the time, along with Italy, they were the least affluent member states and needed the money. In addition, the UK saw the regional fund as a lever for getting back from the EC budget some of its excessive contribution to the Common Agricultural Policy. Regional development was incorporated formally as an EC policy in the Single European Act of 1987.

Regional and social policies have evolved as the EU has tripled its membership since 1975 to include remote regions of northern Scandinavia, mid-Atlantic Islands like the Azores, as well as poor regions and indeed entire countries in eastern Europe. Previously active industrial regions in 'older' member states accelerated their decline during this time. The role of the so-called structural funds has therefore grown significantly. What is now termed 'economic, social and territorial cohesion' accounts for one in every three euro spent by the EU budget. It represents €325 billion from a total EU budget spend of €960 billion for the period 2014–20. It now has three structural funds; the ERDF, the ESF, plus a Cohesion Fund used essentially for the benefit of countries which have joined the Union since 2004. These three funds, together with the European Agricultural Fund for Rural Development (see Chapter 21) and the European Maritime and Fisheries Fund (see Chapter 22) make up the European Structural and Investment Funds (ESIF). All five operate under a set of common rules.

The structural funds

The European Regional Development Fund

The ERDF dominates the funding (2014–20 budget €196.58 billion). It covers all member states and invests under all ESIF thematic objectives. It has a strong focus on four key priority areas – research and innovation, the digital economy, support for SMEs and the low-carbon economy. The ERDF also finances cross-border, trans-national or interregional cooperation. Money from the ERDF and the other structural funds is modulated according to three categories of region. The outermost regions form a separate category of their own.

- More developed regions whose GDP per capita is above 90 per cent of the EU average.
- Transition regions whose GDP per capita is between 75 and 90 per cent of the EU average.
- Less developed regions whose GDP per capita is below 75 per cent of the EU average.

The amount of co-financing awarded under the ERDF is geared to the level of development of the regions concerned. In the less developed regions (and outermost regions) the ERDF can finance up to 85 per cent of the cost of a given project. In transition regions this can go up to 60 per cent while the ceiling in the more developed regions is 50 per cent.

The European Social Fund

The ESF (2014–20 budget €80.32 billion) invests in people, with a focus on improving employment and education opportunities across the European Union. It also aims to improve the situation of the most vulnerable groups at risk of poverty. The ESF investments cover all EU regions. They are earmarked for human capital investment in member states, with an extra €3.2 billion allocated to the Youth Employment Initiative. For the 2014–20 period, the ESF will focus on four of the cohesion policy's thematic objectives:

- promoting employment and supporting labour mobility;
- promoting social inclusion and combating poverty;
- investing in education, skills and lifelong learning;
- enhancing institutional capacity and an efficient public administration.

In addition, 20 per cent of ESF investments will be committed to activities improving social inclusion and combating poverty. The ESF projects address a wide variety of target groups. There are projects aimed at education systems, teachers and schoolchildren; at young and older job-seekers; and at potential entrepreneurs from all backgrounds.

The Cohesion Fund

The Cohesion Fund (2014–20 budget €63.40 billion) targets countries whose Gross National Income per inhabitant is less than 90 per cent of the EU average. It aims to reduce economic and social disparities and promote sustainable development via projects to improve transport and energy and environmental protection. The Cohesion Fund concerns the 13 countries which have joined the Union since 2004, plus Greece and Portugal. It covers the following sectors:

* Trans-European transport networks, notably priority projects of European interest as identified by the EU. The Cohesion Fund will support infrastructure projects under the Connecting Europe Facility.
* The environment: here, the Fund can also support projects related to energy or transport, as long as they clearly benefit the environment in terms of energy efficiency, use of renewables, developing rail transport, supporting inter-modality, strengthening public transport, etc.

Priority regional objectives

For the 2014–20 period, the European Commission has listed 11 priority objectives for the three funds.

1 Strengthening research, technological development and innovation.
2 Enhancing access to, and use and quality of, information and communication technologies.
3 Enhancing the competitiveness of SMEs.
4 Supporting the shift towards a low-carbon economy.
5 Promoting climate change adaptation, risk prevention and management.
6 Preserving and protecting the environment and promoting resource efficiency.
7 Promoting sustainable transport and improving network infrastructures.
8 Supporting sustainable quality employment and labour mobility.
9 Promoting social inclusion, combating poverty and any discrimination.
10 Investing in education, training and lifelong learning.
11 Improving the efficiency of public administration.

Table 24.1 How the ERDF spends its money 2014–20

Activity	Amount (b)
Research and innovation	41.10
Competitiveness and SMEs	33.28
Low-carbon economy	31.63
Network infrastructure and transport & energy	25.80
Sustainability & environment	18.20
Information & communications technology	13.31
Social cohesion	11.90
Education & vocational training	6.75
Technical assistance	5.55
Climate change & adaptation	4.19
Sustainable & quality jobs	3.33
Efficient public administration	1.38
Outermost regions	0.67
TOTAL	**196.58**

Note: Totals may not add up because of rounding.

Source: European Commission.

The ERDF will support all 13 objectives, but 1–4 are its main priorities (see Table 24.1). The leading priorities for the ESF are 8–11, although the fund also supports 1–4. The Cohesion Fund supports objectives 4–7 and 11.

The updated regional policy rules require beneficiaries in more developed regions to allocate at least 80 per cent of their ERDF resources to at least two of the three top priorities and at least 20 per cent to the low-carbon economy. Transition regions are to allocate at least 60 per cent of their ERDF resources to two or more of these priorities and at least 15 per cent to the low-carbon economy. Less-developed regions are to allocate at least 50 per cent to at least two of these priorities and at least 12 per cent to the low-carbon economy. The ERDF also supports sustainable urban development. At least 5 per cent of the ERDF allocation for each member state has to be earmarked for integrated actions for sustainable urban development that will tackle the economic, environmental, climate, demographic and social challenges affecting urban areas. Details of the allocation and future use of ERDF funds are determined in the Partnership Agreements. These are strategy documents drawn up by each member state with the assistance of regional and social partners.

The new period also sees a number of other changes to raise the effectiveness and efficiency of all five funds and make them easier to access and more user-friendly for member states and participants from the private and public sectors.

- Stronger focus on results: clearer and measurable targets for better accountability.
- Simplification: one set of rules for five funds.
- Conditions: introduction of specific preconditions before funds can be mobilised.
- Strengthened urban dimension and fight for social inclusion: a minimum amount of ERDF earmarked for integrated projects in cities, while the ESF is to support marginalised communities.
- Link to economic reform: the commission may suspend funding for a member state which does not comply with EU economic and fiscal rules.

Structural Fund and Cohesion Fund support always involves co-financing. The rates of co-financing by the ERDF may be reduced from standard levels in accordance with the 'polluter pays' principle or where a project generates income.

As Table 24.2 shows, Poland is far and away the biggest beneficiary from the structural funds with an allocation of €77.57 billion for the 2014–20 period out of a total of €325 billion. It is followed at a distance

Table 24.2 Cohesion policy: indicative financial allocations 2014–20 (€bn – current prices)

Country	Allocation/ b	Country	Allocation/ b
Austria	1.24	Italy	32.82
Belgium	1.28	Latvia	4.51
Bulgaria	7.59	Lithuania	6.82
Croatia	8.61	Luxembourg	0.06
Cyprus	0.74	Malta	0.73
Czech Republic	21.98	Netherlands	1.40
Denmark	0.55	Poland	77.57
Estonia	3.59	Portugal	21.47
Finland	1.47	Romania	22.99
France	15.85	Slovakia	13.99
Germany	19.23	Slovenia	3.07
Greece	15.52	Spain	28.56
Hungary	21.91	Sweden	2.11
Ireland	1.19	United Kingdom	11.84

Note: Totals may not add up due to rounding.

Source: European Commission.

by Italy, Spain, Romania, the Czech Republic, Hungary and Portugal. Most regional spending is reserved for regions with a GDP below 75 per cent of the Union average to help improve their infrastructures and develop their economic and human potential.

Setting social policy priorities

The commission and EU countries in partnership set the ESF's priorities and how it spends its resources. One priority is to boost the adaptability of workers via new skills, and enterprises via new ways of working. Other priorities focus on better access to employment: by helping young people make the transition from school to work, or training less-skilled job-seekers to improve their work prospects. Indeed, vocational training and lifelong learning opportunities to give people new skills form a large part of many ESF projects. Another priority targets disadvantaged groups – for whom getting a job is crucial in helping them integrate better into society and everyday life. From 2008, the financial crisis led to a redoubling of efforts to keep people in work, or help them return to work quickly if they lose their jobs. Joblessness peaked at the height of the crisis in late 2013 with overall EU jobless at 11.0 per cent, but at 12.1 per cent in the eurozone. A total of 24 million people were out of work across the EU. The figures had dropped a little by late 2015 to 9.3 per cent in the EU and 10.7 per cent in the eurozone. But even then youth unemployment still exceeded 20 per cent in 12 of the 28 EU countries.

As one of the EU's first common policies, the ESF was set up under Article 123 of the Rome treaty. Its purpose was defined thus:

> To improve employment opportunities for workers in the common market and to contribute thereby to raising the standard of living ... it shall have the task of rendering the employment of workers easier and of increasing their geographical and occupational mobility within the Community.

In the most recent in a series of modifications, the role of the ESF was reinforced in 2014 by making sure each country got a guaranteed minimum amount (see Table 24.3), and by focusing more narrowly on youth unemployment, gender equality and disadvantaged groups. In concrete terms, this means funding for projects to train people and help them get work. The ESF may also provide entrepreneurs with start-up funding and support companies who need to cope with restructuring or a lack of qualified workers. Across the EU, the ESF finances initiatives to improve education and training and ensure young people complete their

Table 24.3 ESF allocations per country 2014–20

Country	Allocation/ b	Country	Allocation/ b
Austria	0.43	Italy	8.25
Belgium	1.03	Latvia	0.63
Bulgaria	1.46	Lithuania	1.12
Croatia	1.44	Luxembourg	0.02
Cyprus	0.13	Malta	0.11
Czech Republic	3.40	Netherlands	0.51
Denmark	0.16	Poland	12.82
Estonia	0.44	Portugal	7.05
Finland	0.52	Romania	4.77
France	6.03	Slovakia	1.99
Germany	6.72	Slovenia	0.62
Greece	3.34	Spain	7.48
Hungary	3.71	Sweden	0.73
Ireland	0.49	United Kingdom	4.94
Total	**80.32**		

Note: Totals may not add up due to rounding.

Source: European Commission.

schooling and get the skills that make them more competitive on the job market. Reducing the school drop-out rate is a priority here, along with improving vocational and tertiary education opportunities.

Employment strategy

The European employment strategy (EES) was introduced in 1992 by the Treaty on European Union and since then has been the cornerstone of the EU's employment policy. Its main aim is the creation of more and better jobs throughout the EU. It now constitutes part of the Europe 2020 growth strategy and is implemented through the European semester, an annual process promoting close policy coordination among member states and EU institutions.

25 Workers' rights

Under Article 117 of the Rome treaty the member states agreed on the need to promote improved living and working conditions for workers, while Article 118 gave the commission the task of promoting close cooperation between member states in the social field, particularly in matters relating to:

- employment;
- labour law and working conditions;
- basic and advanced vocational training;
- social security;
- prevention of occupational accidents and diseases;
- health and safety at work;
- the right of association, and collective bargaining between employers and workers.

As regards labour law, the EU complements policy initiatives taken by individual EU countries by setting minimum standards. Individual EU countries are free to provide higher standards if they so wish. For instance, while the European Working Time Directive entitles workers to 20 days' annual paid leave, many countries have opted for a more generous holiday allocation. EU labour law goes hand in hand with the single market. The free flow of goods, services, capital and workers needs to be accompanied by labour law rules, to make sure that countries and businesses compete fairly on the strength of their products and their technical skills – not by lowering labour standards in a race to the bottom.

In practice, the EU has made most progress in areas like working conditions, equal pay for men and women (see p. 247) and worker mobility – the right of a national of one EU country to work in another. EU legislation also covers the right for a service provider established in one EU country to post its workers to another member state temporarily in order to provide a service there (the so-called posted workers directive of 1996). Attempts to harmonise social security systems have enjoyed only partial success, and commission initiatives to provide a wider framework for worker participation in management decisions have been slowed by the unwillingness of some member governments (notably that of the UK) to agree to legislation in this field.

Better working conditions

The improvement of working conditions was an early target. In 1975 the European Foundation for the Improvement of Living and Working Conditions was established in Dublin. The major emphasis has been on safety and health in the workplace, where more than 100,000 people die in accidents each year and millions are injured. The European Agency for Safety and Health at Work (EU-OSHA) was set up in 1996 in Bilbao, Spain with the mission to gather and provide reliable and relevant information, analysis and tools to advance knowledge, raise awareness and exchange occupational safety and health (OSH) information and good practice.

In its second action programme on work safety, adopted in 1984, the EU concentrated on:

* rules for the use of dangerous substances;
* ergonomics and preventing accidents and dangerous situations;
* improvements in organisation, training and information;
* problems posed by new technologies.

Several directives have been adopted on safety signs, on electrical equipment used in mines, and on protection against chemical, physical or biological agents such as lead, asbestos, noise and vinyl chloride. Under the Single European Act, agreement on new directives or regulations to improve the work environment and on health and safety provisions no longer required unanimity within the Council of Ministers. Decision-making speeded up as a result.

Free movement of workers (internal migration)

Free movement of workers (and their families) is a fundamental principle of the EU's founding treaties, consolidated by EU secondary legislation and the case law of the European Court of Justice. A national of one EU country is entitled to:

* look for a job in another EU country;
* work there without needing a work permit;

Table 25.1 Non-national population in EU countries 2015 (% of total pop.)

	EU citizens	Migrants from outside EU		EU citizens	Migrants from outside EU
Austria	6.1	6.3	Italy	2.4	5.7
Belgium	7.4	3.9	Latvia	0.3	14.9
Bulgaria	0.2	0.6	Lithuania	0.1	0.5
Croatia	0.2	0.5	Luxembourg	39.0	6.3
Cyprus	12.9	5.6	Malta	3.2	2.7
Czech Republic	1.6	2.5	Netherlands	2.4	2.0
Denmark	2.8	4.1	Poland	0.1	0.2
Estonia	0.6	14.2	Portugal	1.0	2.9
Finland	1.5	2.2	Romania	0.1	0.3
France	2.2	4.1	Slovakia	0.8	0.2
Germany	3.8	4.8	Slovenia	0.8	3.9
Greece	1.7	5.9	Spain	4.3	5.8
Hungary	0.8	0.6	Sweden	3.0	5.0
Ireland	8.1	3.7	United Kingdom	4.1	3.8

Source: Eurostat.

- reside there for that purpose;
- stay there even after employment has finished;
- enjoy equal treatment with nationals in access to employment, working conditions and all other social and tax advantages.

Transitional periods of several years before the freedom of movement fully applies is a regular condition of the entry of new EU members. The accession of Croatia in 2013 was no exception. Nationals of the three countries of the European Economic Area (EEA), Iceland, Norway and Liechtenstein, plus Switzerland, have the same rights of free movement as EU citizens (and vice-versa in the EEA and Switzerland). The right of free movement does not apply to migrants from other countries outside the EU even if they are legally resident in an EU member state.

In 2014, citizens of one EU country living in another totalled 14.8 million, or 2.97 per cent of the EU population. Nationals of a non-EU country (so-called third-country nationals) numbered 19.6 million (3.9 per cent of the total population)(see Table 25.1).

Mutual recognition of professional qualifications

It took a long time for the member states to agree on the mutual recognition of professional qualifications, so that for years it was not possible for many workers to practise their professions in EU countries other than their own. However, a series of directives, most recently in 2013, now provide for the mutual recognition by member states of each other's professional qualifications. There are three systems of recognition:

- *automatic recognition* – for professions with harmonised minimum training conditions, i.e. nurses, midwifes, doctors (general practitioners and specialists), dental practitioners, pharmacists, architects and veterinary surgeons;
- *general system* – for other regulated professions such as teachers, translators and real estate agents;
- *recognition on the basis of professional experience* – for certain professional activities such as carpenters, upholsterers, beauticians etc.

The Social Charter of Workers' Rights

A central element in the EU's social policy is the Social Charter of Workers' Rights, signed at Strasbourg in December 1989 by 11 of the then 12 heads of government. Margaret Thatcher, the UK prime minister, refused to sign, arguing that it would lead to higher unemployment by deterring employers from hiring new workers. The Social Charter was originally conceived by Jacques Delors, as a modest counterweight to the decidedly liberal nature of the single market, set to deliver a string of benefits to European companies whose profits would rise as barriers to the Europe-wide market fell. The charter itself had no more than a declaratory effect; but it was to be followed by a Social Action programme, containing 47 pieces of legislation which, once adopted by the Council of Ministers, would be binding on the member states including the UK.

Much of the Social Action programme could be approved by qualified majority voting and would therefore be adopted despite UK opposition. The draft Treaty on European Union, presented to the Maastricht summit in December 1991, would have made the remaining proposals also subject to majority voting rather than unanimity. Thatcher's successor, John Major refused to accept this, however, so the other 11 member states signed a Protocol on Social Policy (also known as the Social Chapter), which enabled them to decide these matters by qualified majority voting among themselves. The UK would not take part in the deliberations nor be bound by the outcome. This extraordinary decision, whereby 11 member states could use the institutions, procedures and mechanisms of the EC for taking decisions that did not apply to the twelfth member, was unprecedented and many observers doubted whether it would last long. It was effectively terminated when the Labour Party won the UK general election on May 1st 1997. The newly elected government pledged to adhere to the protocol, which was formally incorporated in the Amsterdam treaty the following month.

The main directives adopted under the Social Action programme have concerned protecting the employment rights of pregnant women; limiting the number of hours that employees could be required to work within a fixed period; special provisions for restricting night work; guaranteeing subcontracted workers from other countries the same rights (on health and safety, equal opportunities and dismissal) as local workers; and giving part-time workers the right to written contracts.

The Working Time Directive

The 1993 EU Working Time Directive, which took effect in June 1996, sets provisions for a maximum 48-hour working week (including overtime), rest periods and breaks and a minimum of four weeks paid leave per year, so as to protect workers from health and safety risks. It applies to all sectors of activity, both public and private. A number of areas, such as air, rail, road, sea, inland waterway and lake transport, sea fishing, other work at sea and doctors in training, which were exempt from the 1993 directive, were brought within its scope in an amendment agreed in 2000. The directive was further amended in 2003. Several categories of workers are still excluded from the directive:

- management executives or other persons with autonomous decision-making powers;
- domestic workers;
- workers officiating at religious ceremonies in churches and religious communities.

The directive defines working time as 'any period during which the worker is working, at the employer's disposal and carrying out his activities or duties, in accordance with national laws and/or practice'. A rest period is defined as 'any period which is not working time'. The directive does not allow for any interim category. In 2000 and 2003, the European Court of Justice ruled on two cases involving the definition of working time. Both turned on whether time spent on call constituted working time, and both concerned the health-care sector: the *SIMAP* case in primary health care and the *Jaeger* case in hospitals. In both cases the ECJ ruled that time spent on call should be regarded as working time.

The UK government, along with 14 other member states, negotiated an opt-out at the level of individual workers from the directive. Attempts by the European Parliament to cancel the opt-out have been unsuccessful. So the current directive and opt-out remain in force.

Workers' rights in companies

The European Union has moved slowly to promote workers' rights and protect their interests in the companies they work for. A first directive in 1975 defined procedures for negotiations with workers whose employers were forced to make large-scale redundancies. A second directive in 2001 sought to safeguard workers' rights if their company was involved in a transfer or merger which could affect their interests. A third directive in 2002 set out procedures for protecting workers' rights to be informed and consulted on economic or employment issues affecting their workplace.

Separate legislation has been negotiated over the years for the creation of European Works Councils for worker consultation and participation in multinational companies operating in more than one member state. Initial attempts were blocked – partially – by British opposition. Part of the statute was, however, adopted under the Protocol on Social Policy, which meant that, initially at least, it was applicable only in the other member states. Thus when the Council of Ministers adopted the relevant directive later in 1994, it did not apply to workers in the UK. But British companies with employees located in other EU countries were required to comply. In practice, the directive was largely applied in the UK, despite the 'opt-out' insisted on by the Major government, and which was quickly given up by the newly elected Labour government in June 1997. An updated directive covering all member states took effect in June 2011. It affects cross-border companies operating in at least two member states and with at least 1,000 employees and sets rules for worker information and consultation. The powers of the European Works Council and the scope of the information and consultation procedure concern all establishments of the undertaking or all establishments of a wider multinational group situated in the member states. The central management of the undertaking or the group is responsible for establishing a council or an information and consultation procedure.

Revised European company statute

The role of works councils also features in the revised European Company Statute. The statute was formally adopted by EU social affairs ministers in October 2001, after more than 30 years of negotiation. The European Company (known by its Latin name of *Societas Europaea* or SE) gives companies operating in more than one member state the option of setting up as a single company under EU law, operating with one set of rules and a unified management and reporting structure. It obliges SE managers to provide regular reports to a body representing the company's employees, detailing current and future business plans, production and sales levels, implications of these for the workforce, management changes, mergers, divestments, potential closures and lay-offs.

26 Energy

A modern economy and society cannot thrive without abundant and reliable supplies of energy. It was no surprise therefore that energy sources – coal and nuclear – were the object of two of the EU's three founding treaties: for the Coal and Steel Community in 1951 and the Atomic Energy Community (Euratom) in 1957. Yet energy policy *per se* did not feature in the Rome treaty. It is still not a fully fledged EU policy. Responsibility is shared between the Union and the individual member states. Each country is free to decide its own energy mix and the structure of its national energy market. Nowhere is this clearer than in the role ascribed to nuclear energy in electricity production across Europe. In some countries nuclear has gone, or is being phased out. In others it is a central source of generation as in France, but also to a lesser degree in countries like the UK, Finland, Hungary and Slovakia. Moreover, individual member states also offer a range of local incentives to support electricity from renewable sources and its integration into the national transmission grid.

But it became inevitable over the years that national energy responsibilities would get caught up in wider EU policy issues in fields like competition policy, free movement of goods within the single market, the provision of cross-border interconnections for electricity and gas networks, trade issues (including security of supply and import dependence), price volatility, climate change and the reduction of greenhouse gas emissions. A delicate balance for decision-taking involving areas of Union competence and those of national responsibility (and subject to intergovernmental procedures) was devised by the negotiators of the 2009 Lisbon treaty. Article 194 of the TFEU reads:

> In the context of the establishment and functioning of the internal market and with regard for the need to preserve and improve the

environment, Union policy on energy shall aim, in a spirit of solidarity between Member States, to:
(a) ensure the functioning of the energy market;
(b) ensure security of energy supply in the Union;
(c) promote energy efficiency and energy saving and the development of new and renewable forms of energy; and
(d) promote the interconnection of energy networks.

Import dependence

The EU covers just over half its energy needs from internal output. This makes it heavily dependent on imports, especially of oil and gas. In turn this becomes a factor of political risk, firstly because of the need to transport oil and gas over long distances, and because of the political risk associated with some suppliers, notably Russia and the Middle East. Table 26.1 sets out the level of import dependence of the EU (figures for 2013) and lists the main outside suppliers of gas, oil and coal. While there has been some diversification of import sources in recent years, the level of dependence remained steady at 52–54 per cent in the period 2008–13. In 2013, five member states – Cyprus, Malta, Ireland, Italy and Luxembourg – had levels of import dependence in excess of 80 per cent. Six remained nearly wholly dependent on Russia for gas supplies: Finland, the three Baltic states, Slovakia and Bulgaria.

A wake-up call

The first 'oil shock' of 1973, which caught the EC woefully unprepared, served as a wake-up call for the need for common action at EU level. But the initial response revealed deep intra-European fault lines. The 1973 crisis, which saw the quadrupling of oil prices virtually overnight and an Arab oil embargo on the Netherlands, was followed by the fiasco of the December 1973 Copenhagen summit, which singularly failed to

Table 26.1 EU import dependence for energy

Import dependence by source (2013 in %)		*Import share of main suppliers (2013 in %)*
Oil	86	Russia (32), Saudi Arabia (10), Libya (9)
Natural gas	65	Norway (31), Russia (30), Algeria (12)
Coal	42	Russia (27), Columbia (23), United States (21)
Total	**53**	

Source: European Commission.

produce a joint response to the Arab countries. France and the UK went behind the backs of their partners to pursue bilateral deals with oil suppliers rather than to present a united European front. It was only in September 1974 that the Council of Ministers adopted a programme drawn up by the European Commission called 'Towards a New Energy Policy Strategy'. This formed the framework for most subsequent moves on energy policy. The overriding priority was to reduce dependence on imported oil and diversify the sources of supply. It led to the first measures to create strategic energy stocks. A certain convergence in policy and common objectives have been defined without, however, a central mechanism being established to ensure that they are pursued in a coordinated manner.

Energy and the single market

Like other economic sectors, energy products were subject to the general EU rules governing the free movement of goods and services within the European single market. They were also covered by EU requirements on free competition and the restrictions on state subsidies to national industries and companies which might distort competition across EU frontiers. This led to a case where the Dutch gas industry was prevented from supplying cheap gas to horticulturalists which would have allowed them to heat their greenhouses more cheaply than their competitors in other EU countries. In 1990 a directive was adopted enforcing transparency in the pricing policies of electricity and gas suppliers.

Three packages for a single market

But given the specific issues linked to utilities markets in member states' generally state-controlled monopolies prior to liberalisation in the late 1980s, it became clear that special legislation would be needed to create functional single markets for electricity and gas. The legislation was contained in what became known as the three energy packages.

The first energy package

This consisted of two separate directives for electricity (1996) and gas (1998), and made way for the opening of the electricity and gas market with a gradual introduction of competition. Moreover, it imposed broad unbundling requirements on integrated companies, which controlled generation, transmission, distribution and sales. In particular, transmission systems operators needed to be independent and treat all users equally. National authorities would monitor the system to prevent abuse and predatory behaviour.

The second energy package

This legislation package, of 2003 and its two additional directives, focused further on the concepts of unbundling and third party access to the transmission and distribution systems and parsed the requirement for independent national regulatory authorities. This package set two different deadlines for the liberalisation of electricity and gas retail markets, namely July 2004 for industrial customers and July 2007 for private households. It allowed for public service obligations to be imposed on electricity companies and required the publication of network tariffs.

The third energy package

The package of 2009, along with a further two directives, established a new unbundling regime and more clearly defined the duties of national regulatory authorities, including the cooperation with the EU's Agency for the Cooperation of Energy Regulators (ACER). Consumers' rights were significantly strengthened, especially with regard to switching between suppliers. Member states must take action to protect vulnerable customers, first of all by defining the concept of vulnerability and secondly, by prohibiting disconnection of these customers in critical times. The directives also provided a number of measures for the functioning of the internal electricity and gas market, and promoted regional solidarity and national emergency measures in the event of severe disruptions of gas supply.

Fumbling unbundling

Unbundling transmission from generation activities and the related issues of third party access and the independence of transmission grid managers proved to be the most controversial and therefore the most difficult elements to define and implement. Initial difficulties came from Germany, because of its regionalised generation and transmission structure, and France. French opposition was more ideological and aimed at preventing foreign firms entering and competing in its national electricity market, where the state-controlled Electricité de France (EdF) was by far the dominant player. The French chauvinism was in no way attenuated by the fact that the correct application of the energy packages by other EU countries had enabled EdF to enter the UK and German electricity markets. It has since withdrawn from the latter. The upshot was that despite the three energy packages the EU market for electricity and gas was still prone to badly understood and applied rules, and hindrances of many kinds. It was to create order and clarity that on February 4th 2011, the European Council set an ambitious objective to complete the internal energy market by 2014. But as the deadline slipped by, a commission report noted that much still remained to be done concerning investments in smart grids, the need for more interconnections and for better links between wholesale and retail electricity markets so that consumers too could benefit from lower prices.

Environmental protection

Since 1989 the EU, in response to strong pressure from public opinion, has adopted a series of measures designed to reduce environmental damage caused by the energy sector. They have concerned the introduction of lead-free petrol, the reduction of toxic emissions from automobiles and large combustion plants, and the reduction of the sulphur content of heating oil and diesel fuel.

Technological innovation

Since the 1980s, energy has been a prominent plank in the EU's successive R&D programmes. This is confirmed in the Horizon 2020 programme which features 'secure clean and efficient energy' as one of seven societal challenges. The energy challenge has a budget of €5.93 billion for the 2014–20 period and is structured around seven specific objectives and research areas:

- reducing energy consumption and carbon footprint;
- low-cost, low-carbon electricity supply;
- alternative fuels and mobile energy sources;
- a single, smart European electricity grid;
- new knowledge and technologies;
- robust decision making and public engagement;
- market uptake of energy and ICT innovation.

Three priority areas have been identified: energy efficiency, low carbon technologies and smart cities and communities.

The four research centres directly established by Euratom, at Karlsruhe in Germany, Ispra in Italy, Geel in Belgium and Petten in the Netherlands, known collectively as the Joint Research Centre (JRC), do important work mainly in nuclear safety and environmental protection. To lead its research into nuclear fusion as a clean energy source, the EU set up the Joint European Torus (JET) at Culham in the UK. This is one of only four major programmes in the world, the others being in Russia, the United States and Japan. Successful cooperation and exchange of information agreements have led the four to come together to build the International Thermonuclear Experimental Reactor (ITER) at Cadarache in France. This is seen as the next major step in a programme whose ultimate goal is the generation of abundant electricity by nuclear fusion, which is a cheaper, cleaner and safer energy source than nuclear fission.

Energy and climate change

After the Kyoto protocol in 1997 to reduce greenhouse gas emissions and limit global warming, the EU's energy policy was intricately linked with its climate change commitments (for more details, see Chapter 29). In a policy paper in August 2006, the European Commission identified three main objectives for EU energy policy. It should:

- be sustainable with an emphasis on environmentally friendly forms of energy;
- allow healthy competition that delivers affordable prices for consumers;
- ensure a secure and continuous energy supply, and decrease dependence on foreign sources.

The production of electricity from fossil fuels – hard and brown coal, oil and gas – is central to the EU's emissions trading scheme (EU ETS). This is a market-based mechanism, first introduced in 2005, to reduce CO_2 emissions from electricity generation. Emissions are capped and generators exceeding their allotted ceilings pay a penalty. Companies which do not use all their emissions allocation can sell unused emissions allowances on the market to those who have exceeded their CO_2 limits.

Energy targets for 2020 and 2030

An energy and climate change package was confirmed at a landmark EU summit in December 2008. Despite hostile lobbying by business and various EU member states, the so-called 2020 strategy which set targets in three areas was confirmed (see Chapter 29):

- 20 per cent cut in greenhouse gas emissions by 2020 (from 1990 levels);
- 20 per cent share of EU energy from renewable sources by 2020;
- 20 per cent improvement in energy efficiency by 2020.

Then in 2014, as part of its preparations for the UN climate conference (COP21) in Paris the following year EU countries agreed the following objectives for 2030:

- a binding EU target of at least a 40 per cent reduction in greenhouse gas (GHG) emissions by 2030, compared to 1990;
- a binding target of at least 27 per cent of renewable energy in the EU energy mix;
- an energy efficiency increase of at least 27 per cent, to be reviewed by 2020, potentially raising the target to 30 per cent, by 2030;
- the completion of the internal energy market by reaching an electricity interconnection target of 15 per cent between EU countries by 2030, and pushing forward important infrastructure projects.

By these decisions, the EU sought firstly to confirm its position in the vanguard of countries seeking a global agreement to reduce GHG emissions and, secondly, to provide the EU with a stable policy framework on GHG emissions, renewables and energy efficiency in the interests of governments, consumers, industry and investors alike.

European Energy Charter

As communism collapsed, the EC launched the initiative in 1989 to set up a European Energy Charter to trade EC support for the development and modernisation of the energy sector in the Soviet Union in exchange for guaranteed long-term access to Soviet oil and gas supplies. The charter was signed in The Hague in December 1991 by the EU, 37 European and OECD states and 12 former Soviet republics. Its objective was to create a structure to facilitate western investment and technology transfer in Russia and other former Soviet republics by applying market-economy principles to the field of energy. It would also target energy efficiency and environmental protection, as well as safety issues, R&D, and education and training. To give the charter legal force, the participants went on to sign the European Energy Charter Treaty in 1994. The treaty came into force in 1998. However, the US and Canada did not sign up to the treaty. Russia did, but suspended its provisional application in 2009. Since then a new broader document, the International Energy Charter which reached out beyond Europe and updated the provisions of the original charter, was signed by 65 countries from around the world in The Hague in May 2015. Russia and Canada did not sign the new charter. The US did. One of the difficulties since the outset of this process has been to strike an acceptable balance of interests in the charter between consuming and producing countries.

The ECSC treaty expires

When the European Coal and Steel Community was established in 1951, coal and steel, the 'basic industries', dominated the European economy. This is no longer the case, though both industries remain significant factors. The steel industry, in particular, has been transformed in the past three decades, and the Community was involved, first in its rapid growth and subsequently in its sharp decline. The ECSC treaty expired on July 23rd 2002. Well before the treaty ran out, the levies on coal and steel production had been phased out, as they were yielding far more than was needed to meet the social costs of the run-down of the two industries. By 2001, the total budget of the ECSC was €168 million, compared with €339 million 14 years earlier.

However, despite the treaty's expiry, the commission decided to maintain the strict rules on state aid for the European coal and steel industry. The demise of the ECSC meant its assets were transferred to the EU, as provided for in a protocol annexed to the Nice treaty. The revenue from these assets is now used exclusively for research in the sectors related to the coal and steel industries.

27 Transport

Dereliction of duty

The Rome treaty, in Article 74, provides for the creation of a common transport policy, but for the first 24 years of the EC's existence progress was so slow that in September 1982 the European Parliament took the Council of Ministers to the Court of Justice for failing to carry out its treaty obligation. The action was partially successful. The court held that the council had infringed the treaty by failing to ensure freedom to provide services in cross-border transport or to set conditions for allowing non-resident EC carriers access to national transport markets in other member states. It did not confirm, however, the absence of a common transport policy as such, on the grounds that the treaty did not define that policy with sufficient clarity for the court to make a judgement. But the court did recommend that the council work continuously towards the progressive attainment of a common transport policy.

Speed-up after court ruling

Following the court's ruling, council decision-making speeded up, partly in the context of the programme to complete the EC's internal market by 1992. In 1991, a report entitled 'Transport 2000 and Beyond' was adopted, setting objectives for an integrated continent-wide transport system, involving EC support to link national networks and improve links with central and eastern Europe. Transport is estimated to contribute 4.9 per cent of gross value-added in the EU and provides 11 million jobs. It accounts for 31.6 per cent of total energy consumption. Its relevance for the economic integration of Europe can hardly be overestimated.

Overall transport priorities

The European Commission has sought to build a common transport policy through a series of white papers. The most recent of these was issued in

March 2011. Called the 'Roadmap to a single transport area', it aims to create, by 2050, a competitive transport system that will increase mobility, remove barriers in key areas, and fuel growth and employment. At the same time, the proposals set out to reduce EU dependence on imported oil and cut carbon emissions in transport by 60 per cent by 2050. Key goals for 2050 include:

- No more conventionally fuelled cars in cities.
- Forty per cent use of sustainable low carbon fuels in aviation; at least 40 per cent cut in shipping emissions.
- A 50 per cent shift of medium-distance intercity passenger and freight journeys from road to rail and waterborne transport.
- All of which will contribute to a 60 per cent cut in transport emissions by the middle of the century.

The proposed single European transport area, with a fully integrated network linking the different transport modes, will facilitate a profound shift in transport patterns for passengers and freight (relevant national statistics are shown in Table 27.1). The Transport 2050 roadmap sets different goals for different types of journey – within cities, between cities, and long-distance. It covers all transport modes – road and rail, air, sea and inland waterways. On safety, it confirms the aim of halving road accidents by 2020, moving close to zero fatalities by 2050 and making sure the EU is a world leader in safety and secure transport by air, rail and sea. It identifies the main modal priorities:

- remove the technical, administrative and legal barriers which still impede entry to national rail markets;
- further integrate the road freight market to make it more efficient and competitive;
- create a 'blue belt' for sea routes around Europe to simplify formalities for ships travelling between EU ports;
- build a suitable framework for handling the European aspects of inland waterway transport.

Earlier, in September 2001, the commission issued a white paper on a common transport policy for the following decade. The underlying aim was to reduce congestion on roads caused mainly by increasing freight volumes and to transfer part of it to more environment-friendly means of transport such as maritime routes and railways. It pinpointed uneven growth in the different modes of transport, with congestion on some main roads and rail lines but not on others, a negative impact on the environment or citizens' health, and poor road safety. The paper targeted investment in the trans-European transport networks (TEN-T). The 2001 white paper led to a series of actions:

- A regulation reinforcing air passengers' rights.
- The creation of a European Road Safety Action Programme.
- To reduce congestion by promoting inter-modality, through the 'Marco Polo' programmes.

Table 27.1 Modal breakdown of inland passenger and freight transport, 2012

	Passenger transport (% of total inland passenger-km)			Freight transport (% of total inland freight-km)		
	Car	Bus	Rail	Rail	Road	Waterway
Austria	78.5	10.0	11.5	32.7	63.7	3.7
Belgium	80.4	12.4	7.1	11.9	71.5	16.5
Bulgaria	89.1	16.9	3.0	16.6	52.9	30.5
Croatia	85.8	10.7	3.5	22.2	70.6	7.3
Cyprus	81.3	18.7	–	–	100	–
Czech Republic	74.8	16.8	8.4	30.5	69.4	0.1
Denmark	80.2	9.7	10.1	10.9	89.1	–
Estonia	82.6	14.5	1.8	66.9	33.1	–
Finland	84.9	9.8	5.3	28.6	71.9	0.4
France	85.1	5.4	9.5	10.8	86.2	3.0
Germany	85.4	5.7	9.0	19.1	70.7	10.2
Greece	81.6	17.1	0.7	1.5	98.5	–
Hungary	67.7	22.2	10.1	29.8	63.8	6.4
Ireland	82.5	14.4	2.8	1.0	99.0	–
Italy	78.9	15.0	6.1	12.7	87.3	0.1
Latvia	76.9	18.3	4.6	84.1	15.9	–
Lithuania	91.0	8.2	0.8	70.3	29.7	–
Luxembourg	83.0	12.4	4.6	7.1	84.0	8.9
Malta	82.5	17.5	–	–	–	–
Netherlands	88.2	3.0	8.8	6.0	47.5	46.5
Poland	84.6	10.7	4.8	27.6	72.3	0.1
Portugal	89.2	6.6	4.1	12.8	87.2	–
Romania	82/2	12.9	4.9	31.4	39.4	29.2
Slovakia	77.8	15.1	7.1	36.5	58.7	4.7
Slovenia	86.7	11.1	2.3	32.8	67.2	–
Spain	80.7	13.7	5.6	5.3	94.7	–
Sweden	84.7	6.7	9.1	35.8	64.2	–
United Kingdom	86.0	5.5	8.2	11.6	88.3	0.1
EU–28	**83.3**	**9.2**	**7.4**	**18.5**	**74.7**	**6.8**

Note: Totals may not add up due to rounding.

Source: Eurostat.

- The revision of the Eurovignette directive for charging heavy goods vehicles on European motorways, so as to reflect the 'external costs' of transport and promote the modal shift.
- To improve infrastructure via trans-European networks and integrate new member states into the network.
- To reinforce the position of railways, with the adoption of three packages of measures aimed at market liberalisation and harmonisation.

Roads

It is in road transport that the commission has made the most persistent attempts to apply EU policies. It is also a sector where the Council of Ministers has been slow to act.

Road safety

Some 40,000 people are killed and 1.7 million injured each year in road accidents in the EU. A series of directives has harmonised standards for vehicle brakes, lighting, windscreens, sound levels, and so on. Agreement was reached in 1984 on common standards for weights and dimensions of commercial vehicles. The maximum lorry weight was set at 40 tonnes (38 tonnes in the UK and Ireland). A further agreement on maximum axle weights for articulated vehicles was reached in 1986 (11.5 tonnes, but 10.5 tonnes in the UK and Ireland). National authorities are free to fix higher weights and dimensions for trucks operating only on their national road network. Down the years, some flexibility for cross-border haulage has been introduced, most recently by a directive of April 2015 adopted by the Council of Ministers and the European Parliament. This allows, for instance, exceptions to the maximum length if it makes trucks more aerodynamic and therefore greener. Derogations on weights are also allowed for vehicles powered by alternative fuels. The latest directive takes effect in May 2017. Earlier directives have concerned:

- technical vehicle inspection;
- lorry suspension systems;
- fitting speed limitation devices in lorries and coaches;
- limiting the risks involved in the carriage of dangerous goods;
- limiting drivers' hours.

Maximum driving periods have been established per day and per week as well as obligatory rest periods. Observance of these rules is controlled by a tachograph (known pejoratively as 'the spy in the cab') which records the driving and rest time and speeds of heavy goods vehicles.

Frontier crossing

Delays and bureaucratic checks at internal frontier crossings were removed under the 1992 single market programme. National quota restriction also disappeared. But it was only in June 1998 that carriers were granted full freedom to operate transport services within other member states (so-called cabotage).

Railways

In recent years, the commission's efforts have concentrated on three major areas:

1   Opening the rail transport market to competition, including the separation of train operators from network infrastructure managers.
2   Improving the interoperability and safety of national networks.
3   Developing rail transport infrastructure.

Rail could become the default mode for passenger transport for distances up to 300 kilometres and even beyond. Moreover, rail is one of the most energy-efficient modes of transport and should be at the heart of any efficient inter-modal structure. The 2011 white paper set the following goals:

1   Thirty per cent of road freight over 300 kilometres should shift to other modes such as rail or waterborne transport by 2030, and more than 50 per cent by 2050, facilitated by efficient and green freight corridors. To meet this goal will also require appropriate infrastructure to be developed.
2   By 2050, complete the European high-speed rail network. Triple the length of the existing high-speed network by 2030 and maintain a dense rail network in all member states. By 2050 the majority of medium-distance passenger transport should go by rail.
3   Create a fully functional and EU-wide multimodal TEN-T 'core network' by 2030, with a high-quality and capacity network by 2050 and a corresponding set of information services.
4   By 2050, connect all core network airports to the rail network, preferably high-speed; ensure that all core seaports are adequately connected to the rail freight and, where possible, inland waterway system.

In October 2007, EU member states agreed the third railway package of reforms. It introduced open access rights for international rail passenger services including cabotage. Train operators may pick up and set down passengers at any station on an international route, including two points both located in the same member state.

Inland waterways

Inland waterways play an important role in bulk trade in several parts of the EU. Of the 28 member states, 21 have inland waterways, 13 of which have cross-border interconnections. The main inland waterway networks are formed by the Rhine, Rhone and Danube basins and their tributaries. The potential for increasing the share of inland waterway transport is significant. Since 1976, member states have agreed to a mutual recognition of each other's decisions on the navigability of waterways. Technical specifications have been set for inland waterway vessels, which have been updated regularly, most recently by the Council of Ministers in June 2015. Earlier directives have liberalised cabotage, introduced the mutual recognition of boat masters' certificates, cockpit crew licences and driving licences. The commission has taken the initiative in:

- moves to eliminate overcapacity, financed by national governments;
- setting up a market-monitoring system;
- drawing up an international agreement for free competition on the Rhine–Main–Danube canal.

Inland waterway transport is a competitive alternative to road and rail, offering an environment-friendly option in terms of energy consumption and noise. Its energy consumption per tonne-kilometre (tkm) of transported goods is 17 per cent that of road transport and 50 per cent that of rail.

Shipping

Ships carry 90 per cent of the EU's international imports and exports and 40 per cent of its internal trade. The EU priorities are to provide very strict safety rules preventing sub-standard shipping, reducing the risk of serious accidents and minimising the environmental impact of maritime transport. It also works actively against piracy and terrorism threats at sea. Another important activity concerns working conditions, health and safety issues and professional qualifications of seafarers. In December

1986 the Council of Ministers agreed most elements of a common shipping policy which would enable the EU to use its collective bargaining power to strengthen its chances to compete on the world market. Regulations took effect in July 1987 to:

• ensure EU competition rules applied to the sea transport sector;
• impose anti-dumping measures on third countries which practice predatory pricing or reserve cargos for national vessels;
• guarantee freedom for EU vessels to ply between EU ports and outside destinations.

Several other EU initiatives were adopted in 1998, including common safety rules for roll-on, roll-off ferries and high-speed passenger craft; a proposal to improve port reception facilities for ship-generated waste and cargo residues; and directives to impose on all vessels operating in EU waters (including those flying the flags of third countries) the working hours laid down by the International Labour Organisation. They were also required to apply certain international safety standards for passenger vessels, and to register all persons sailing on board passenger ships.

Tougher prevention and clean-up rules were announced in 2000 in the wake of the Erika oil tanker spill off the French coast, when the 25-year-old single-hull vessel broke in two, releasing up to 100,000 tonnes of oil and damaging 400 kilometres of the Brittany coast. The first package of measures, known as Erika I, was aimed at tougher port inspections, better controls for ship-classification societies and the gradual phase-out of single-hull tankers. The second package, Erika II, emphasises training for crews, establishes a European pollution damage fund to provide compensation of up to €1 billion for victims and sets up a European Maritime Safety Agency.

Airways

Air transport is a strategically important sector for the EU economy. According to the commission, it provides 5.1 million jobs and contributes 2.4 per cent to European GDP each year. But for years, air transport was a closed shop, firmly in the hands of governments and state-owned national flag-carriers. Competition was non-existent. Fares in Europe were sky-high, particularly when compared to North American levels. The system has changed dramatically. In April 1986 a ruling from the Court of Justice enabled the commission to force the pace of liberalisation. The case involved a French travel firm Nouvelles Frontières, which had challenged price-fixing regulations under the French Civil Aviation

Code. The court ruled that the EC general competition rules also applied to air transport.

As a result, the EU aviation market was liberalised through three successive packages of measures which covered air carrier licensing, market access and fares. Decades of restrictions, protected markets and price-fixing disappeared. Airlines were free to enter new markets and make cross-border investments. Regional air travel was opened up. The arrival of low-cost airlines did the rest. Since March 1997 airlines have been free to set their own fares and to operate anywhere within the EU. The principal beneficiaries have been the low-cost operators and the travelling public.

Row over emissions control

But the sector faces other problems linked to congestion, delays and pollution. Aviation was included in the EU Emissions Trading System (see pp. 218–20) in January 2012, after four years of negotiations. It initially covered all flights to and from destinations within the EU and flights to and from third countries. But the same year the EU ETS was suspended for flights to and from non-EU countries after massive protests from the US, China and a number of other countries at what they considered unilateral action by the EU. The suspension is ostensibly to allow the International Civil Aviation Organisation (ICAO) time to come up with an alternative global mechanism for emissions control to be effective by 2020. In the meantime, the EU ETS will continue to apply to internal EU flights and flights to and from EEA countries Iceland, Norway and Liechtenstein.

Single European Sky

Overcoming heavy airspace congestion and the strain on airport capacity as traffic increases is the aim of the ambitious initiative for a Single European Sky (SES), launched by the Council of Ministers in 2004. A second package of measures, known as SES II, followed in 2009 and had a greater emphasis on environment and cost efficiency.

The EU also created the European Aviation Safety Agency (EASA) in 2002. It was initially mandated to guarantee the air-worthiness and environmental compatibility of aircraft, but its mandate was extended to cover all other fields of aviation safety to 'ensure precise, uniform and binding rules for airport safety, air traffic management and air navigation services'. The EU and Eurocontrol, an inter-governmental agency for air traffic management, set up the Single European Sky ATM Research (SESAR), a public-private research and development partnership to link all air assets together via common data-exchange networks to provide a mobile, real-time overview at all times. However, despite continuing efforts by the commission, the European sky remains broadly divided into 28 different pieces of airspace under the control of national governments.

In December 2015, the commission published a new strategy for the aviation sector in Europe. Its four targets are:

1   Negotiate new international agreements at EU level, while guaranteeing free competition.
2   Tackle limits to growth in the air and on the ground.
3   Maintain high EU standards for safety, security, environment, social issues and passenger rights.
4   Make progress on innovation, digital technologies and investments.

Galileo

Launched in March 2002, the Galileo satellite programme offers a European and primarily civil alternative to the dominant American global positioning system (GPS) which was developed largely for military purposes. Galileo, initially based on 30 satellites, will pinpoint the locations of users such as car drivers and airline pilots to within 1 metre, compared with the 100 metres offered by GPS.

Galileo is due to offer three navigation and positioning services from 2016:

- *Open service*: Galileo provides free-of-charge open signals for navigation and time services.
- *Public regulated service*: a special navigation service using encrypted signals for critical transport and emergency services, better law enforcement, improved border control, and safer peace missions.
- Search and rescue service: Europe's contribution to COSPAS-SARSAT, an international satellite-based search and rescue distress alert system.

A commercial service that gives access to two additional encrypted signals has been under test since 2015 and will be provided when the system reaches full operational capability.

Galileo should cover extreme latitudes that GPS misses, overcome the poor availability that GPS suffers in urban areas and make it possible to study from space tectonic movements in earthquake zones or analyse the level of rivers and lakes. It is expected to create 150,000 jobs and generate over €11 billion in annual revenue for EU companies.

28 The environment

Today, environment policy is seen as one of the most effective in the EU, covering issues from air, water and ground pollution or chemical registration to eco-labels and climate change. But it was not a priority for the EU's founding fathers. There was no provision in the Rome treaty for a common policy on the environment. The gap, reflecting the low level of environmental awareness in the 1950s, was filled by the Single European Act of 1987, whose Article 25 sets out three aims for action on the environment:

• to preserve, protect and improve the quality of the environment;
• to contribute towards protecting human health;
• to ensure a prudent and rational utilisation of natural resources.

Programmes adopted from 1973

In the absence of any definition of EC competence in this area, early action on the environment was inevitably *ad hoc* and piecemeal. It was not until 1985, for example, that the Council of Ministers drew up a work programme for obtaining information on the state of the environment and natural resources. Nevertheless, from 1973 onwards the council adopted a series of action programmes which gradually broadened out from immediate responses to serious pollution problems to an overall preventive strategy for safeguarding the environment and natural resources. The most recent, the Seventh Environment Action Programme, was agreed in November 2013. The main areas where EU measures have been adopted are described in this chapter.

Water pollution

A number of directives have been approved for the protection of water, surface and underground, fresh and salt. Quality standards have been set for bathing water, drinking water, fresh water suitable for fish life and water used for rearing shellfish. The discharge of toxic substances is strictly controlled, with limits for mercury, cadmium, lindane, DDT, pentachlorophenol and carbon tetrachloride, and specific rules for the control and gradual reduction of dumping of titanium dioxide, which causes 'red sludge'. The EU is a participant in several conventions to reduce pollution in international waterways such as the River Rhine, the North Atlantic, the North Sea and the Mediterranean. The Water Framework Directive of 2000 commits EU members to achieve good qualitative and quantitative status of all water bodies – including marine waters up to 1 kilometre from the shore – by 2015. The directive requires the production of a number of key documents over six-year planning cycles. Most important among these are the river basin management plans published in 2009 and 2015 and those due to be published in 2021.

Atmospheric pollution

Despite a series of directives on the discharge of sulphur dioxide, the use of chlorofluorocarbons (CFCs) in aerosol cans and the control of pollution from certain industrial premises, progress has been slow in what are widely regarded as the two key areas: pollution from large combustion plants, particularly power stations, and the exhaust gases of motor vehicles. Both are blamed for widespread damage to forests through acid rain and for a variety of threats to public health. In March 1985 the council reached agreement that unleaded petrol would be generally available from October 1st 1989. But it was only in July 1987, thanks to the majority voting provisions of the Single European Act, that a series of regulations on automobile exhaust emissions was agreed. A directive was adopted in November 2001 requiring large combustion plants to upgrade emissions standards or shut down by 2015 at the latest.

Carbon dioxide, the main greenhouse gas, is now at the heart of industry and government agendas to curb car emissions as part of the climate change package. However, other emissions have long been targeted for their polluting effects. These include nitrogen oxides (NO_x: NO and NO_2), which contribute to smog and acid rain, and carbon monoxide (CO), a product of incomplete combustion, which reduces the blood's ability to carry oxygen and so is dangerous for people with heart disease. Hydrocarbons (HC) are an important ingredient of acid rain, as are sulphur oxides, and particulate matter (PM). They can cause respiratory diseases and cancer. The first attempts to curb these vehicle exhaust emissions originate from the 1970s. The latest EU exhaust standards, Euro 5, and the even stricter Euro 6, took effect in 2009 and 2014 respectively.

Noise

Directives have been adopted fixing maximum noise levels for cars, lorries, motorcycles, tractors, subsonic aircraft, lawnmowers and building-site machinery. The noise level of household equipment must be stipulated on its packaging, and proposals are under consideration concerning helicopters and rail vehicles.

Chemical products

Particularly since the Seveso accident in northern Italy in 1977, which resulted in the contamination of a large area by a highly toxic dioxin, increasingly stringent measures have been taken to reduce the risks arising from the manufacture and disposal of chemical substances. As early as 1967 a directive was adopted for the classification, packaging and labelling of dangerous substances. Two 1973 directives control the composition of detergents, while a European Inventory of Existing Chemical Substances was set up in 1986 to list all chemical products on the market, enabling them to be part of a general procedure for notification, evaluation and control. Other measures ban the use of certain substances in pesticides, and strictly control the manufacture and use of PCBs and PCTs (the substances involved in the Seveso accident), and of asbestos. In an attempt to prevent further major accidents and to limit their consequences, a directive of June 1982 imposes on manufacturers in all member states the obligation to inform the authorities about substances, industrial plants and possible locations of accidents.

Following the 1984 Bhopal tragedy in India, there has been strong pressure, particularly in the European Parliament, for tighter controls on chemicals. Concern at the depletion of the ozone layer, which protects the Earth from ultraviolet rays, led the EU to adopt a series of measures to bring about a substantial reduction of CFCs and other substances thought to be responsible for this phenomenon. Another environment initiative was the commission's 2003 proposal to regulate the chemicals found in many everyday household items: companies would be responsible for checking the safety of chemicals used in their products. The commission said the move was necessary because of growing concerns over a rise in cancers, birth defects and other illnesses which may be caused by exposure to chemicals. Despite active opposition from manufacturers, the commission's proposal became part of the 2007 REACH regulation. This replaced 40 pieces of earlier legislation. REACH (Registration, Evaluation and Authorisation of Chemicals) requires about 30,000 substances to be registered by 2018 with the new Chemical Agency in Helsinki which was created as part of the regulation. The new law puts the onus on the chemical industry to prove that its products, including those that have been on sale for years, are safe. Previously it was national authorities who had to prove that a given substance was hazardous. A safety report now has to be drawn up for chemicals produced or imported in quantities of more than 1 tonne per year.

In December 2008, the Council of Ministers and the European Parliament agreed to tighten rules on pesticide use and ban at least 22 chemicals deemed harmful to humans. The law bans substances that can cause cancer or harm human reproduction or hormones. In addition, any use of pesticides near schools, parks or hospitals is banned or severely restricted. Large-scale aerial crop-spraying is also banned.

Waste disposal

Since 1975 rules have been in force for the collection, disposal, recycling and processing of waste, of which the EU produces more than 2 billion tonnes a year. Specific measures have also been taken in individual areas, such as waste from the titanium oxide industry, waste oils, the dumping of waste at sea and radioactive waste. Recommendations have been made on the reuse of paper, cardboard and drinks containers. Two pieces of legislation concern collecting, treating and recycling waste from cars and household appliances were introduced in 2002 and 2003 and have been updated several times since. The Waste Electrical and Electronic Equipment (WEEE) directive ensures electrical goods manufacturers will have to pay for recycling their products and prevent them from ending up in landfill sites and incinerators. The End of Life Vehicle (ELV) directive involves taking back and recovering the annual 9 million tonnes of ELVs, and requires all hazardous substances such as oil, brake fluid and coolant to be removed from all vehicles before they are scrapped.

Nature protection

The EU belongs to the 1979 Berne Convention on the conservation of wildlife, the 1950 Paris Convention on the protection of birds and the 1971 Ramsar Convention on Wetlands. The Council of Ministers has adopted several directives on the conservation of wild birds, on banning imports of products made from the skins of baby seals (following a mass campaign in which the European Parliament played a crucial role) and on the control and restriction of scientific experiments on animals.

Broadening the scope of environmental policy

By the early 1990s there was a widespread feeling that the EU should adopt a much more determined and systematic approach to environmental management. The creation of a European Environmental Agency was agreed, but its establishment was delayed by failure among the member states to agree on where it should be sited. In 1991 the scope of EC environmental policy was extended, in light of its links to other policy areas including agriculture, the internal market, transport and energy. Also in 1991 the Council of Ministers adopted the LIFE programme, designed to provide financial incentives for priority projects in the environmental field. The most recent LIFE programme, for 2014–20, is worth a total of €864 million. It focuses on the environment and climate action.

The Maastricht summit in December 1991 incorporated a new section on the environment into the Rome treaty (now the TFEU) substantially extending EU competence. The Amsterdam Treaty of June 1997 elevated the promotion of 'a high level of protection and improvement of the quality of the environment' into a specific EU objective.

Making polluters pay

The EU has taken other environmental initiatives. After ten years of preparation, a directive on Environmental Liability was agreed in 2004. It makes polluters pay for the damage they cause. Member states are required to prevent and restore environmental damage by ordering economic operators to take full liability, or by suing. The directive aims to prevent and remedy environmental damage defined as damage to protected species and natural habitat. However, it does not require polluters to repair economic loss or damage relating to private property, while marine pollution incidents and nuclear damage are excluded. In 2006, the European Commission produced an action plan to halt biodiversity loss by 2010. Little came of it. It proposed a long-term strategy in January 2010 with four priorities. These were endorsed by the Council of Ministers in June 2011.

29 Climate change

At the cross-over between environment and energy policies, climate change, including related issues like greenhouse gas emissions and energy efficiency, has become a policy area in its own right. It burst onto the global agenda at the June 1992 UN Earth Summit in Rio de Janeiro, although the EU had already highlighted the need for a worldwide approach to cutting carbon dioxide emissions. When the UN Framework Convention on Climate Change produced the 1997 Kyoto protocol to limit global GHG emissions, the EU was its most ardent proponent, even if other Kyoto signatories like the US did not ratify the protocol, or like Australia subsequently withdrew from it.

The EU and Kyoto

The Kyoto Protocol established a legally binding commitment to reduce greenhouse gases. These are acknowledged on the basis of available scientific evidence and observation to be a primary cause of climate change and global warning. Kyoto commits participants to strive to keep the rise in global temperatures to less than 2°C above preindustrial levels. This target was confirmed – and reinforced – at the COP21 world climate conference in Paris in December 2015 which was tasked with setting the framework for global climate action once the Kyoto protocol runs out in 2020. Like other leading industrial powers at Kyoto, the EU accepted a target for reducing its GHG emissions, principally of carbon dioxide. It pledged to cut them to 8 per cent below 1990 levels by 2008–12 – a target it comfortably achieved. It then proceeded to set even more ambitious reduction targets for 2020 and beyond.

However, the overall 8 per cent cut agreed for the EU at Kyoto masked big differences in the efforts individual member states were asked to make. Some less-advanced countries would be able to go on increasing their emissions so as not to stymie their economic development. The brunt

Table 29.1 Allocation of Kyoto commitments within EU

	Percentage change from 1990
Austria	−13.0
Belgium	−7.5
Denmark	−21.0
Finland	0.0
France	0.0
Germany	−21.0
Greece	+25.0
Ireland	+13.0
Italy	−6.5
Luxembourg	−28.0
Netherlands	−6.0
Portugal	+27.0
Spain	+15.0
Sweden	+4.0
UK	−12.5
EU commitment	**−8.0**

Source: Council of the European Union.

of the reductions would be borne by the most economically advanced members. This intra-EU burden-sharing facility irritated many developing countries at Kyoto who had no access to this kind of flexibility. Notwithstanding, they argued, against strong western opposition, that they too were entitled to emit more to support their industrialisation.

For many in Europe, the burden-sharing formula showed the solidarity the EU is capable of on a good day. Portugal, Greece, Spain and Ireland were allocated big emissions' increases, while Germany and the UK accepted the biggest reductions. Their task was made easier by the fact that the industrial collapse of the former east Germany was lowering German emission levels anyway. For the UK, the 'dash for gas' (and away from coal) which followed electricity privatisation brought windfall cuts. France, whose CO_2 levels were lower than the rest because of its heavy dependence on nuclear power, was rewarded with a business-as-usual scenario. This is how the Council of Ministers carved up the 8 per cent burden among the then 15 member countries in a decision of June 1998 (see Table 29.1).

Cap-and-trade

After Kyoto, the EU published its European Climate Change Programme (ECCP) in June 2000 to identify and develop a strategy to implement the protocol. The flagship initiative was the EU's Emissions Trading

System (EU ETS), the largest of its kind in the world. It is what is called a 'cap-and-trade' scheme. A ceiling is set on the amount of CO_2 to be emitted. This is then doled out in the form of emissions permits to industrial emitters (power plants, steel mills, oil refineries, cement producers, aluminium smelters and so on) on the basis of their historic emissions: emit more than your quota, then you have to buy extra permits on the market to cover the difference; generate fewer emissions than your entitlement, and you can sell the surplus permits to emitters who have exceeded their limit. The emission ceiling (or cap) is reduced each year, making the market tighter and, hopefully, raising the cost of buying extra permits on the EU ETS market. The overall aim of the scheme is to encourage industrial plants to invest in low-carbon technologies by pushing up the cost of emitting CO_2. In the first Kyoto commitment period up to 2012, permits (known as European Emissions Allowances) were issued free of charge. In the second commitment period (2013–20), the intention was gradually to introduce an auctioning process whereby most permits would be subject to competitive bidding by emitters. Emitters in ten low-income EU countries, mainly in central and eastern Europe, will continue to receive permits free of charge.

The EU launched the ETS in 2005, covering about 10,000 heavy industrial plants across the EU, which together account for almost half the EU's CO_2 emissions. Since 2012, it has also covered the air transport sector – but only for internal flights starting and ending within the EU (see pp. 214–16). Other sectors, including sea transport, are expected to be brought under the ETS eventually and the scheme will also include other greenhouse gases such as nitrous oxides and perfluorocarbons. The overall CO_2 emissions cap under the EU-ETS is reduced by 1.74 per cent each year. The rate of annual reduction is due to accelerate post-2020. The faster pace is essential if the EU is to achieve its own 40 per cent reduction target for 2030.

Since its inception, however, the EU ETS has underperformed. In the running-in period from 2005 to 2007, too many permits were handed out, flooding the market and depressing prices. But even afterwards, the price of emissions allowances on the ETS languished at low levels – well under the minimum of €20 or even €30 per tonne of carbon forecast by its progenitors – as the global recession reduced industrial activities around the world, including the EU. The falling price of coal and other fossil fuels also lowered carbon prices. European emitters therefore found it cheaper to go on buying ETS allowances, and go on emitting CO_2, than to fund investments in low-carbon technologies. Would-be investors were also unsettled by mixed signals from governments on the promotion of renewable sources and their privileged position as a source in electricity generation.

Three times twenty

In parallel with its Kyoto targets, the EU set climate action goals of its own. An energy and climate change package was confirmed at an EU summit in December 2008. It set the triple targets for 2020:

*   20 per cent cut in greenhouse gas emissions (from 1990 levels);
*   20 per cent share of EU energy from renewable sources;
*   20 per cent improvement in energy efficiency.

The EU is on track to meet the 20 per cent emissions reduction target. In 2014, total estimated EU emissions were 4 per cent down on 2013 – and therefore about 23 per cent below 1990 levels. On an unchanged business-as-usual trajectory, the forecast reduction in 2020 will be 24 per cent lower than 1990. Achieving the renewables target is not only important in the context of climate change. Renewables make a significant contribution to reducing EU dependency on imported energy sources as well as to creating new jobs in high-tech sectors of the economy. On energy efficiency, governments are free to introduce promotional schemes so long as they do not breach EU competition rules.

In October 2014, with an eye on the coming UN climate conference (COP21) in Paris and as a token of their involvement in the international climate action process, EU countries agreed the following objectives for 2030. They build logically on the targets set for 2020:

*   A binding 40 per cent reduction in greenhouse gas emissions by 2030, compared to 1990.
*   Increasing the share of renewables in the EU energy mix to at least 27 per cent.
*   Increasing energy efficiency by at least 27 per cent, to be reviewed by 2020.
*   The completion of the internal energy market with an electricity interconnection target of 15 per cent between EU countries by 2030.

'Burdens' become 'efforts'

Sectors not covered by the ETS account for nearly 60 per cent of all EU greenhouse gas emissions. Chief among these are road and sea transport, buildings, services, agriculture and smaller industrial installations. A decision of the Council of Ministers and the European Parliament of March 2009 calls for an overall cut of 10 per cent of these emissions by 2020, compared with 2005 levels. The European Commission estimates that beyond 2020, burden-sharing can achieve a reduction by 2030 of 30 per cent over 2005. The 2009 decision sets binding national targets for emission cuts for each of the 28 member states within the overall envelope of the 10 per cent EU reduction. Here again, as for Kyoto, burden-sharing allows for a wide range of national targets, including some substantial emissions' increases. But the term burden-sharing has now been renamed as the less onerous 'effort sharing'. Eighteen member states are to cut their emission by between 4 per cent and 20 per cent while less advanced economies can go on increasing their emissions by amounts which are as high as 19 per cent for Romania and 20 per cent for Bulgaria.

Open to abuse

The automobile sector – which accounts for about 14 per cent of CO_2 emissions in the EU – was set an average emission target of 120 grammes of CO_2 per kilometre by 2012 for new cars, compared with previous levels of 160g/km. The target for 2020 is 95g/km. However, the car industry across the EU received a severe jolt in summer 2015 when US regulators discovered that German carmaker Volkswagen had installed devices on 11 million diesel-powered vehicles worldwide which ensured they complied with emissions standards under test conditions, but exceeded them by wide margins under normal driving conditions. The harm done to the reputation, reliability and quality claims of the EU auto sector was not limited to Volkswagen. In addition, national governments and EU authorities stood accused of being easy victims of the EU's powerful car lobby. Specialists at the Commission's Joint Research Centre also learned about the scam and had been warning the EU well before the American regulators went public.

30 Justice and home affairs

Underpinning free movement

The right of EU workers to live and work in the member state of their choice goes back to the Rome treaty (Article 48). Personal mobility is also one of the four freedoms enshrined in single market legislation. One purpose is to ensure workers (and their families) enjoy the same level of legal, civil, social and economic rights and protection in their new host country as they did at home. For this, the EU needs to harmonise standards of justice, security and home affairs management in all member states. Personal mobility also required the removal of frontier controls at internal EU borders. One of the first concerns was to ensure equality before the law, not only for law-abiding citizens on the move, but also so that law-breakers could not escape their home criminal justice system by slipping into a next-door member state. It is said that criminals are usually one step ahead of the law; and it is true that in the complex and interrelated areas of free movement, justice, frontier controls, immigration, asylum, cross-border crime and terror, the EU has oft-times been behind the curve.

One problem has been, of course, that most issues of civil and criminal law, justice, public security and policing are the prerogative of national governments. An attempt to codify this was included in the Maastricht treaty which created the three-pillar structure for the EU, where pillars two (foreign and security policy) and three (justice and home affairs) were regarded as areas to be handled by member states cooperating on an intergovernmental basis with only a small supporting EU role.

It soon became clear that the pillar structure did not fit with reality. Border controls, aspects of civil law (like cross-border custody of children of divorced parents of different EU nationalities), immigration and asylum, increasingly touched directly on areas of EU responsibility. Some procedures were unwieldy and inefficient. A first remedy was applied by the 1997 Amsterdam treaty which transferred civil law matters, asylum and immigration to pillar one (where normal EU procedures applied), with police and judicial cooperation in criminal matters remaining within the third pillar. The 9/11 terror attacks in the US in 2001 added another dimension. The short-lived pillar structure was abolished altogether by the 2007 Treaty of Lisbon. Like a number of other policies, justice and home affairs and their related sub-policies became mixed responsibilities shared by the EU and the member states.

However, the difficulties and contradictions remained – and got worse over time. The challenge now is to guarantee free movement within the Schengen passport-free area (see pp. 134–6), while promising public security by combating terrorism and organised crime, including human trafficking, sexual exploitation, arms and drug trafficking, corruption and fraud. Sorting out legal from illegal immigration and applying fair and humane rules for dealing with refugees and asylum seekers from the world's many trouble zones also pose huge problems. The result has been to hoist justice and home affairs to the top tier of EU activities alongside managing the eurozone and trying to put in place a coherent foreign and security policy. The massive refugee influx from Libya and then Syria in 2015 starkly revealed the limits of EU capabilities.

Informal beginnings

At the outset, freedom of movement was viewed essentially in economic terms and concerned only workers. But by the 1970s, the desire to extend this freedom to everyone and the growing importance of certain problems – such as cross-border organised crime, drug trafficking, illegal immigration and terrorism – encouraged member states to seek informal cooperation in justice and home affairs. Member states were already cooperating at various levels: bilaterally, regionally (within the Council of Europe, for example) and globally (Interpol and the UN).

From 1975 onwards, intergovernmental cooperation slowly began to develop outside the Community's legal framework for dealing with immigration, the right of asylum and police and judicial cooperation. Informal arrangements were set up to swap experiences, exchange information and expertise, and develop networks to improve contacts between member states. The Trevi Group, an informal forum for justice ministers set up in 1975, met initially to discuss terrorism and internal security, but it extended its scope in 1985 to cover illegal immigration and organised crime. In parallel, 1984 saw the first regular informal meetings of justice and home affairs ministers, every six months, to discuss issues such as police, judicial and customs cooperation, and the free movement of people.

The Single European Act of 1986 marked a turning point in inter-governmental cooperation, when it created the single market and its four fundamental freedoms: the free movement of goods, capital, services and persons. But freedom of movement for all – European citizens and non-European nationals present on their territory – obviously implied scrapping border controls. Resistance from certain member states was overcome by promises of parallel measures to strengthen external frontiers and draft European asylum and immigration policies. But the initial hesitancy on the part of some, prompted France, Germany and the Benelux countries to sign the Schengen Agreement in 1985 and the Schengen Convention in 1990. This was designed to abolish internal border checks, improve controls at external borders and harmonise arrangements relating to visitors' visas, asylum, and police and judicial cooperation.

The dance of the treaties

The Maastricht treaty revived the process. Besides creating the third pillar, it identified nine areas of common interest: asylum policy; the crossing of external borders; immigration; combating drug addiction; combating international fraud; judicial cooperation in civil matters; judicial cooperation in criminal matters; customs cooperation; and police cooperation. But the third pillar's decision-taking mechanism threw up many questions. Should drug abuse come under Community health policy (pillar one) or cooperation on justice and home affairs, which covers trafficking and drug dependency (pillar three)? Should questions of asylum, immigration and external frontiers be dealt with in the context of free movement of persons, i.e. in a Community framework?

The Treaty of Amsterdam, negotiated in 1997, defined the area of freedom, security and justice more precisely, and brought external border controls, asylum, immigration and judicial cooperation in civil matters under the first pillar, where they can be the subject of EU directives, regulations, decisions, recommendations and opinions. This included the Schengen agreement.

The treaty changes provided for opt-outs, and the UK, Ireland and Denmark indicated in protocols to the Treaty of Amsterdam that they do not wish to participate fully in all the measures relating to the area of freedom, security and justice (all have since adopted the Schengen rules). The treaty also provided for opt-ins which have enabled Norway, Switzerland and Iceland, although outside the EU, to be part of the Schengen area.

The Treaty of Nice negotiated in December 2000 brought further changes, including the Charter of Fundamental Rights for EU citizens (see also Chapter 4). It also shifted voting in the Council of Ministers to qualified majority on asylum, civil law, the free movement of legal third-country nationals, frontier controls, illegal immigration and repatriation. In 2000, the EU also set up a €216 million four-year European Refugee Fund to help member states cope with the influx of displaced people. In May 2001, justice and home affairs ministers agreed penalties of no less than eight years in prison for people convicted of smuggling and harbouring illegal immigrants. They also agreed to swap information among criminal investigation agencies to combat money-laundering, allowing foreign investigators access to bank accounts in countries with strong banking secrecy laws if they can demonstrate the information they are looking for has substantial value.

Practical tools

From the 1990s onwards, a panoply of practical instruments was created.

- *Europol* is the European Union's law enforcement agency whose main goal is to help make Europe safer for all EU citizens. It is modelled on Interpol, the international police agency. It assists member states in their fight against serious international crime and terrorism. Based in The Hague, Europol was created in 1995 under the Maastricht treaty and became operational in October 1998.
- *Eurojust* coordinates investigations and prosecutions of cross-border crimes between the competent authorities in the member states by facilitating the execution of international mutual legal assistance and the implementation of extradition requests. Set up in 2002, it is also based in The Hague.
- *The European arrest warrant* is valid throughout all member states. Issued by the national judicial authority in one country, it requires another member state to arrest and extradite a criminal suspect or sentenced person to the issuing state so that the person can be put on trial or complete a detention period. Agreed by a council decision of 2002, it became operational in January 2004. It applies to 32 diverse crimes, including terrorism, trafficking in human beings, corruption, rape and racism, and was followed in June 2006 by a system to speed up the transfer of evidence (an 'evidence warrant') for criminal investigations from one member state to another. This was hailed as an important step in fighting terrorism and organised crime.
- *The Charter of fundamental rights* of the EU brings together in a single document the fundamental rights protected in the EU. They come under six headings: Dignity, Freedoms, Equality, Solidarity, Citizens'

Rights and Justice. Drawn up in 2000, the charter became legally binding on the EU with the entry into force of the Treaty of Lisbon, in December 2009.

*   *Frontex* is the EU external border management agency. Created in 2004 and based in Warsaw, Frontex helps border authorities from different EU countries work together. It applies the concept of integrated border management, while respecting the principles set out in the fundamental rights charter. Its full title is the European Agency for the Management of Operational Cooperation at the External Borders of the Member States of the European Union.

Immigration

Given Europe's aging population, unfavourable demographics and skills shortage, immigration is a standard feature of EU policy-making and medium-term planning. The EU measures on legal immigration cover the conditions of entry and residence for certain categories of immigrants from outside the EU. The EU has the competence to lay down the terms for third-country nationals but member states still retain the right to determine admission rates for non-EU incomers seeking work. Categories where conditions are set at EU level include highly-qualified workers subject to the EU Blue Card Directive and students and researchers. Family reunification and long-term residents are also provided for. In this way, immigration can make a valuable contribution to the EU's economic development and performance in the long term. To ensure EU countries get their share of available highly-skilled workers from outside, the blue card scheme was introduced in 2009. Like the American green card, the EU blue card operates on a points system for skills and languages, with some weight given to family ties within the EU. An engineer who speaks English and French, and who has family in France, would have a better chance of getting a permit than an unskilled labourer who speaks only a little English and has no family in the EU. The legislation also allows member states to set quotas on blue card holders or to ban them altogether if they see fit.

Illegal immigrants

Often called economic migrants, they come to Europe in the hope of obtaining better living conditions than in their home countries. The majority consist of young men. According to the European Commission, 276,000 migrants entered the EU illegally in 2014, an increase of 138 per cent over 2013. To enter the EU clandestinely via land, air and sea routes, most migrants have recourse to criminal networks of smugglers. Migrant smuggling is a fast growing global criminal activity, feeding on the poverty, social and political instability affecting would-be migrants, as well as unavailability or limited access to legal channels. The EU has enacted legislation to crack down on people smugglers. At the end of 2010, the so-called Return directive entered into force. It applies to those who entered the EU illegally or stayed on after their temporary visa expired. It provides for clear, transparent and fair common rules for the return and removal of the illegal migrant. Of those ordered to leave the EU every year, only about 40 per cent actually do so. Voluntary returns are also encouraged.

Asylum and refugees

Since 1999, the EU has been working to create a Common European Asylum System (CEAS) and to improve the legislative framework. The EU rules have gradually been improved and strengthened, with the aim of setting common high standards and stronger cooperation to ensure that asylum seekers are treated equally in an open and fair system – in whatever member state they apply. The main components of the system are the following. All items of legislation were revised and updated in 2013 with most new rules taking effect in mid-2015. The main aim is to set clearer rules and simpler and faster procedures:

- The Asylum Procedures Directive harmonises asylum procedures and aims at fairer, quicker and better quality asylum decisions.
- The Reception Conditions Directive ensures that there are humane material reception conditions (such as housing) for asylum seekers across the EU and that the fundamental rights of the persons concerned are fully respected.
- The Qualification Directive clarifies the grounds for granting international protection.
- The Dublin Regulation contains the rules establishing the state responsible for examining asylum applications.
- The Eurodac Regulation establishes the Eurodac fingerprint database system in order to allow comparison of fingerprints with the aim of assisting the application of the Dublin Regulation.

Under the Dublin Regulation, asylum seekers have to apply for asylum in the first EU country they enter and, if they cross borders to another country after being fingerprinted, they can be returned to the country of arrival. Justice and home affairs ministers set up Eurodac in 2002 as an important tool against illegal immigration and 'asylum shopping' whereby would-be asylum seekers submit applications in more than one country. The new Eurodac system allows immigration services to check the fingerprints of asylum seekers against records held by other EU countries.

Overwhelmed by the 2015 refugee crisis

But the revamped CEAS was tested beyond its limits from day one by the massive influx of refugees in 2015, initially from Libya to Italy which was followed by a second wave, consisting largely of Syrians, from Turkey to Greece. Many of the latter moved overland to central Europe in the hope of reaching Germany and Sweden, traditionally the most welcoming member states for asylum seekers. For, despite common rules and standards, EU member states apply their own rules for actual reception conditions, recognition rates, and integration measures. Greece and Italy were unable to apply the Dublin regulation on registration and fingerprinting because of the numbers involved. The Dublin system as it stands places an unfair burden on them, although its stated purpose is to foster the onward movement of asylum seekers to other resettlement countries.

Schengen under threat

According to Eurostat, 942,000 claims for asylum were made in 2015, by far the largest number in Germany which had said it would accept up to one million refugees. Of those making perilous crossings in often unseaworthy vessels, 150,000 reached Italy from Libya and 818,000 reached Greece over the Aegean Sea from Turkey. More than 3,500 died en route. To ease the burden on Greece, Italy and Hungary (the most frequently used transit country), the EU agreed to resettle 160,000 refugees from these countries to other member states. Not all accepted. The EU also agreed to pay Turkey €3 billion, along with other sweeteners, to help it look after the more than two million Syrian refugees it was hosting, and dissuade then from trying to reach Europe. So-called hotspots were set up in Italy and Greece, by drafting in specialists from other member states, to expedite the registration process. To reduce massive flows onto their territory several EU countries brought back border controls inside the EU's frontier-free Schengen area. There are provisions for this under Schengen rules, but only in emergencies, involving issues of public policy and public security, and only for limited periods – normally a maximum of six months.

Responding to terror

The Schengen system of open borders also fell victim to the jihadist terror attacks in Europe, particularly in France, in 2015. Internal frontier checks were reintroduced temporarily between France and its neighbours. Following the mass killings in Paris on November 13th 2015, the Council of Ministers took a series of steps to reinforce controls at the EU's external frontiers, upgrading electronic and other controls, reinforcing the exchange of information, introducing systematic checks on all border-crossers including migrants and refugees, and focusing on the most exposed border areas. Frontex would step up cooperation with Europol and Eurojust, exchanging data on processing hotspots. A European Counter Terrorism Centre was to be set up within Europol. Dealing with radicalised young fighters from Europe on their return from Syria and Iraq was another priority.

Terrorism is not a new phenomenon in the EU. It has had a counter-terrorism coordinator since 2004 following the Madrid train bombings that killed some 200 people – the single biggest terror incident in Europe – and a counter-terrorism strategy since 2005. Previous efforts to combat terrorism inside the EU were hampered by differences in the laws of member states: only six had laws referring to terrorism or terrorists; the rest used more general laws to prosecute suspects. The new agreement defines terrorism broadly, also covering cyber and environmental attacks, and included a two-tier penalty system of 8 years' imprisonment for those who commit terrorist acts and 15 years' for the leaders of terrorist groups. The EU also agreed measures to force courts to freeze and transfer criminals' assets on request from a court in another member state.

Programmes and budgets

As the legal scope has expanded, so have programmes and budgets, in particular for managing immigration and asylum on the one hand and EU internal security on the other. In the 2014–20 budgetary period, The EU has set aside €6.9 billion for what it calls 'an open and secure Europe'. The money will be channelled through two funds, rather than six as previously:

- The Asylum, Migration and Integration Fund (AMIF) with a 2014–20 budget of €3.1 billion, which replaces the European Refugee Fund (ERF), the Integration Fund (EIF) and the Return Fund (RF).
- The Internal Security Fund (ISF) with a budget of €3.8 billion, which will replace the External Borders Fund (EBF), the Prevention,

Preparedness and Consequence Management of Terrorism and other Security-related risks programme (CIPS) and the Prevention of and Fight against Crime (ISEC). The ISF has been divided into two programmes: ISF–Borders and ISF–Police.

The total amount is little changed from the €7.1 billion allocated to the six previous funds for 2007–13. The bulk of both funds – €4.5 billion from a total of €6.9 billion – will go to support national programmes in the priority areas identified by the council in November 2015. Another €1.1 billion will be invested in IT systems to help control migrant flows across the EU's external frontiers.

31 Consumers

Cinderella of the EU

To some extent consumer policy has been the Cinderella of the EU. It was not mentioned in the Rome treaty, and it took years of campaigning by consumer organisations, often backed by pressure from the European Parliament, before practical steps were taken to ensure that consumer issues were taken seriously. The turning point came at the summit meeting in Paris in 1972, when the leaders decided that economic development must be accompanied by an improvement in the quality of life. This meant that the Community should pursue an active consumer policy. Three important steps followed over the next few years:

- The creation of a service, and then a full directorate-general, for the environment and consumer protection, within the European Commission.
- The creation of a Consumers' Consultative Committee (CCC).
- The adoption by the Council of Ministers, in April 1975, of a first consumer information and protection programme. It listed five basic consumer rights: the right to safeguards for health and safety; the right to economic justice; the right to redress for damages; the right to information and education; and the right to consultation. These rights were to be implemented by concrete measures and also taken into account in other Community policies, such as agriculture, the economy, social affairs and the environment.

Consumer consultation

The body which consults consumer organisations has changed titles over the years, but remains essentially the same. Initially the Consumer Consultative Committee, it was reconstituted as the Consumer Committee in

1995, and in 2003 became the European Consumer Consultative Group (ECCG). The ECCG gives opinions on consumer issues, advises the commission when it drafts policies, and acts as a source of information and a sounding board on EU action. It consists of:

- one representative of national consumer organisations per country;
- one member from each European consumer organisation (BEUC and ANEC);
- two associate members (EUROCOOP and COFACE);
- two EEA observers (Iceland and Norway).

Extending consumer choice

An important judgment by the Court of Justice in 1979 was of major significance in extending consumer choice. This was in the '*Cassis de Dijon*' case, and it reaffirmed in principle that all goods legally manufactured in a member country must be allowed into others (see Chapter 10, p. 97). The judgment found that national technical regulations, even if applied equally to domestic and imported goods, must not be allowed to create a barrier to trade except for overriding reasons such as the protection of public health or consumer interests. Ministers responsible for consumer affairs met for the first time in 1983. They are now established participants in the Council of Ministers, meeting several times a year and addressing a steady stream of legislative proposals put up by the commission. Decisions taken so far in the consumer field can be divided into three broad categories:

- the health and safety of consumers;
- protecting consumers' economic interests;
- consumer information and education.

Health and safety

It is in this category that most progress has been made. Measures adopted have covered the following areas:

Foodstuffs

European lists of permitted substances and purity standards have been established for foodstuff additives, such as colourings, anti-oxidants, preservatives, emulsifiers, stabilisers and gelifiers. Tight limits have been set for pesticide residues in fruit and vegetables and erucic acid in oils and fats for human consumption. Regulations also govern the production of honey, fruit juice, tinned milk, cocoa and chocolate, coffee and chicory extracts, mineral waters, jams and marmalades and chestnut purée, and specialist foodstuffs such as products for special diets. Directives are in force relating to the labelling of foodstuffs, specifying ingredients, quantity and the date by which they should be consumed. A ban has been imposed on the use of animal growth promoters which contain certain substances with hormonal or thyrostatic effects.

Agricultural products

Down the years, the common agricultural policy has taken important steps to protect consumers. One was the introduction of detailed traceability of farm products and animals. Another was the creation in 2002 of the European Food Safety Agency after a series of food scares. The EFSA provides independent scientific advice to the decision-makers who regulate food safety in Europe, thereby helping to protect consumers, animals and the environment from food-related risks.

Dangerous substances

Directives control the classification, marketing and labelling of dangerous substances as well as the use of many toxic substances such as pesticides, solvents, paints, varnishes, printers' ink, glues and asbestos.

Pharmaceuticals

The testing, patenting, labelling and marketing of pharmaceutical products are all controlled by EU directives.

Other products

EU directives regulate, for safety reasons, such products as cosmetics, textiles (where the main concern is to prevent the use of inflammable material), toys and a number of other manufactured products. Several hundred directives have been approved for the purpose of standardising tools, component parts and finished products in the manufacturing industry, with a view to increasing the efficiency and competitiveness of European firms, but since 1985 a new approach to standardisation has been adopted. Since then new directives have concentrated only on laying down safety specifications and have relied on the mutual recognition of national standards where no European standards exist. The commission does, however, give financial support to the two bodies responsible for setting European standards, CEN and Cenelec, and has given them remits to draft European standards concerning, in particular, toys, pressure vessels, gas appliances and IT equipment.

Warning system

In March 1984 the Council of Ministers established a system for the rapid exchange of information on dangerous products, allowing the authorities of one member state rapidly to draw the attention of all the others to serious incidents and take action to protect the health and safety of consumers. The 2001 directive on general product safety created the rapid alert system for non-food dangerous products (RAPEX). There were 2,341 RAPEX notifications in 2014: 650 for toys, 530 for textiles and clothing, 292 for motor vehicles and 217 for electrical appliances. Some 1,462 notifications concerned products made in China.

Protection of consumers' economic interests

Action to protect the economic interests of consumers has been slower because of difficulty in achieving agreement within the Council of Ministers. A number of directives have, however, been adopted in recent years on the following:

- *Misleading advertising*. Consumers can complain to the courts, which are empowered to require advertisers to prove the accuracy of their claims.
- *Consumer credit*. All credit agreements are to be in writing, be easily understandable and clearly indicate the real interest rate charged.
- *Door-to-door sales*. This directive is designed to protect consumers against hard selling techniques, and allow them time to change their mind.
- *Airlines*. A regulation of April 1991 requires airlines to pay financial compensation to passengers who are delayed through overbooking on commercial flights. A package of airline passenger compensation rules came into effect in 2005, providing greater compensation for cancellations, delays and overbooking. Since 2007, the EU has taken action against websites that fail to indicate clearly the total price of airline tickets (for example, not mentioning taxes, or imposing mandatory insurance). In 2008, the commission threatened airlines with legal action if their websites continue to 'mislead and rip off' consumers.

- *Product liability.* Potentially the most important EC decision affecting consumers was the adoption in August 1985 of a directive on product liability, which came into force in 1988. It imposed a strict liability on producers for damage caused by defects in their products, and it was adopted only after several years of campaigning on behalf of the victims of unforeseen side effects of pharmaceutical products. Under the directive member states may impose a limit to the liability, but this must be at least €70 million.

Consumer information and education

In addition to the directives for labelling foodstuffs and dangerous substances, others require electrical household appliances to be marked with their estimated energy consumption, and food to be marked with unit prices (by the kilogram or litre). Measures are also proposed to extend price marking to goods other than food. Multiannual action plans have been launched over the years. The most recent is the EU consumer programme 2014–20 with a budget for that period of €188.8 million. It aims to help citizens fully enjoy their consumer rights and actively participate in the single market.

The commission has been active in promoting a wider awareness of the results of comparative tests on consumer goods, better cooperation between the testing organisations and more information for consumers on the action taken on their behalf. It sponsors frequent conferences on consumer issues, supports experiments on consumer education in schools and gives subsidies to national consumer groups to support local consumer information programmes.

One area of particular action is in combating smoking. In 2002, the EU agreed a wide-ranging ban on tobacco promotion that prevents cigarette companies using ashtrays, umbrellas and other goods to promote their products. It also applies to publicity on the Internet and has put an end to sponsorship by tobacco companies of cross-border events such as Formula One motor racing. The commission also launched a €72 million campaign against smoking that included a series of hard-hitting images showing the damage it can do to people's health.

Roaming meets its gloaming

Another area is digital rights. The commission has been active in setting guidelines for business over the Internet, and offering guidance for consumers in areas like online shopping and auctions, social networking

Table 31.1 Maximum tariffs (excluding VAT) for mobile calls, texts and data

	July 1st 2014	April 30th 2016	June 15th 2017
Outgoing voice calls (per minute)	€0.19	domestic price + up to €0.05	no extra roaming fee, same as national rate
Incoming voice calls (per minute)	€0.05	€0.0114	no extra roaming fee, same as national rate
Outgoing texts (per SMS message)	€0.06	domestic price + up to €0.02	no extra roaming fee, same as national rate
Online (data download, per MB)	€0.20	domestic price + up to €0.05	no extra roaming fee, same as national rate

Source: European Commission.

and digital downloads. And in October 2015, the European Commission, backed by the European Parliament, finally won a high-profile ten-year battle with mobile telecoms operators to end extra 'roaming' charges on mobile phone calls sent and received by citizens on holiday or during short stays in another EU country. The commission led the attack with gusto, knowing its popularity among consumers, already looking askance at the mark-ups charged by mobile operators. Price caps were imposed on additional roaming charges in 2007, 2012 and 2015. Under the 2015 regulation adopted by the council and parliament, roaming charges will disappear by July 2017 (see Table 31.1). Domestic tariffs in the subscriber's home country will then apply wherever he or she is on EU territory.

Food labelling

Another area is food labelling. Legislation was approved in 2006 to standardise food product labels to prevent misleading claims. The new rules target the use of health or nutritional claims, such as 'low fat', 'high fibre' and 'helps lower cholesterol'. The legislation bans vague claims for foods, such as 'preserves youth', along with slimming or weight control claims and health claims on beverages with more than 1.2 per cent alcohol content.

32 Education

Education policy was, and still is, mostly in the hands of national governments. It is an area where national traditions and methods, which are extremely varied, should be respected and, indeed, fostered. This is also in line with the principle of subsidiarity or devolved responsibility (see p. 111). Any attempt to standardise teaching, structures, methods or syllabi, it is accepted, would be misplaced. The role of the EU is therefore one of support and coordination.

There was little reference to education in the Rome treaty, except for the need for mutual recognition of diplomas (Article 57) and vocational training (Articles 41 and 118). Despite the EU's limited role, education was formally recognised as an area of EU competence in the Maastricht Treaty of 1992. This stated that

> the Community shall contribute to the development of quality education by encouraging cooperation between member states and, if necessary, by supporting and supplementing their action, while fully respecting their responsibility for the content of teaching and the organisation of education systems and their cultural and linguistic diversity.

Six-point programme adopted in 1976

Since 1974, there has been increasing recognition of the need for closer cooperation between the member states in educational matters. Accordingly, in February 1976 the Council of Ministers adopted a six-point programme:

1 Improved cultural and vocational training for migrant workers and their children.
2 Better mutual understanding of the different European educational systems.
3 The collection of basic documentary information and statistics.
4 Cooperation in higher education.

5   The improvement of foreign-language teaching.
6   Equal access to all forms of education throughout the Community.

Subsequently, the programme was extended to include measures to improve the vocational training of young people and to ease the transition from school to workplace. Since 1980 there has been increasing concern about youth unemployment. With a few notable exceptions, EU policy has taken the form of recommendations to member states rather than of legislation requiring action by them. The main exception concerned efforts to facilitate freedom of movement in jobs and professions, involving special training and other requirements. The adoption of a series of directives ensured that by the beginning of 1993 a comprehensive formula existed for the mutual recognition of educational diplomas and the right to practice any trade or profession in all member states. Another directive, adopted earlier, in 1977, concerned the schooling of the children of migrant workers.

More typical, however, was promoting a wider knowledge of EC languages. In June 1984, ministers from the member states committed themselves to a programme to encourage a working knowledge of two languages apart from the mother tongue before the statutory school-leaving age. There was no guarantee, however, that all member states would make an equivalent effort to achieve this objective. Similar agreements have been reached to promote:

- student and teacher mobility;
- education in European current affairs;
- the transition from school to working life;
- education for those with special needs;
- literacy campaigns;
- new information technologies.

Education and training programmes

Many education and training programmes have been launched since the first student exchange programme, Erasmus, was conceived in 1985. The various initiatives were integrated under a single umbrella, the Lifelong Learning Programme, which had budget of nearly €7 billion for 2007–13. There are four sub-programmes focusing on different stages of education and training:

Erasmus

This €3.1 billion flagship programme enabled 200,000 students to study and work abroad each year, as well as supporting cooperation between higher education institutions across Europe. It caters not only for students, but also for professors and staff who want to teach abroad and for university staff who want to be trained abroad. Around 90 per cent of European universities take part in Erasmus and 2 million students have participated since it started in 1987. An international dimension was added to extend the programme to third countries in 2004 (Erasmus Mundus).

Comenius

Designed for schools, the €1.05 billion programme aimed to improve the quality and maintain the European dimension of school education by supporting transnational cooperation between schools and institutions active in the field of education. The main goal in the current programme is that at least 1 pupil in 20 – around 3 million pupils – will become involved in joint educational activities during the programme.

Leonardo da Vinci

All aspects of vocational training were concentrated within this €1.73 billion programme, which aimed to improve mobility, make participation more accessible and boost cooperation between businesses, unions, NGOs, research centres and other groups.

Grundtvig

With a €358 million budget, this programme aimed to strengthen the European dimension in adult education and lifelong learning.

Rebranding the programmes

But the whole group of programmes was recast and integrated into one greatly expanded Erasmus+ for the EU's 2014–20 budget period. What had been the EU's highly successful flagship programme for student mobility and exchanges was reborn in a regulation of the Council of Ministers and the European Parliament on December 11th 2013 as 'Erasmus+: the Union programme for education, training, youth and sport'. With total funding for the seven-year period of €14.7 billion, Erasmus+ brings together seven existing programmes, offering a simplified one-stop shop for up to 4 million potential users. In addition to the above four programmes, the others are

- *Youth in Action*, associated with non-formal and informal learning in the field of youth;
- *Sports*, associated with activities in the field of sport.

The Erasmus+ budget represents an increase of 40 per cent in these programmes compared with 2007–13. Its main function will still be to provide opportunities to study, train, gain work experience or volunteer abroad. Of the total budget, 77.5 per cent is earmarked for education and training. One notable innovation in Erasmus+ is a loan guarantee facility for master's degree students to finance their studies in another EU country.

In a broader context, Erasmus+ will support trans-national partnerships among education, training, and youth institutions and organisations to foster cooperation and bridge the worlds of education and work in order to tackle the skills gaps facing Europe. It will also support national efforts to modernise education, training and youth systems. It will for the first time provide support for sport. Here, Erasmus+ will fund grassroots projects and cross-border actions to combat match-fixing, doping, violence and racism. As an integrated programme, Erasmus+ offers more opportunities for cooperation across the education, training, youth and sports sectors and is easier to access than its predecessors, with simplified funding rules.

Education and training structures

Down the years, the EU has created a number of education and training structures. They include the following:

The European Training Foundation

Established in 1990, operational since 1994, the European Training Foundation (ETF) is located in Turin, Italy, and helps improve vocational training systems in non-EU countries, mostly in neighbouring regions such as candidates for membership, North Africa, the Middle East, the Balkans and the former Soviet Union.

The European Institute of Innovation and Technology

The European Institute of Innovation and Technology (EIT) aims to be a flagship research university for excellence in higher education, research and innovation. The initial concept was based on the example of the Massachusetts Institute of Technology (MIT) and its combination of world-class education, research and deep engagement in effective innovation processes. The regulation came into force in April 2008. Based in Budapest, the EIT became operational in 2010. It operates mainly by setting up networks of universities and research institutions, without building any new education or research institutions or granting EU diplomas.

Euridice

This information service network has been in operation since 1980, with access to educational administrators in all member states. It consists of a databank, containing a mass of information about educational developments throughout the EU. It now covers the EU's 28 member states, plus Iceland, Liechtenstein, Norway and Turkey.

European University Institute

This post-graduate institution, set up in Florence in 1976, offers courses in economics, law, political and social sciences, history and civilisation.

European Centre for the Development of Vocational Training

Established in Berlin in 1975, the purpose of the European Centre for the Development of Vocational Training (Cedefop) is to foster the development of vocational training and in-service training of adults.

The European Schools

Although mainly intended for the children of people working in EU institutions, the schools are open to other pupils. Fifteen schools offer an international syllabus, in which part of the teaching is in a language other than the pupil's native tongue, leading to a European baccalauréat, which provides admission to universities throughout the EU. The schools are in Luxembourg (two); Brussels (four) and Mol in Belgium; Varese in Italy; Frankfurt, Karlsruhe and Munich in Germany; Bergen in the Netherlands; Alicante in Spain; Strasbourg in France; and Culham in the UK.

33 Women's rights

The position of women within the Union has substantially improved since the EEC was first established, although they still face many disadvantages and are still therefore some way from achieving full equality with men. By 2012, the employment rate for women was 62.4 per cent (up from 53.6 per cent in 2000), while that of men was 74.6 per cent (up from 70.7 per cent in 2000). It was only 35 per cent in the 1970s. But women are still concentrated in certain sectors and job categories that are often vulnerable, less highly qualified, lower paid and with fewer promotion prospects. According to the European Commission, women accounted for 4 per cent of the CEOs in the biggest companies in the 28 member states in 2015. They occupied 14 per cent of board functions and 22 per cent of senior management positions in these companies. Above all, women predominate in part-time employment (30.7 per cent, compared with 6.5 per cent for men), and there is a higher proportion of unemployment among women than among the working population as a whole.

How the EU has helped improve women's status

There can be little doubt that the Union has done its bit to improve the status of women. Article 119 of the Rome treaty stipulates that 'each member state shall . . . ensure and subsequently maintain the application of the principle that men and women should receive equal pay for equal work'. It then spells out the principle in some detail, stipulating that 'pay' means 'the ordinary basic or minimum wage or salary and any other consideration, whether in cash or in kind, which the worker receives, directly or indirectly, in respect of his employment from his employer'. The article goes on to state that:

Equal pay without discrimination based on sex means:
- that pay for the same work at piece rates shall be calculated on the basis of the same unit of measurement;
- that pay for work at time rates shall be the same for the same job.

Despite the relative simplicity and lack of ambiguity in these provisions, it was necessary for the Council of Ministers to adopt several further measures before all the member states took adequate action to ensure their implementation. However, in its regular monitoring reports, the commission acknowledged that the wage gap was slow to close. At an average of 16 per cent it is still little changed from the 17 per cent registered in 1995 – despite women being better educated than 20 years ago. Actions taken by the council, in the form of directives, include:

- *February 1975.* Member states were obliged to revise their laws so as to exclude all discrimination on grounds of sex, particularly in systems of occupational classification. Workers believing themselves to be victims of discrimination must have the right and the possibility to take their case to a tribunal, and be protected against any wrongful dismissal if they do so.
- *February 1976.* The Equal Treatment Directive requires that there shall be 'no discrimination whatsoever on grounds of sex, either directly or indirectly by reference in particular to marital or family status'. In 2002, it was amended to include definitions of sexual harassment, harassment, and direct and indirect discrimination.
- *December 1978.* Any discrimination in statutory social security schemes is now illegal.
- *End 1986.* Direct or indirect discrimination against self-employed women workers (including agricultural workers) to be eliminated by the end of 1989 (or 1991 in some cases). The directive also included further provisions regarding maternity and social security. This directive achieved only limited results and was replaced by a recast and improved directive in July 2010.
- *November 2000.* The Employment Equality Directive prohibits discrimination, harassment and victimisation in employment and training on grounds of race, religion, ethnic origin or sexual orientation.
- *December 2004.* A directive implementing the principle of equal treatment between women and men in the access to and supply of goods and services aims to provide clearer information, for example, on how insurance premiums and benefits are calculated.

Action programmes

In addition to these directives, the European Commission has put forward a series of action programmes to the Council of Ministers, which have been adopted in the form of recommendations (that is, they are not mandatory on the member states). The most recent covering 2010–15 targets several specific actions:

- Support the promotion of gender equality in implementing the Europe 2020 strategy, especially as regards relevant national measures, through technical support as well as funding from specific EU programmes (structural funds and R&D initiatives).
- Monitor closely the national policies adopted to improve gender equality in the labour market and boost the social inclusion of women.
- Promote female entrepreneurship and self-employment.
- Assess remaining gaps in entitlement to family-related leave, notably paternity leave and carers' leave, and the options for addressing them.
- Report on the member states' performance with regard to childcare facilities.
- Promote gender equality in all initiatives on immigration and integration of migrants.

Actions taken also include a European Institute for Gender Equality to help raise awareness. Based in the Lithuanian capital, Vilnius, and inaugurated in 2007, it had a budget of €52.5 million for 2007–13. It is tasked with promoting gender equality, combating sex discrimination, and gathering reliable research data and information.

At a broader level, the EU opened a Fundamental Rights Agency in Vienna in 2007 to help combat discrimination on the basis of race, gender or religion. It replaced the EU's Monitoring Centre on Racism and Xenophobia. With a budget of €30 million, its purpose is to collect data on violations of fundamental rights, provide advice to the EU and its member states and raise public awareness. At the same time, 2007 was named the European Year of Equal Opportunities for All. Some 430 national actions were launched and there were over 600 events raising awareness about non-discrimination. In 2008, the commission set up an advisory committee on equal opportunities for women and men, with 68 government and NGO members.

Educational initiatives to encourage equal opportunities

In the belief that the roots of sexual discrimination may lie in the educational system, the commission has launched several initiatives to encourage sexual equality. The aim is to remove elements which both stereotype the sexes from an early age and cut off girls from career choices more readily open to boys.

Violence against women

In 1997 the European Parliament adopted a resolution on the violation of women's rights and another on the need for a Europe-wide campaign of zero tolerance of violence against women. It called for 1999 to be designated 'European Year against Violence against Women' and for respect for women's rights to be written into all EU agreements with non-member countries. The EU's Daphne III programme, whose 2007–13 budget was €117 million, tackles all forms of violence against women and children.

Sexual harassment

In April 2002, tough new rules to combat sexual harassment at work were agreed, and a number of other changes were made to the EU's sex equality laws. The new rules oblige employers to introduce preventive measures against sexual harassment in the workplace and to provide information to workers about equal treatment of men and women in the organisation.

'Cherchez la femme'

Given its early and fulsome commitment to sexual equality, the EU singularly failed as a role model. For 30 years, from its creation in 1958 to 1988, there was no woman member of the European Commission. Tokenism began in 1989 with the second Delors Commission, which had two women members, the first ever – Vasso Papandreou from Greece and Christiane Scrivener (France) – alongside 15 men. Real change had to wait until 1995, spurred by egalitarian Nordics from Sweden and Finland who joined the Union that year and who considered the Brussels sexual imbalance as an aberration. The Santer Commission, which took office in January 1995, included 4 women among its 20 members. This rose to five in the Prodi Commission (1999–2004). The Barroso Commission that followed in 2004 included eight women among its 25 commissioners, which rose to 9 out of 27 in Barrroso's second term (2009–14) – exactly one third. The commission headed by Jean-Claude Juncker, whose mandate runs from 2014 to 2019, kept 9 women members, out of a total complement of 28. Below commissioner level, the same pro-male bias was early on a permanent feature among senior and middle managers. The Nordics made the first inroads at this level too, but since then the higher proportion of women among the successful recruits from central and eastern Europe has considerably improved their presence among middle and senior managers.

34 Culture and the media

A cultural union

Europe was a cultural union long before it was anything else. Its name was Christendom. It lasted for centuries. Christianity built on the cultural, social, economic and scientific affinities among the peoples of Europe. The papacy, the 'Brussels' of yore, could exercise some centralising influence. The continent had been converted from the south via Rome, but also from the west. In 664 AD, bishops from northern England met at the Synod of Whitby to decide between the Celtic and Roman rites. They chose the latter. But Christendom was also able to accommodate the schisms, first with Orthodoxy, and then the Protestants. Then, as now, people could study and work where they liked. They moved freely across Europe – passports were a much later invention. Education and learning were integrated as scholars moved from one great university to another – from Krakow to Coimbra or from Oxford to Bologna. The same was true of painters, musicians, weavers, artisans and tradesmen. English prostitutes were said to be favourites at many inns in continental Europe. When on the move, people could use Latin as the European common language. Travellers and merchants could pay their way with a single currency in the form of gold and silver coins that were readily acceptable and convertible, even if they were variously called florins, marks, guilders, shillings or reals. Into the nineteenth and early twentieth century, the silver Maria-Theresa Thaler[1] from Austria, first minted in 1780, was a virtual world currency, accepted across the globe. It was still in circulation in Arabia in the 1960s.

Today's EU faces very different challenges. Culture takes a back seat. In fact, in the early years, the EEC deferred to the Council of Europe, as the guardian and promotor of cultural values. But new technologies of mobility, communications, production, storage and delivery techniques in the audiovisual sector and films forced a reassessment. National frontiers disappeared. Cultural goods became eminently tradeable. Competition grew, particularly from the US and Japan.

Culture programmes

Giving work to more than 5 million people, the cultural sector makes a substantial contribution to EU growth and employment. It accounts for about 2.6 per cent of the Union's GDP, with above-average growth compared to other sectors of the economy. Although it had started promoting culture in a limited way in the 1980s (the highly successful programme of cultural capitals launched in 1985 and still going strong), it was only in 1998 that the EU agreed its first culture programme. In the latest multi-annual budget period (2014–20), European cultural and creative sectors, including cinema, television, music, literature, performing arts, heritage and related areas, will benefit from increased support under the EU's new Creative Europe programme, with a budget of €1.46 billion during this period (9 per cent more than before). Creative Europe will support:

- culture sector initiatives to develop cross-border cooperation, platforms, networking and literary translation;
- audiovisual sector initiatives to promote the development, distribution or access to audiovisual works;
- a cross-sectoral strand, including a guarantee facility for SMEs and transnational policy cooperation.

The programme consists of two sub-programmes; the Culture sub-programme to promote the culture sector, and the MEDIA sub-programme to support the audiovisual sector. In recent years, MEDIA has supported more than 50 European films distributed outside their countries of origin – including *Le Fabuleux Destin d'Amélie Poulain, Volver, La Vita e Bella, La Môme* and *The Wind that Shakes the Barley*.

The aims of the new programme are to:

- safeguard and promote Europe's cultural and linguistic diversity and cultural richness;
- contribute to the EU's goal of smart, sustainable and inclusive economic growth;

- help the arts and creative sectors adapt to the digital age and globalisation;
- open up new international opportunities, markets and audiences.

This will, specifically, provide funding for 250,000 artists and cultural professionals, 2,000 cinemas, 800 films and 4,500 book translations.

Films, television and the 'cultural exception'

EU legislation here was largely motivated in the 1980s by the prospects offered by the development of direct broadcasting by satellite and the extension of cable networks. The key directive, entitled 'Television without Frontiers', was adopted in 1989 and came into force in October 1991. Member states could no longer impede the transmission of programmes from other EC countries provided they conformed to the directive's requirements on advertising, sponsorship, the protection of minors, ethical questions including the right of reply. It also invoked the so-called cultural exception secured by the EU from the World Trade Organisation, whereby cultural goods, given their non-material aspects, need not be treated as tradeable commodities. The directive, denounced as protectionist by the US government, called on member states to try to ensure that at least 50 per cent of air and screen time is devoted to programmes originating within the EC and that at least 10 per cent of their programming budgets is devoted to European works from independent producers.

The directive was revised in 2006 to reflect and encompass the enormous pace of change in broadcasting and the Internet, and renamed the Audiovisual Media Services Directive. It retains the cultural exception, first introduced at France's insistence, to protect European audiovisual markets from being flooded by works from the US, by far the dominant outside supplier. The notion of cultural exception was replaced by 'cultural diversity'; the Americans were unimpressed. The issue re-surfaced in 2013 during early stages of the negotiations between the EU and the US for a new Transatlantic Trade and Investment Partnership (TTIP). It was one controversial item among many.

The updated directive covers the growing market of video-on-demand services and Internet-based broadcasters. It allows new forms of advertising, such as split-screen, virtual and interactive advertising. And it aims to create a level playing field between traditional TV-based broadcasts and less-regulated broadcasts on the Internet and other social media.

The audiovisual media services directive requires EU countries to coordinate national legislation with each other to create comparable conditions in all countries for emerging audiovisual media as well as to safeguard media pluralism and the independence of national media regulators. They are also obliged to combat racial and religious hatred, and to preserve cultural diversity. Each country is encouraged to apply minimum standards for the following:

- Advertising: rules and restrictions to be in place for certain products (e.g. alcohol, tobacco, medicines) and no more than 12 minutes' advertising per hour.
- Major events: events like the Olympic Games or the football World Cup must be available to a wide audience on free-to-air channels, not just to pay-tv subscribers.
- Protecting children: violent or pornographic programmes to be scheduled late at night or with limited access through parental controls.
- Promotion of European films and audiovisual content: at least half of TV broadcasting time should be allocated to European films and television programmes. Video-on-demand services should also promote European works.
- Accessibility: media companies should make their audiovisual content accessible to people with visual or hearing impairments.

Copyright and enforcement

The audiovisual sector is also the main target for two directives, on copyright and enforcement. The 2004 enforcement directive for intellectual property was designed to clamp down on music, movies and software copying, with provisions for pirates and counterfeiters to be jailed, fined and have their bank accounts frozen. It also allows legal attacks on Internet file-sharing networks. The 2001 copyright directive aimed to improve protection across the EU in the digital environment, allowing companies to defend their products with copy-protection technology and made it illegal for anyone to circumvent such technology. These have been complemented by several more recent directives including the 2014 directive on collective management of copyright and related rights and multi-territorial licensing of rights in musical works for online use in the internal market.

Efforts to widen the cultural audience

The EU supports regular prizes for cultural heritage, architecture, literature and music which highlight Europe's artistic achievements. Besides regular funding for cultural events, exhibitions and festivals, the EU also sponsors a highly successful programme to promote every year two cities as Europe's Capitals of Culture. It started with the designation of Athens in 1985 and now covers two cities each year. The pairings to 2020 are:

2016: Wroclaw (Poland) and San Sebastian (Spain)
2017: Aarhus (Denmark) and Paphos (Cyprus)
2018: Valletta (Malta) and Leeuwarden (Netherlands)
2019: Plovdiv (Bulgaria) and Matera (Italy).

The EU also sponsors years dedicated to specific issues. The European Year of Intercultural Dialogue was in 2008, while 2009 was the European Year of Creativity and Innovation. Proposals have been made to designate 2018 as the European Year of Cultural Heritage and Tourism.

Sport

The EU has become increasingly involved in sport. The 1995 Bosman ruling on football transfers is the most widely known ruling by the European Court of Justice. It outlawed transfer fees for out-of-contract players, thus aligning football rules with standard EU employment contracts. UEFA and FIFA, respectively the European and world football authorities, were slow to accept the ruling, but finally complied. In March 2001, FIFA'S package covering transfers, training and compensation for breached contracts was approved by the European Commission. The Bosman ruling also ended the quotas of national players in club teams, heralding a spectacular growth in foreign-player transfers throughout Europe. Other EU actions in sport include:

•   Participation in the launch of the World Anti-Doping Agency (WADA), the body set up by the International Olympic Committee to drive out drug cheats. As well as being instrumental in providing funding, the commission took observer status in the agency.
•   Making 2004 the European Year of Education through Sport.
•   Working with UEFA to ensure that the broadcasting rights for the European Champions League are sold on a fair basis and do not constitute a market-sharing carve-up among rights-holders.

Note

1   The name Thaler (pronounced 'ta-ller') lives on in today's dollar.

35 Citizens' rights and symbolism

Jacques Delors, the best-ever president of the European Commission said 'You can't fall in love with the single market'. The remark could stand for the whole EU – especially today. Remote, yet meddlesome, and run top-down by bureaucrats and officials, are frequent criticisms. But the EU is closer to its citizens than they think. In 19 of the 28 members, it gave them the euro in their pocket. In 22 of them, citizens have a frontier-free area stretching from the Atlantic to the borders of Russia and from Lapland to the Canaries and Madeira. As a result, millions of Europeans on holiday or business cross from one EU country to another without showing passports or changing money.

Do it by committee

In its own formalistic way, the EU has done its bit to help citizens identify more with the EU and reinforce a sentiment of belonging and ownership. The EC heads of government, at the Fontainebleau summit in June 1984, appointed a committee for this purpose. Known as the committee for a people's Europe, it was chaired by an Italian, Pietro Adonnino, and produced two reports with a series of ideas for special rights for citizens, culture, information, youth, education, exchanges and sport, voluntary work to assist developing countries, health, social security, drugs and twinning schemes. Among the proposals were:

• *The right to participate in European elections under equal conditions.* Electoral procedures should be made uniform, as set out in Article 138 of the Rome treaty.
• *Permanent residents in another member state.* Numbering about 14 million, they should have the right, after a period of time, to vote and stand in local elections.
• *Border region residents.* Taken in the widest sense, they should have the right to be consulted when the neighbouring country is contemplating

developments with cross-border impact like major public works, reorganisation of transport or measures affecting ecology, safety or health.

- *The right of all Community citizens to enjoy full benefits of EU policies.* In cases where these conflict with national regulations, the citizen can seek redress in the courts.
- *European passport holders.* The holders of EU passports should benefit from the assistance or protection of the embassy or consulate of another member state when visiting a foreign country where their own country is not represented.

During 1986 and 1987 the commission tabled proposals to meet most of the points listed in the two Adonnino reports, and the major part of the programme was implemented by the target date of 1992 for the completion of the internal market.

Areas of particular difficulty

Frontier controls

Fears about drug traffickers, terrorism and illegal immigrants made some member states, particularly the UK, reluctant to ease or abolish controls at internal EU frontiers. This led five countries – France, Germany and the three Benelux states – to sign the first Schengen Agreement in 1985 (see pp. 134–6) to eliminate their own frontier controls before the 1992 deadline and to align their immigration and visa requirements for citizens of non-EU countries. The majority of member states, and even outsiders like Iceland, Norway and Switzerland, subsequently subscribed to the Schengen Agreement, although Ireland and the UK remain outside, and are likely to stay there for the foreseeable future. So will the divided island of Cyprus. The latest newcomers to the EU, Bulgaria, Romania and Croatia, are eager to join. Under the Amsterdam treaty, the Schengen Agreement was incorporated in the European Union and it is now mandatory on all member states except the UK and Ireland, which have secured opt-outs.

Euro-election procedures

The demand for a uniform procedure for elections to the European Parliament has still not been fully met. A big hurdle was overcome, when a British Labour government elected in May 1997 accepted a form of proportional representation (PR) refused by the previous Conservative administration. This means elections to the European Parliament from June 1999 onwards have been held under one form or another of PR in all the member states. As a result, pressure for a unified PR system eased, and it seems unlikely that one will be adopted in the near future.

EU citizenship

Despite progress in implementing the Adonnino proposals on citizenship, the Spanish government wanted a specific treaty commitment whereby all persons holding the nationality of a member state would have citizenship of the European Community. The Maastricht Treaty on European Union, agreed December 1991, duly contained provisions establishing citizenship of the EU. It guaranteed the rights of free movement and residence, the right of EU citizens to vote and stand as candidates in municipal elections and European Parliament elections, in countries of residence other than their home country, and to equal consular protection in third countries where their own countries were not represented.

Ombudsman

Another Adonnino proposal, for a European ombudsman, was also part of the Maastricht treaty. Appointed by the European Parliament, the ombudsman is empowered to receive complaints from any EU citizen or any person residing or having a registered office in a member state concerning maladministration on the part of EU institutions.

Common symbols

One factor which has retarded the development of popular loyalties to the EU, according to some governments, has been the absence of common symbols, which the EU has subsequently sought to rectify.

An EU flag

Since 1986 the EU has had its own flag, which is flown at national and international functions and ceremonies, as well as on other occasions with EU significance. This flag, which contains a circle of 12 five-pointed gold stars on an azure background, had already been used since 1955 by the Council of Europe, and is now common to both.

Anthem

The Council of Europe also shares the European anthem with the EU. The words are Schiller's 'Ode to Joy', set to the last movement of

Beethoven's Ninth Symphony. This is a cut above most national anthems whose words and music are generally banal. May 9th, the date of Robert Schuman's birth in 1886, was also chosen in 1986 as Europe Day. But it is scarcely celebrated beyond the Brussels beltway (*ceinture* in French).

Passport

It took 15 years, from 1974 to 1989, to agree a joint format for a common European passport. In 1981–82, the member states reached agreement on a uniform model. The format is 88mm x 124mm, the colour is burgundy red, and the heading is now 'European Union', followed by the name of the member state. The date set for its introduction was January 1st 1985, but only three countries, Denmark, Ireland and Luxembourg, respected this deadline. Most other member states started issuing the new-style passports (which progressively replaced old national passports on renewal) later on in 1985, but it was only in 1989 that European passports were being issued in all member states.

Driving licence

In 1980 the Council of Ministers adopted a directive for a Community driving licence, which was implemented in two stages. Since 1983 there has been mutual recognition by member states of each others' licences, which since then have been issued on the basis of theoretical examinations, practical tests and medical requirements conforming to common specifications. Since January 1st 1986 driving licences issued by member states conform to a Community model, which meets the requirements of the 1968 Vienna International Road Traffic Convention, so that they are also valid in non-EU countries which subscribe to this convention. A 1991 directive harmonised the categories of driving licences among member states. In 2006, ministers adopted a directive to create a single European driving licence to replace the 110 different models then in existence across the EU. The format, in force since January 2013 but with a long transition period, is a credit-card-style, plastic-coated document. Member states have the option to include a microchip containing information about the card holder.

36 Development assistance

This chapter is devoted essentially to the EU's relationship with former colonial territories of member states, principally in Africa, but also in the Caribbean and Pacific regions for whom the Union has assumed special responsibility. Its relations with other emerging or developing countries in Asia and Latin America are described in Chapter 16.

Part Four of the Rome treaty, (Articles 131–136) obliged the original Six to create an association of the former colonial territories of Belgium, France, Italy and the Netherlands. It said:

> This association shall serve primarily to further the interests and prosperity of the inhabitants of these countries and territories in order to lead them to the economic, social and cultural development to which they aspire.

Collective agreements and conventions

Initially, this provision applied mainly to former French-speaking territories in Africa, nearly all of which became independent in the early 1960s; subsequently, former UK, Spanish and Portuguese territories also became eligible. The first agreement, which dates from 1963, concerned only 18 countries, known collectively as the Associated African States and Madagascar (AASM). Now 79 in number, they have been known since the mid-1970s as the African, Caribbean and Pacific (ACP) states (see Appendix 7). Cuba is a member of the ACP group but does not take part in EU–ACP activities. South Africa, on the other hand, is not an ACP country and has a separate trade, development and cooperation agreement with the EU. It takes part in some regional ACP activities

The AASM agreement, contained in the first and second Yaoundé conventions of 1963 and 1969, set the pattern for the wider EU–ACP conventions that were to follow. Signed in the Cameroon capital of Yaoundé, they were followed by four EU–ACP conventions signed in the Togolese capital of Lomé in 1975, 1979, 1984 and 1989. The Lomé conventions made provisions on the one hand for duty-free access to the EU for almost all the products of the ACP countries, without any reciprocity being required. On the other hand, development aid was made available, both in the form of grants from the European Development Fund (EDF), which was set up for this purpose, and of low-interest loans from the European Investment Bank. About 20 per cent of the total aid programmes of the EU member states is channelled through the Union, and the bulk of it goes to the ACP countries, although India is the largest single recipient in absolute terms.

The EU–ACP conventions broke new ground in four ways. They have:

• given stability to cooperation links by creating a legal framework, based on fixed-term contracts between two groupings, each comprising a large number of independent states;
• established a single contract between regional blocs, excluding economic and ideological discrimination and taking account of the special problems of least-developed, land-locked and island countries;
• created common institutions largely responsible for the implementation of the development programmes: a joint assembly of MEPS and ACP representatives, an ACP–EU Council of Ministers and a Committee of Ambassadors;
• instituted a global approach covering all aspects of cooperation: financial aid, trade concessions, stabilisation of export earnings, agricultural and industrial assistance.

Big changes bring big problems

The fourth Lomé convention was rolled over for a second five-year period from 1995 to 1999 when the system of Lomé conventions was brought to a close. The time for benign paternalism was over. Lomé was replaced by a 20-year agreement signed in Cotonou, the capital of Benin in June 2000. It took effect in April 2003 and comes up for revision every five years from 2005. It changes the Lomé model in several ways. The political changes reset a better balance between the EU and the ACP group as partners by:

• giving ACP countries more responsibility and more say on national development programmes and implementation, and strengthening their ownership of strategies for economic and social development;

- including other national stakeholders in this process: non-state actors, the private sector, trade union, civil society and NGOs;
- introducing mutual obligations which the EU and ACP countries must respect;
- streamlining EDF funding operations and making it more flexible;
- including a human rights clause, which evokes the possibility of temporary suspension of part or all of the agreement for ACP countries which fail to respect its essential and fundamental elements.

But the driver for operational changes to Lomé came in the form of pressure from the WTO. The Lomé system of unilateral trade preferences was seen as discriminatory against other developing countries. So were the special deals the EU offered for ACP exports of sugar and bananas. Time was also being called on the ACP sugar deal by the imminent liberalisation of the European sugar market which would make ACP producers uncompetitive anyway.

You can't fall in love with an EPA

If ACP countries were unhappy with the WTO, they did not much like the remedy put forward by the EU to bring the ACP trading system in line with WTO rules. This forced ACP countries to form regional groupings to promote their economic integration. Each regional group would sign and implement an Economic Partnership Agreement (EPA) with the EU devised so as to be WTO-compliant. Special arrangements would apply to vulnerable ACP countries: those that were least-developed or land-locked or islands.

The timetable for negotiating EPAs was 2002–08. By end-2015 none was fully operational. Some EPAs were being partly applied on a provisional basis; in some regions individual ACP countries struck interim EPAs with the EU in the absence of regional consensus. The EU had divided the ACP group into seven regions, five in Africa plus the Caribbean and Pacific. At end-2015, agreements had been reached, but not yet signed, with three of the five African regions: West Africa, East and Central Africa and the Southern Africa Development Community (which includes non-ACP member South Africa).

A 2015 European Commission presentation said the EPAs:

- are a part of a commitment entered into with the signing of the Cotonou Agreement;
- are 'tailor-made' to suit specific regional circumstances;
- are WTO-compatible, but go beyond conventional free-trade agreements, focusing on ACP development, taking account of their

socio-economic circumstances and including assistance to help ACP countries benefit from them;

- open up EU markets fully and immediately, but allow ACP countries long transition periods to open up partially to imports from the EU while protecting sensitive sectors;
- provide scope for trade cooperation on areas like sanitary norms and other standards;
- create joint institutions to monitor implementation of the agreements and address trade issues in a cooperative way;
- are designed to be drivers of change that will help kick-start reform and contribute to good economic governance. This will help ACP partners attract investment and boost their economic growth.

The European Development Fund

Together the EU and its member states are the world's biggest donor of overseas development funding. In recent years, around 30 per cent of total EU spending on external assistance has been channelled through the European Development Fund. The EDF is the tool for implementing the financial aspects of the Yaoundé, Lomé and Cotonou agreements with the ACP countries. It is an intergovernmental fund financed by member states outside the EU budget, but most of its resources are managed by the European Commission. The eleventh EDF runs from 2014 to 2020. It has a budget for this period of €30.5 billion. The budget of the tenth EDF (2008–13) was €22.7 billion. Cotonou streamlined the fund and introduced a system of rolling programming, making for greater flexibility and giving the ACP countries greater responsibility. As well as managing part of the EDF's resources under the European Investment Facility, the EIB contributes low-interest loans to ACP countries from its own resources.

Other aid instruments

The total Official Development Assistance (ODA) of the 28 member states alone, without EU input, rose to €56.1 billion in 2014 from €54.0 billion a year earlier, remaining at 0.41 per cent of GNI. Additional ODA from the European Investment Bank contributed another €2.1 billion to the collective EU amount, bringing it to €58.2 billion. The 2014 figures were based on a new methodology for calculating GNI. Under the old system the EU's GNI level in 2014 would have been 0.44 per cent. In 2014, 16 member states increased their ODA while the amount fell for the other 12. Also in 2014, the UK joined for the first time the

Table 36.1 External financial instruments, 2014–20

Instrument	Funds available
Instrument for Pre-accession Assistance	€11.70 billion
European Neighbourhood Instrument	€15.43 billion
Development Cooperation Instrument	€19.66 billion
Partnership Instrument	€955 million
Instrument contributing to Stability and Peace	€2.34 billion
European Instrument for Democracy & Human Rights	€1.33 billion
Instrument for Nuclear Safety Cooperation	€225 million
Instrument for Greenland	€217 million
European Development Fund	€30.5 billion

Source: European Commission.

group of EU countries whose ODA exceeds the UN target of 0.7 per cent of GNI. The others are Denmark, Luxembourg and Sweden. The EU had set itself a target for all 15 'older' members (pre-2004) to achieve 0.7 per cent by 2015.

Only about 51 per cent of ODA from the EU goes to ACP countries. The remainder is destined mainly for countries either negotiating to join the EU or form part of the European Neighbourhood Policy (ENP). Besides the EDF, the EU has eight other so-called external financial instruments (see Table 36.1). Besides candidate countries and near neighbours, they cover assistance operations in Asia and Latin America. Leaving aside the EDF, the combined budget of the other eight for the 2014–20 financing period is €51.86 billion. Some of the instruments are regional; others are horizontal – available for operations in all regions.

The principal instruments covering development cooperation are:

- *The Development Cooperation Instrument (DCI)* The DCI covers geographic cooperation with South and Central America, Asia, Central Asia and South Africa, as well as the thematic programmes benefiting all developing countries: investing in people (social sectors); non-state actors (civil society) and local authorities; environment and sustainable management of natural resources including energy; food security; migration and asylum.
- *The European Instrument for Democracy and Human Rights (EIDHR)* The EIDHR is a global financing instrument which contributes to the development and consolidation of democracy and respect for human rights in third countries.
- *The Instrument for Stability* This contributes to stability in situations of crisis or emerging crisis, thereby preserving, establishing or

re-establishing the conditions for development cooperation; it also helps build capacity to address threats and prepare for pre- and post-crisis situations.

Emergency aid

The EU sends foodstuffs to countries which request assistance in coping with serious food shortages. Emergency aid is also sent to countries devastated by natural or man-made disasters. Such aid, much of it channelled through NGOs, is administered by the European Community Humanitarian Office (ECHO), created in 1991. Its total available funding for 2014–20 is €6.6 billion.

37 Foreign, security and defence policy

Although not a priority for the authors of the Treaty of Rome (unlike foreign trade policy), foreign policy cooperation has been a permanent feature of EU activity since 1969. Progress towards a proper foreign policy has been ragged, but real. It started, informally, at the landmark Hague summit of December 1969.

Davignon Report provided basic framework

At The Hague, EEC leaders launched foreign policy cooperation (long known as 'political cooperation' in Brussels jargon) when they asked top national officials to see how the Six could cooperate in foreign affairs. A committee under Etienne Davignon (then political director of the Belgian foreign ministry and later a prominent member of the European Commission) drew up a report which recommended a system to 'harmonise points of view, concert attitudes and, where possible, lead to common decisions'.

The Davignon Report, variously adapted down the years, provided the framework for political cooperation among EC countries during the 1970s and 1980s. It proposed that foreign ministers should meet at least twice a year to discuss foreign policy matters. In practice, they now meet monthly, and more often at times of crisis. For a number of years, largely at French Gaullist insistence, a sharp distinction was drawn between meetings on political cooperation (convened in the country holding the rotating presidency of the Council of Ministers and therefore outside the EC institutional framework) and those on 'normal' EC business,[1] which were in Brussels or Luxembourg. Nowadays both types of business are transacted at the same meeting.

Under the Single European Act, which formalised political cooperation for the first time, a small secretariat was established in Brussels in 1987 to provide back-up support and ensure greater continuity in political cooperation. This presence grew over the years until the Lisbon treaty created the European External Action Service (EEAS) with aspirations to become a virtual EU foreign ministry. The EEAS is headed by the High Representative for foreign and security policy who presides over meetings of foreign ministers and who is also a vice-president of the European Commission. A number of EU countries, and not just the bigger ones, are vigilant in ensuring the EEAS will not accumulate too much power.

Hard to speak with one voice

The Single European Act committed the member states to 'endeavour jointly to formulate and implement a European foreign policy' (Article 30). It also (Article 2) regularised the position of the European Council which had been meeting informally three times a year since 1973, and twice yearly since 1986. The European Council played a considerable role in pushing political cooperation, and foreign policy issues invariably occupy a prominent, and sometimes predominant, place on the agenda when they meet. This offers the chance for the European members of the Western alliance to coordinate their positions, and speak with a common voice, especially in dialogue with the United States, which dwarfs each of them on a one-to-one basis.

This was more easily said than done, for several reasons. One has been the neutrality of Ireland, Austria, Sweden and Finland who are not NATO members. Another is the reverse situation: the non-EU membership of NATO partners, Norway, Iceland and Turkey. Between them, they prevent the EU from acting as the European wing of NATO. Furthermore, both Denmark and Greece, although they belong to NATO, had strong inhibitions about discussing matters of western security within an EU framework.

The elusive phone number

Seen from the outside, particularly from America, the absence of a single European voice on foreign and security issues, and indeed a lack of transparency on decision-taking structures and procedures, caused frustration. This led the then secretary of state Henry Kissinger to ask famously at a 1974 NATO meeting in Ottawa which issued a *Declaration on Atlantic Relations*: 'Whose number do I call if I need to contact Europe in a hurry?' He had to wait 25 years for his answer, which came in 1999 with the appointment of the first High Representative for foreign and security policy.

Other obstacles to speaking with a single voice came from the three larger EU members – Germany, France and the UK – who have on occasion been reluctant to subordinate their independent national interests to those of the Union. Before German unification in 1990 the West German government, because of its economic links with East Germany and in the context of eventual reunification, often took a slightly softer position towards Russia and eastern Europe than other member states. After unification it continued to be more accommodating to Russia and other post-Soviet republics. By 1992, however, the cost of unification had become so great that German resistance hardened to paying the lion's share of financial aid to eastern Europe. France and the UK both have worldwide interests, which means their foreign policy priorities can, and do, diverge from those of other Europeans.

Maastricht defined the CFSP

But security and defence issues have, inevitably, moved onto the EU agenda. A comprehensive common foreign and security policy (CFSP) was codified in the Maastricht treaty of 1992. It was to be handled on an intergovernmental basis, with member states in charge under the short-lived Maastricht three-pillar structure (see p. 56). The Maastricht treaty committed the 'Union and its member states' to put in place a CFSP. This was to be pursued by establishing systematic cooperation between member states, gradually implementing joint action. They were required to inform and consult each other within the Council of Ministers on matters of foreign and security policy, and the council would adopt common positions where necessary. Member states were to ensure that their national policies conformed to the common positions, and to coordinate their action within international organisations. The European Council was to define general guidelines for joint action and the council would decide, by unanimity, whether an area or issue should be the subject of joint action. The detailed arrangements for the implementation of joint action would be decided by qualified majority. The treaty stated that the CFSP should include all questions relating to the security of the EU, including the eventual framing of a common defence policy, which might in time lead to a common defence.

Left outside the EU framework altogether following the rejection by the French parliament of the European Defence Community (EDC) treaty in 1954, defence cooperation had been consigned to the low-key Western European Union until Maastricht, which made it an integral part of the CFSP. Since becoming operational in 1999, the European Security and Defence Policy (ESDP) ran numerous missions (see also p. 274) in sectors like policing, military training, peace-keeping and the rule of law. Two of the most significant were in the Balkans, where an EU-led peace-keeping force (EUFOR) took over from the previous NATO-led international force (I-FOR) in Bosnia and Herzegovina in 2004. In 2008, after Kosovo declared its independence, the EU sent its biggest-ever external mission to support the establishment and extension of a functioning judicial system. Its mandate runs until 2016. At its height it had 2,800 international and local staff. Its average annual budget is €120 million.

Defining relations with NATO

The Lisbon treaty in 2009 renamed the ESDP as the Common Security and Defence Policy (CSDP), broadening its scope and context. Lisbon recognised that the deployment of military resources of the CSDP is only one of a wide range of available foreign policy instruments. It is precisely through this diversified approach that the EU may be better equipped than, say, NATO to tackle the consecutive stages in a crisis management process (from prevention to stabilisation and reconstruction). It was to clarify EU–NATO relations, particularly following the Anglo-French declaration on European Defence in St-Malo in 1998, that the three 'Ds' were agreed which fixed the contours of CSDP actions. They should not *duplicate* what is done effectively under NATO, there should be no *decoupling* from the US and NATO, and no *discrimination* against non-EU members like Turkey.

Three areas of CFSP progress

The CFSP decisions generally take one of three forms; adopting a common position, imposing sanctions or taking initiatives. They can also be combined so as to reinforce their impact.

Adopting a common EU position

A serious effort was made to get member states to speak with one voice in international fora. The foreign minister of the country holding the presidency now speaks on behalf of all the member states at the annual opening session of the UN in September. During the course of the year the 28 EU ambassadors to the UN are in constant conclave and make a big effort to ensure that all EU countries vote together in the General Assembly. As well as in the UN, it has become the practice for the country holding the presidency to present a common EU position at other international conferences. Agreeing common positions on routine issues is relatively easy. It is harder when the stakes are higher. The split among EU members over support for the US-led war on Iraq in 2003 was a case in point. And then in March 2011, Germany split from its EU partners over Libya when it abstained, along with Russia, China and India, in the UN Security Council vote on a resolution to create a no-fly zone over Libya co-sponsored by France and the UK.

Imposing sanctions

Common action has been taken many times over the years to impose economic, political and personal sanctions as an instrument of foreign policy. These have been imposed by all or most EU members, in concert. Target countries included:

- Southern Rhodesia in 1965 after its unilateral declaration of independence;
- Argentina during the Falklands War in 1982 (Italy and Ireland discontinued the sanctions halfway through the war);
- Israel after the invasion of Lebanon in 1982;
- South Africa in 1986 (the UK initially declined to participate, but did so after the original package of measures had been considerably watered down);
- Iraq, following its invasion of Kuwait in August 1990, in accordance with the resolutions of the UN Security Council;
- Serbia and Montenegro during the fighting in Croatia and Bosnia-Herzegovina in 1991–95;
- Serbia before, during and after the Kosovo conflict, from 1998 onwards;
- Zimbabwe in 2002, following evidence of violence and massive irregularities in the presidential election;
- Belarus in 2006, for political oppression and jailing of opposition leaders. Most sanctions were lifted in October 2015;
- Russia in 2014 first for its annexation of Crimea and subsequently for its actions to destabilise the situation in eastern Ukraine (see also pp. 47–8).

The fragility of agreeing a common position, especially when leading to sanctions, was demonstrated in the case of Russia. Germany had already been criticised by several member states for using its size and economic power to strike a separate gas supply deal with Russia. There were fears it would try to tone down the EU's reaction to events in Ukraine and the Russian annexation of Crimea. But Germany agreed and applied anti-Russian sanctions along with the other member states. France also went along with the sanctions, although this meant blocking the delivery of two warships for the Russian navy under construction in France. It could be argued that EU sanctions might have been tougher, had Germany and France not built close economic ties with Russia in sensitive sectors. But the sanctions package, however modest, sent out the correct signals, while maintaining the EU's fragile unity. In any case, a sanctions package can only represent the lowest common denominator acceptable to all member states so long as the unanimity requirement remains in place.

Taking initiatives

Initiatives on international issues of the day in regions like the Middle East, Afghanistan, Central America, Africa and Asia have had little effect, despite being widely publicised at the time. A persistent weakness of these statements is that they have generally been purely declamatory, with little serious attempt made to follow them through. There have been significant exceptions.

- *Georgia* After mediation by President Nicolas Sarkozy of France, whose country held the rotating EU presidency at the time, to stop fighting in August 2008 between Georgian and Russian forces, the EU sent a mission to monitor compliance with the ceasefire. The fighting broke out after an incursion by Georgian forces in a part of South Ossetia controlled by the Russians, and the Russian riposte.

- *Iran* The EU played a significant part, thanks to the mediating role by its high representative for foreign and security policy, in negotiating an agreement with Iran over modification in its nuclear policy to remove its potential for military applications. Following verification of Iranian compliance, the EU announced on January 16th 2016 that, along with the UN and the US, it was lifting its nuclear-related economic and financial sanctions.

Maastricht did not go far enough

The treaty specifically gave authority to the country holding the rotating presidency of the Council of Ministers to act on the EU's behalf, which it had often done informally in the past. It gave it the responsibility for organising the CFSP, assisted where appropriate by the preceding and successive presidencies (the so-called 'troika') and by the commission. It also required that the European Parliament be kept regularly informed by the presidency, be consulted on broad policy questions and be able to question the council and make recommendations. There was widespread disappointment when the Maastricht treaty provisions did not prove effective, and a number of changes were incorporated in the Amsterdam treaty in June 1997. They included:

- The appointment of a High Representative for Common Foreign and Security Policy, intended to be a major political figure. He or she would act as secretary-general of the Council of Ministers, with a new Policy Planning and Early Warning Unit at their disposal.
- A new 'troika', consisting of the president of the Council of Ministers, the high representative and the president of the commission (or his or her nominee).
- Unanimity would be retained for substantive decisions, but there would be a possibility for 'constructive abstention by member states which do not want to participate in a joint action, but have no wish to prevent a 'willing majority' from acting together'.

Europe gets a rapid reaction force

The appointment in September 1999 of Javier Solana, formerly secretary-general of NATO and foreign minister of Spain, as the EU's first high representative, gave a new impetus to the CFSP. This was followed up at the Helsinki summit the following December with a series of decisions to boost the overall power and influence of the EU in international affairs. The principal of these was for the Union to have its own military force to back up the CFSP. The aim was to assemble within three years a rapid reaction force (RRF) of 60,000 troops, which would be available within 60 days for deployment to a crisis area up to 2,500 miles away, with the ability to stay in place for at least a year. The missions that the force would fulfil were the so-called Petersberg tasks, enumerated at a WEU conference at Petersberg, Germany, in June 1992:

- humanitarian and rescue tasks;
- peacekeeping tasks;
- tasks of combat forces in crisis management, including peace-making.

Such missions are normally carried out by NATO. The largely unspoken justification for having a separate EU force was to cover situations in which NATO (and, more particularly, the United States) did not wish to be directly involved, but was nevertheless sympathetic. A new institutional basis was established for controlling the RRF. The Political and Security

Committee (PSC) was set up at ambassador level, with twice-weekly meetings in Brussels. It replaced the former Political Committee, which met far less frequently and whose members were based in national capitals. The PSC is flanked by a military committee, chaired for a three-year term by a four-star general, initially General Gustav Hägglund from Finland. The 140-strong military staff was headed by General Rainer Schuwirth from Germany.

The objective was to have the RRF operational within three years, but, despite a dispute with Turkey about the conditions under which NATO equipment and planning resources could be loaned to the new force, it was declared 'partially operational' at the Laeken summit one year early, in December 2001.

The member states held two 'capabilities conferences' in 2000 and 2001, at which pledges were made of troops and equipment for the force. There was little difficulty in finding the numbers of troops needed, but there were significant shortfalls on the equipment side, mainly of air-lift and sea-lift capacity, communications equipment and headquarters units, intelligence-gathering satellites and aircraft, and precision-guided weapons. It was clear that, for the foreseeable future, the RRF would be heavily dependent on NATO assistance in any large-scale combat missions.

Further changes

The changes since Amsterdam should help to bring greater coherence to European foreign policy. So long as the unanimity rule is maintained for the CFSP, however, it is always going to be hard for the EU to play as effective a part on the world stage as its economic power, military potential and wealth of democratic experience would warrant. This became embarrassingly clear in the run-up to the US intervention in Iraq in 2003, when the EU failed to reach a common position: the UK, Spain, Italy and Poland led those supporting the US plans, while France and Germany were the most vocal opponents. Amid bitter exchanges within the EU, Donald Rumsfeld, the US defence secretary, chose to characterise France and Germany as 'Old Europe' and the US allies – including most of central and eastern Europe – as 'New Europe'.

Although EU leaders were unable to patch up their differences, they did confirm a 15-page European Security Strategy in December 2003 outlining areas where they felt the EU should be a more effective actor in world affairs and prevent divisions like those over Iraq. Although the document, the so-called 'Solana doctrine', says nothing about the use of force, and references to pre-emption were excised from the final text, it focuses on 'effective multilateralism' and containing proliferation through export controls and other political pressures. Also in December 2003, the EU's main military powers – France, Germany and the UK – agreed a deal on a military planning cell for crisis management operations. It showed that despite high political tensions, there was strong cooperation on foreign and defence policy between London, Paris and Berlin.

From CFSP to the Lisbon treaty

In the ten years between the appointment of Javier Solana as high representative and the application of the Lisbon treaty in December 2009, the EU embarked upon no fewer than 22 overseas operations of a military or civilian nature, many of them in the immediate neighbourhood of the EU, but some many thousands of miles away, reflecting greater interest in, and sense of responsibility for, the outer world. Among these interventions were:

- The civilian monitoring mission in the Indonesian province of Aceh in 2006 that oversaw the implementation of the peace agreement negotiated by the former Finnish president, Martti Ahtisaari.
- The military operation in the Democratic Republic of the Congo in support of the UN mission during the election process in 2006.
- The deployment of 3,000 soldiers to Chad and the Central African Republic to protect refugees from the Darfur region of Sudan.
- The dispatch of 300 monitors to Georgia in 2008 to oversee the ceasefire negotiated by Nicolas Sarkozy as president of the EU Council of Ministers.
- The stationing in Kosovo of 1,800 police, judges and customs officers (the Eulex mission) to help build an effective justice system and to protect the Serb minority.
- The deployment of a naval force (EUNAVFOR) off the coast of Somalia to protect international shipping from pirate attacks.
- The dispatch of police missions to Afghanistan and the Palestinian territories, including manning the Rafah crossing point between the Gaza strip and Egypt.

Although it took more than two years from agreement in 2007 to entry into force in December 2009, the Lisbon treaty was worth waiting for as far as CFSP is concerned. It reinforced the position of the high representative, set up the European External Action Service (EEAS) and created the permanent post of president of the European Council. The renamed High Representative of the Union for Foreign Affairs and Security Policy would run the EEAS which became operational in 2012, chair sessions of EU foreign ministers, and be a vice-president of the European Commission.

The first president of the European Council was former Belgian premier Hermann Van Rompuy, who handed over to ex-Polish prime minster Donald Tusk in December 2014. The first high representative in the post-Lisbon context was Catherine Ashton of the UK, formerly the European Commissioner for trade. She was succeeded in November 2014 by Italian foreign minister Federica Mogherini. Both women played significant roles in the successful international nuclear negotiations with Iran.

Note

1 The foreign ministers form the so-called 'general affairs council', which is regarded as the most senior of the various manifestations of the Council of Ministers. As such they often meet to discuss matters unrelated to foreign affairs, sometimes arbitrating on issues which overlap the competences of departmental ministers, sometimes discussing particularly knotty problems, sometimes acting as direct deputies to the heads of government.

Part IV

Special problems

38 Enlargement

The European Union was never going to be a closed shop. Article 237 of the Treaty of Rome stated: 'Any European state may apply to become a member of the Community.' This general invitation was, however, qualified by the preamble to the treaty which referred to the original members' resolve to strengthen peace and liberty and called upon 'the other peoples of Europe who share their ideal to join in their efforts'. This boiled down to the simple formula whereby any country in Europe could join the EU provided it was democratic and had the economic and administrative capacity to handle the rights and obligations of membership. The purpose of entry negotiations was to help the newcomer(s) with the adaptation process and transition to full membership over a set period. Thus from 1973 the six-nation EEC grew nearly five-fold to a 28-member European Union 40 years later.

During this time, four countries applied to join but did not become members. Morocco applied in 1987, with the support of the then French President François Mitterrand. But the bid was rejected immediately for obvious reasons of geography. Three European countries applied for membership but did not join. Switzerland and Iceland submitted bids but let them lapse. Norway applied twice; first with the UK, Denmark and Ireland in 1967, and then with Sweden, Finland and Austria in the early 1990s. Although the negotiations were concluded successfully both times, the outcomes were rejected by Norwegian voters in referendums.

Despite the catch-all wording of Article 237, not all European countries were accepted as possible members. Mikhail Gorbachev was told soon after communism collapsed that Russia was too big to fit into the EU. Smaller east European countries, Ukraine, Georgia, Armenia and Moldova, were also considered as not eligible for membership although the EU has negotiated close trade and cooperation agreements with each of them. Some EU member states would, for instance, like Ukraine, particularly since Russian interference there, to join the EU. Others would not. Turkey, although only 4 per cent of its land-mass lies in Europe, has been reluctantly accepted as a candidate, despite initial hesitation from Germany, France and Austria. But Turkey's negotiations have been erratic and intermittent since they started in 2005. Turkey's application dates from 1987.

Successful applicants

In 1961, and again in 1967, the UK, Denmark, Ireland and Norway applied to join. De Gaulle vetoed the first application by putting an end to the ongoing entry negotiations in January 1963. The UK and the other three reapplied in 1967. This time, the UK application was opposed by de Gaulle but not vetoed. It was put on hold, and dusted down when de Gaulle resigned in 1969. New negotiations began with the four applicants which resulted in treaties of accession being signed in 1972. The three smaller applicant countries submitted the treaties to referendums, which produced majorities in favour in both Denmark and Ireland. France also held a referendum which showed a majority in favour of enlargement, but the Norwegian referendum resulted in a narrow majority against joining the Community (53 to 47 per cent). Denmark, Ireland and the UK became full members on January 1st 1973, with a five-year transition period for adjusting tariffs, and for staggering various other membership provisions, notably on agriculture and budget contributions. The UK did not hold a referendum on its entry to the Community, but following the election in 1974 of a Labour government the entry terms were partially renegotiated, and UK voters subsequently confirmed membership by a majority of more than 2:1 in a referendum on June 5th 1975.

The democracy rule effectively excluded Greece, Portugal and Spain from membership during their time under dictatorships. Greece, which had already negotiated associate status with the EC several years before the military coup which overthrew its democratic regime in 1967, lost no time in applying for full membership after democratic government was restored in 1974. Its application was tabled in 1975, and Greece became the Community's tenth member on January 1st 1981. Given the reputedly weak Greek administrative capacity, the European Commission proposed a trial period prior to full EC membership. But it was overruled by the Council of Ministers, under pressure from the US, keen, it was said, to reinsert Greece into western democratic structures as quickly as possible.

Portugal and Spain also applied for membership within a year or two of the Portuguese 'carnation' revolution of 1974, and the death of General Franco in 1975. Their membership negotiations were a great deal longer and more complicated than those of Greece, partly because of initial French reluctance in the face of Spain's competitive agriculture sector. European political foundations, led by the Social-Democratic Friedrich-Ebert Foundation of West Germany, were enlisted to fund, groom and advise traditional parties from the centre-right to the centre-left so as to limit communist participation in the 'new' Iberian democracies. Negotiations were completed in May 1985 and Spain and Portugal joined the EC on January 1st 1986. In this case the transitional period was for seven years, ending on January 1st 1993, but for a number of sensitive agricultural products it lasted for ten years up to January 1st 1996. Freedom of movement for workers did not come fully into effect for seven years.

Two events gave a strong impetus to expanding EU membership, which had looked as though it would stabilise after the accession of Spain and Portugal in 1986: the 1992 programme to complete the single European market and the collapse of Soviet communism.

Negotiations with EFTA countries

The impending launch of the single market programme in January 1993 (see Chapter 16) caused big problems for the seven EFTA countries. They had all negotiated industrial free trade agreements with the EC in the 1970s, but they needed to make sure they would also benefit from the enhancements provided by the single market. Between 1990 and 1992 they therefore negotiated an agreement to set up the European Economic Area (EEA) in which EFTA countries would become de facto part of the EU's single market. The EEA was to start on January 1st 1993. But the EFTA countries realised that the EEA was an unsatisfactory halfway house. It gave them access to the single market, but in return they had to contribute to the EU budget. Furthermore they had no say in EU decision-taking on the single market – or anything else. Five of the seven drew the obvious conclusion and applied for full EU membership: Sweden and Austria already in 1991; Finland, Switzerland and Norway in 1992. Iceland and Liechtenstein did not. Swiss voters rejected the EEA in a referendum in December 1992, leading Switzerland to put its EU application on ice – where it remains. Without the EEA, Switzerland's relations with the EU are contained in a complex maze of bilateral agreements between it and the EU. Making the necessary adjustments to disentangle Switzerland delayed the EEA by one year.

Membership negotiations with Austria, Finland, Sweden and Norway took a year, ending successfully in March 1994. Referendums duly followed: Austria in June, Finland in September and Sweden and Norway in November 1994. The first three produced majorities in favour, but Norwegian voters for the second time rejected EU membership (by 52.5

to 47.5 per cent), so the number of member states rose from 12 to 15 in January 1995.

Few problems arose during the negotiating process, given the degree of coordination inherent in the EEA process. The main adjustments required of the EFTA countries concerned agriculture, the environment, regional policy, transport (in particular the Alpine transit of goods across Austria) and alcohol monopolies (in the three Nordic countries). Expected difficulties stemming from the traditional neutrality policies of Austria, Finland and Sweden largely disappeared with the end of the Cold War. In the event, each of these countries declared that, from the time of its accession, it would 'be ready and able to participate fully and actively in the Common Foreign and Security Policy as defined in the Treaty on European Union' (the Maastricht treaty). To complete the EFTA story, Iceland, previously reluctant to join because of the need to protect its fishing interests, submitted an EU application in July 2009 after it was overwhelmed by the global financial tsunami. Entry negotiations began in 2010 but Iceland withdrew its bid in March 2015 as financial recovery took root.

Central and eastern Europe

No sooner had the countries of central and eastern Europe broken free from the Soviet yoke in 1989–91 than they began to see their future as members of the European Union. Some EU voices were raised against this, but in December 1991 association agreements were concluded with Czechoslovakia, Hungary and Poland which specifically foresaw eventual membership. Similar agreements were later negotiated with Albania, Bulgaria, Romania, Slovenia and the Baltic states of Estonia, Latvia and Lithuania. The agreement with Czechoslovakia was later replaced by separate agreements with the Czech Republic and Slovakia after they split. Slovenia also negotiated a similar agreement.

At the Copenhagen summit in June 1993 it was specifically affirmed that any central or east European country that so wished could become a member of the EU 'once it was able to fulfil the obligations associated with membership and meet the economic and political requirements'.

The first countries to apply were Hungary and Poland in March 1994, and over the next two years they were followed by Bulgaria, the Czech Republic, Estonia, Latvia, Lithuania, Romania, Slovakia and Slovenia.

The commission produced a policy paper in May 1995, setting out the preliminary steps the applicant countries should take to prepare for membership. This bulky document, with hundreds of recommendations under 23 different policy headings, was intended as a checklist for the adaptation and adjustment process. At the same time, a great deal of technical assistance was provided to each country under the EU's Phare programme, to help minimise the pain that the process would inevitably entail. It was subsequently decided at the Florence summit in June 1996 that membership negotiations with the central and east European applicants could start, at the same time as those with Cyprus, which had applied to join the EU in 1990. But, in an Opinion assessing the level of preparedness of each candidate, the European Commission split them into a fast-track group of six consisting of Cyprus, the Czech Republic, Estonia, Poland, Hungary and Slovenia, and a second-tier group of Bulgaria, Latvia, Lithuania, Malta, Romania and Slovakia. Malta applied for membership at the same time as Cyprus in 1990, but let its bid lapse under a Labour government in 1996–98 when it was reactivated upon a change of government.

Negotiations with the fast-tracked candidates began in 1998 with each of them individually, and in 2000 with the second group of six. However, talks were complex and hard, and by the end of 2001 four of the second-tier candidates (Latvia, Lithuania, Malta and Slovakia) had caught up with the early starters. Negotiations were over in late 2002. All the new member states, except Cyprus, held referendums during 2003 to ratify the membership terms. All ten joined the EU in May 2004 – in time to take part in elections for the European Parliament the following month. The last stumbling block for the negotiations was a deal whereby the new members in central and eastern Europe would receive initially only 25 per cent of the farm subsidies paid to 'older' EU members, but rising to 100 per cent in 2013. They did not like it, but they lumped it. Bulgaria and Romania, clearly behindhand in terms of readiness, entered the EU in January 2007.

Ready for 2004

Only in the case of Cyprus did things go wrong. It had been hoped that the imminent prospect of accession to the EU would stimulate efforts to agree on the reunification of the divided island, on the basis of a compromise plan put forward by Kofi Annan, the UN secretary-general. This plan was put to voters in Cyprus in two separate referendums held on April 24th 2004. The Turkish Cypriots accepted the plan by a two-to-one majority, but the Greek Cypriots, largely influenced by a negative campaign led by the recently elected left-wing president, Tassos Papadopoulos, rejected it by a margin of three to one. So one week later only the Greek-controlled part of the island was able to join the Union. In retrospect, it is clear that the EU made an error of judgment in agreeing in advance to the entry of the Republic of Cyprus in the absence of an agreement on reunification. Its bargaining power with the Greek Cypriots has been reduced virtually to zero now that the current government of Cyprus is part of the EU. In fact, France had insisted prior to the start of the reunification talks that only a reunited Cyprus could join the EU. But Greece threatened to veto the entry of the central and eastern European countries if Cyprus was excluded. Its bluff was never called.

Two days after the referendums, EU foreign ministers acknowledged the change of heart by Turkish Cypriots. In response they sought to open the EU market to goods from northern Cyprus and offer some financial assistance. Papadopoulos responded by threatening to veto these proposals when presented to the Council of Ministers for approval. They were never implemented.

Unsuccessful applicants

Turkey, which signed an association agreement with the EEC in 1963, officially applied for membership in April 1987. The Turkish application was officially referred to the commission, for an opinion on its acceptability, as provided by the Rome treaty and as had occurred with all previous applications. In the past the commission verdict had always been favourable and membership negotiations had subsequently been opened. In this case, however, the commission reported that Turkey was not yet ready for membership, both because its economy was insufficiently developed and because its democracy had not been fully established. It was politely suggested to Turkey that its application should be shelved indefinitely. Faced with this rebuff, the Turkish government announced in November 1992 that it wished to proceed to a full customs union with the EU, as had been foreshadowed in the original association agreement. The target date that the Turks set themselves was 1995.

Despite much scepticism, and some reluctance by the European Parliament to give its approval, the customs union came into effect on December 31st 1995. It would be a severe test for Turkish industry, which would have to face the full effect of competition from manufacturers within the EU. Yet the Turkish government welcomed this challenge as it believed that it would give an essential spur to the efficiency of Turkish enterprises. Turkey had attracted a considerable amount of west European investment in recent years, and – since the end of the Cold War – had been seen as an important trading link with the countries of the former Soviet Union and its satellites in the Balkans, the Caucasus and central Asia. At that time, the Turks were convinced that their economic and ultimately political alignment was with Europe. For its part, the EU was not inclined to contemplate full membership for Turkey unless and until three conditions were met:

1   a sustained improvement in Turkey's human rights record;
2   a solution to the Cyprus dispute, involving the withdrawal of Turkish troops from the northern part of the island;
3   the consolidation of Turkish democracy.

Turkey tries again

At the 1999 Helsinki summit, it was finally signalled to Turkey that it, too, was a candidate for eventual membership, while spelling out the conditions it would have to meet before negotiations could begin. The Turkish government announced early in 2002 that it was embarking on an ambitious programme of political and economic reforms to meet the EU's prerequisites for membership and aimed to begin negotiations during 2003. This proved too optimistic, but the sweeping victory in the general election of November 2002 of the Islamic Justice and Development Party (AKP) brought Recep Tayyan Erdogan to power. His government pursued the reform programme with greatly increased vigour, and at the December 2004 summit EU leaders agreed that negotiations would begin in October 2005. This target was reached, but the serious bargaining began only in June 2006, when an agenda setting out 35 chapters for the negotiation was formally agreed. The first of these, on science and research, was opened and quickly concluded, but in December 2006 the negotiation came to a juddering halt as Turkey had not fulfilled its obligation to open its ports to ships from the Republic of Cyprus. The Turks said this was because the EU had not kept its promise to open up trade with Northern Cyprus. Since then the negotiations have been virtually frozen. The increasingly authoritarian Erdogan went on to win elections in 2007, 2011 and 2015 (twice). The EU engaged with Erdogan in 2015 over problems linked to the massive inflows of Syrian refugees to Europe via Turkey.

The waiting room in south-east Europe

It was agreed, in principle, at the Thessalonica summit in June 2003 that Albania, Bosnia-Herzegovina, Croatia, Macedonia and Serbia-Montenegro would be eligible for membership if they fulfilled the necessary conditions. Croatia submitted a bid in 2003 and Macedonia (known as the Former Yugoslav Republic of Macedonia or FYROM) a year later. Negotiations began with Croatia in October 2005 but were held up by a territorial dispute with Slovenia which lasted until 2009. Negotiations with Croatia were completed in 2011, and it became the EU's twenty-eighth member on July 1st 2013. So far, negotiations have not begun with Macedonia, pending settlement of a dispute with Greece over the country's name, which the Greek government insisted implied a claim on its own northern province of Macedonia (see Table 38.1).

Montenegro, which voted in 2006 to end its union with Serbia, applied for membership in December 2008, followed by Albania in April 2009 and Serbia itself in December 2009. Negotiations with Montenegro began in June 2012 and with Serbia in January 2014. Bosnia–Herzegovina applied in February 2016. Kosovo (which has been recognised as a potential candidate) may not be ready to apply for some time. Kosovo's case may be complicated because its declaration of independence is not recognised by five member states: Spain, Slovakia, Greece, Romania and Cyprus.

Table 38.1 Candidates and negotiation status (February 2016)

Country	Application date	Negotiation start date
Montenegro	2008	2012
Serbia	2009	2014
Macedonia	2004	–
Albania	2009	–
Bosnia-Herzegovina	2016	–
Turkey	1987	2005

Source: European Commission.

39 The UK: In or out?

A troublemaker inside remains a troublemaker outside

There are those in Brussels and elsewhere in Europe who say it will make little difference whether the UK stays in the European Union or leaves. In or out, Britain will remain the local neighbourhood troublemaker. As a premise this is pretty sound. It also serves as a warning to the British political class, that the outcome of David Cameron's 2015–16 negotiations for change may be seen as so modest that anti-EU hostility in the UK media, public opinion and right-wing political groups, could flare up again in a matter of months or rather weeks of the referendum.

The deal negotiated between Cameron and his EU partners in February 2016 is good as far as it goes. It shows understanding and readiness to compromise on both sides. The trouble is it does not go nearly far enough to satisfy a large number of British voters. In fact no conceivable deal would. What has been negotiated concerns only a tiny fragment of a much bigger canvas. Many at the referendum will not be voting on the merits of Cameron's settlement, but on the black-and-white choice of staying in or leaving the EU altogether. This is a question on a vastly different scale. In most referendums the question being asked becomes secondary. Referendums are blunt instruments, which often veer out of control. They are best left, according to Clement Attlee, Britain's first post-war prime minister, to despots and dictators.

Better on the inside

If making trouble means a robust determination to defend, or advance, the UK's national goals and policies, self-interest and common sense show that this is best done from inside the EU. Paradoxically, the thicket of EU legislation, in the form of thousands of directives, regulations and decisions, are the UK's best weapons. As a member, these laws, institutions and systems are at the UK's disposal when pursuing its interests and protecting itself in dealings with EU partners. Discard them, and you cut ground from under your feet. If it leaves the EU, Britain will still have to deal with its European neighbours on a quasi-permanent basis, but weakened by its withdrawal from EU structures. The UK would no longer be an equal among equals. Goodbye level playing field.

Playing as an EU-insider with EU structures and systems at your back, also provides leverage – acres of it. They are the tools of trade-offs and bargains. Agreements in the EU, like elsewhere, are reached on the basis of give-and-take among partners or, on occasion, of threat and blackmail. Chapter 38 showed how a small country like Greece, or even a midget like Cyprus, can use their membership of the EU and the EU legislative context to threaten, blackmail or bluff their way to safeguard vital national interests. How much more powerful and effective would these tactics be when applied by the EU's third biggest country and second largest economy? As a full EU member the UK is able to veto any legislation that is deemed against its national interests in a number of sensitive areas. Outside the EU, the veto over unacceptable Union policies, which could affect the UK, even as an outsider, and all its leverage potential as a member state, would disappear. In any subsequent post-exit negotiations with the EU, the UK would be largely dependent on the good-will of its former partners.

Giving up vital links

Were the UK to leave, it would have to renegotiate its links with a number of EU law enforcement agencies, like Europol, the Schengen Information System and the border control agency, Frontex. In today's uncertain world the case for making any unnecessary administrative adjustments is a weak one. The same goes for the UK's cooperation with its EU partners on terrorism, migration and the massive refugee influx. On foreign policy too, the UK would have to review and revise relations with the EU's European External Action Service. In addition, the UK would have to leave or adopt a new relationship with the EU military committee and the EU's Rapid Reaction Force. There will also be implications for the Union's Common Security and Defence Policy where the UK, along with France, plays a lead role.

Brexit also makes less sense given that the UK's partners have made a considerable effort to meet Cameron's demands for change. This attitude on their part not only demonstrates their solidarity with Cameron to keep Britain in the EU, it also shows great forbearance in the light of the opt-outs (or opt-ins) on fundamental policies, and other examples of special treatment for the UK that have frayed the limits of its EU membership to near breaking point. The terms of the settlement also show the readiness of the UK's partners to overlook the negative role of British media, largely ignorant about the EU, but happy to dole out errors, half-truths and outright lies about Brussels and the rest of the EU.

Terms of the British deal

Although specifically tailored for Britain, the terms of the settlement negotiated with Cameron would be available for any other member state who wished to apply them. The draft settlement will only come into force if the UK votes to stay in the EU. If the UK leaves, the agreement will be withdrawn, and therefore will not be available to others. The agreement does not involve treaty changes; the procedures involved for negotiation and ratification in the latter case would last years rather than months. The deal comes in four parts.

Free movement for EU citizens

The UK will be able to limit in-work benefits for EU workers. This could last for up to four years after they start working in the UK, but would only be allowed on an 'emergency' basis. The UK would have to make a request to the EU which would require approval by the Council of Ministers. The deal would allow the UK to place more restrictions on non-EU family members of EU citizens who apply to come to the UK, and to limit the payment of child benefit to EU workers who have children in another member state. There would have to be three new EU laws, proposed after the referendum, to make all this happen.

Sovereignty

A red card for national parliaments. This would require EU institutions to stop adoption proceedings for a new EU law if a majority of national parliaments (representing at least 55 per cent of registered EU voters) objected to it, on the grounds that the issue should be handled at national, not EU level, under the 'subsidiarity principle'. The proposal also addresses Cameron's demand to exempt Britain from the idea of 'ever-closer union' in the EU. It does so indirectly, spelling out different ways in which the UK can opt out of EU laws or avoid involvement in further political integration. Despite the indirect formulation, this let-out on ever-closer union would have more than just a symbolic effect.

Competitiveness of the EU

This section contains several general statements, and little of substance. But Cameron could simplify the application of EU legislation in the UK by reducing the amount of administrative red tape in the form of national regulations required to bring it into force.

Relations with the eurozone

This provision allows the UK to delay draft laws being proposed for euro-zone countries if it thinks they would affect British banking interests. But the UK would not have a veto. Urgent eurozone legislation would not be delayed in this way.

The reluctant member

Britain is the only member state that has not been able to come to terms with its EU membership. For other countries this issue was settled on joining. Of course, criticism and hostility exist in other countries, but they have been spasmodic, not systemic as with the UK.

Britain never wanted to be part of European integration. In the post-war period, UK political leaders from the Conservative and Labour parties saw this as the solution for long-term reconciliation and peace between Germany and the neighbours it had overrun during World War II. As Europe's sole victor in that war, the UK still saw itself as a world power. Its prestige among its neighbours would have given it a lead role in any initiative. But it declined the invitation of the original Six to help create the European Coal and Steel Community in 1951. For the same reason, it stayed away from the Messina conference of 1955, which set the essential foundations for the European Economic Community two years later. Had it sat down with the Six, the UK would have been able to cast certain aspects of the Treaty of Rome in ways much more favour-able to British interests. Instead, in a deliberate attempt to limit the scope and action of the EEC, Britain created in 1959 the European Free Trade Association (EFTA) as a rival. But the UK was too large in relation to its partners for EFTA to succeed.

Down on its uppers by the early 1960s, the UK was in deep economic and financial trouble. The end of empire and decolonisation were difficult and costing it dear. There were insurrections in its colonies and former territories from Malaya to east and west Africa via the Gulf and Cyprus. British industry was hopelessly uncompetitive when up against resurgent German, French and other Europeans. It was about to call on the IMF for emergency financial support. Witnessing the early and rapid success of the EEC, it applied to join in August 1961. It had nowhere else to go. Given the circumstances, the UK was a sullen, reluctant partner from the outset with little enthusiasm for a project it had not helped to create, and did not particularly like. The fact that de Gaulle vetoed the first attempt after 18 months in January 1963 made the mood worse. Hoping for a change of heart in France, the UK applied again in May 1967. But this only came in 1969 when de Gaulle resigned. In the meantime, the UK had devalued sterling by 14.3 per cent in November 1967, a much more traumatic experience than it is today.

A passenger not a driver

Thus, the UK joined the EU in 1973 on terms and conditions which were much harsher than if it had started the process in Messina as a founder member and had not come late to the party. This was particularly the case concerning the excessive British contribution to the EU budget. The reason was that the common agricultural policy (see Chapter 21) is a one-size-fits-all system which penalises automatically a country like the UK with a small domestic farm base and a heavy reliance on imported foodstuffs.

The Conservative Party of Edward Heath who, as prime minister, brought Britain into the EU felt more comfortable than Labour with the EEC's liberal economic policies. Although it was a Labour prime minister, Harold Wilson, who reapplied to join the EEC in 1967, the party was split on Europe. Wilson, who replaced Heath in 1974, partially renegotiated the UK's terms of entry, including the budget imbalance. The modest result was validated in the 1975 referendum (see p. 14). Yet the party went on to advocate unilateral withdrawal from the EU in its 1983 election manifesto. But this position changed at the TUC conference in 1988 when Jacques Delors reconciled left-wing trade unionists with the single market and the parallel social benefits that went with it. Since then the Labour Party has overall been mildly pro-Europe.

Reluctance turns to resentment

With the exception of the short initial period under Heath, no British government from the left or right has tried genuinely to claim Britain's rightful place at the heart of the EU alongside Germany and France. Margaret Thatcher's European obsession from the day she took office in May 1979 was to staunch the rising outflow of UK taxpayers' money to the EU budget. It had become clear by this time, that the reduction mechanism negotiated by Wilson in 1975 was totally inadequate. Thatcher attended her first European Council in Dublin in November 1979 where she demanded her money back (see p. 18). All other EC activity virtually stopped for more than four years until the Fontainebleau settlement, guaranteeing a permanent rebate on the UK contribution, was brokered by François Mitterrand in 1984. The focus over a long period on a single, and controversial, issue meant that relations between the UK and Europe soured. Reluctance had veered to resentment.

North Sea oil pays off the mortgage

Moreover by the mid-1980s, the world, Europe and the UK had moved on. By 1984, now-abundant North Sea oil and gas released the UK from EC economic bondage. It no longer needed the EC and its hand-outs. Thatcher created a close personal relationship with Ronald Reagan, then US president, rekindling thoughts of a new Atlantic special relationship. This relationship continued with Reagan's successor, George H.W. Bush. In August 1990 in the run-up to the first Gulf war she even warned him: 'George, this is no time to go wobbly'. Together Thatcher and Reagan liberalised their economies and cut taxes. Thatcher launched the privatisation of state-owned utilities, which were sold off at below-market prices to ensure the success of the operation to the great joy of middle-class investors and the annoyance of other taxpayers too poor to profit from Thatcher's largesse. Financial services were freed up on both sides of the Atlantic. The Thatcher 'big bang' of liberalisation in 1986 propelled London into the role of world capital for financial services. Greed was good; tax was bad; and profits would trickle down anyway. Who needed the common market? For the UK, Brussels had become at best an irrelevance, at worst a nuisance.

But things did not stop there. By 1990 Thatcher began opposing or taking a minimalist position on most EU policy initiatives – even those that would clearly benefit the UK. She seemed to relish being in a minority of one against her EU partners. The issue of national sovereignty exercised her and right-wing elements in her party. For them transfer of sovereignty to the EU was a zero-sum: what you transfer to Brussels is lost for you; whereas the reasoning of her partners was that only by pooling their resources in a number of fields would the member states be able collectively to achieve objectives which would be beyond their individual capacity.

It was her harsh attitude both during and after the Rome meeting of the European Council on EMU in October 1990 which shocked even her own Cabinet colleagues, leading to her replacement by John Major. Despite declared intentions to do the opposite, Major widened the rift between London and Europe by demanding opt-outs on the single currency and on the EU Social Chapter of the Maastricht treaty agreed in December 1991.

John Major chooses appeasement

These opt-outs were double-edged so far as Major was concerned. While not really appeasing the growing number of eurosceptics in his own party, they were profoundly distasteful to the Labour Party and the Liberal Democrats, on whom he was going to have to rely during the long and difficult process of getting the Maastricht ratification bill through both Houses of the UK Parliament. This was completed only in July 1993, after repeated alarms and a real risk that the government, with its slender parliamentary majority, might be swept away in the process. Major and his colleagues emerged shell-shocked from the experience and thereafter seemed to give overriding priority to keeping Tory eurosceptics happy. The party leadership has been playing to the eurosceptic gallery ever since.

This led to a resumption of Thatcherite anti-EU rhetoric by ministers, and the UK once again allied itself with those wishing to obstruct further progress towards European integration. Major tried single-handedly in spring 1994 to get the EU to reduce the size of the minority needed to block EU legislation following the entry of Austria, Finland and Sweden in 1995. He was left high and dry by the rest of the EU, and forced into a humiliating climb-down. Otherwise he would have jeopardised the accession of four countries whose membership had been supported all along by the UK.

Worse came in June 1994 at the Corfu summit. There, Major vetoed Belgian prime minister, Jean-Luc Dehaene, to succeed Jacques Delors as president of the commission on the ground that he was a 'federalist'. Yet only weeks later Major agreed without demur to the choice for the job of Luxembourg prime minister Jacques Santer, who blandly announced that his own views were identical to those of Dehaene. His eurosceptic fellow-Conservatives were not impressed. The UK negativism continued on virtually all EU matters until Labour under Tony Blair beat the Conservatives in the May 1997 general elections.

Labour dashes expectations

The newly elected Labour government said it would make a 'fresh start' in relations with the EU, and that, although it would defend vital UK interests, it would adopt a more positive approach than its predecessors. Its first initiative, within a couple of days of the election, was to announce that it would end the UK opt-out and sign up to the Social Chapter at the earliest opportunity. But there was great disappointment later in 1997 when Gordon Brown, the chancellor of the exchequer, announced that the UK would not be one of the founder members of economic and monetary union. He set five economic tests to be met before the UK would consider joining the single currency:

1   Would joining EMU create better conditions for firms investing long-term in the UK?
2   How would adopting the single currency affect UK financial services?
3   Are business cycles and economic structures compatible enough for the UK and others in Europe to live comfortably with euro interest rates on a permanent basis?
4   If problems emerge, is there sufficient flexibility to deal with them?
5   Will joining EMU help to promote higher growth, stability and a lasting increase in jobs?

A political decision

Few of these tests were susceptible to precise measurement, and there was a large subjective – not to say cosmetic – element to them. The government's decision was, in fact, to be made on political rather than economic grounds. However, since the financial and economic crisis of 2009, any prospect of the UK adopting the euro is so distant that it has fallen off the radar screen. Besides pressure from the more sceptical Brown, Blair's cautious attitude was affected by three important factors. First, opinion polls, which consistently showed majorities of two to one, or even more, against entry, even though 80 per cent of voters expected the UK to adopt the single currency at a later date. Second, the hostility of large parts of the press, particularly *The Sun* and the *Daily Mail*. Third, the opposition of the bulk of the Conservative Party. In sum, a bold Blair could have joined the eurozone in 1997, but did not. The rest is history.

The Blair government also participated actively in the ill-starred negotiations for an EU constitution in 2003–04. His main goal was to ensure that certain red lines guarding against the encroachment of EU powers were not crossed. More surprisingly, he even promised a referendum to validate the result of the constitutional conference. The wisdom of this decision was never tested. The constitutional agreement collapsed after its rejection by voters in France and the Netherlands in referendums in May and June 2005. Needless to say, the treaty was stridently opposed by the Conservative Party and the bulk of the British press who saw a federal super-state in the making.

No referendum for Lisbon

At Germany's initiative, the constitutional treaty which sought to make the EU more transparent and effective and to ease decision-making when membership rose from 15 to 27, was replaced by a watered-down Treaty of Lisbon (see Chapter 3). With the exception of the Irish, who had constitutional problems of their own, the EU heads of government agreed to ratify the treaty by a parliamentary rather than popular vote, and this was the view taken by the new British prime minister, Gordon Brown, and his ministers. The earlier referendum pledge, they maintained, applied only to the Treaty Establishing a Constitution for Europe. Lisbon was a different document, if similar in its effect, with no obligation to put it to a referendum. By this time anti-European feeling within the Conservative Party had built up so much – under the successive leaderships of William Hague, Iain Duncan Smith, Michael Howard and David Cameron – that the once powerful pro-European element within the party had been reduced to derisory dimensions. Virtually the whole party was now converted to a eurosceptic, if not europhobic, view – a sad commentary on a party once led by such convinced Europeans as Winston Churchill, Harold Macmillan and Edward Heath.

Outmanoeuvred by UKIP

The Conservative shift to the eurosceptic right was partly a response to the growing success of the UK Independence Party (UKIP). This started in 1991 as a single-issue anti-EU movement, adding action against swelling migration into the UK as the second string to its bow. Many of its early adherents were former conservative supporters. The UK Independence Party deftly used the European Parliament and its party-funding opportunities to break into UK politics via Europe. It entered the European Parliament at the 1999 election winning three seats. Three elections later in 2014, it won 22 seats, making it the largest UK party in the EP.

As conservative leader, Cameron took a consistently negative view towards the EU. How much was conviction and how much fear of being outflanked by UKIP is hard to say. He denounced the Lisbon treaty, and said a future Conservative government would hold a referendum on it, while recommending a 'no' vote. He emphasised his anti-EU position by withdrawing the British Conservative MEPs from the centre-right European People's Party group in the European Parliament, and linking them instead with a motley collection of extreme right-wingers, infuriating the main centre-right leaders within the EU, such as Nicolas Sarkozy and Angela Merkel. When the Irish voters finally endorsed the treaty, in their second referendum in October 2009, enabling it come into force a few weeks later, Cameron conceded that there would be no referendum in the UK despite the 'cast-iron' guarantee he had given. However, he said he would seek to reopen the question by attempting to 'repatriate' certain unspecified powers that had been transferred to the Union. Thus he sowed the seeds for his subsequent bid to renegotiate certain key aspects of the UK's relations with the EU.

When the Conservatives were returned to power at the head of a coalition with the Liberal Democrats in May 2010, their anti-EU rhetoric was translated into action. The most spectacular, but also the least effective, was the veto by Cameron at a European Council in December 2011 of a Fiscal Stability Treaty (see Chapter 3 for details). The others simply did an intergovernmental deal amongst themselves, which did not concern the UK or the EU, except that EU services were made available to implement its policies.

Referendum confirmed

But in January 2013, Cameron came back to his 2009 commitment to repatriate power from Europe. He told a London audience that if the Conservatives won the 2015 election, he would undertake negotiations with Britain's EU partners to repatriate some powers to London and ask UK voters to decide by referendum whether to stay in the EU or leave, in the light of the results obtained. The referendum would take place before the end of 2017. Cameron duly won the May 2015 elections, this time with an absolute majority and no need for a coalition. Things moved fast. An EU referendum bill was adopted on May 27th 2015. On September 1st a negotiating task-force was set up in Brussels under the authority of commission president Jean-Claude Juncker.

On February 2nd 2016, Donald Tusk, President of the European Council, circulated a draft agreement to Cameron and other EU leaders. In between, Cameron criss-crossed Europe to explain his position to other EU heads of government. With minor modifications, the draft was approved by the European Council on February 19th after a ritual night-long final negotiation. Britain's partners, keen to keep the UK inside the Union, gave him nearly everything he asked for. The following day Cameron set June 23rd as the referendum date.

40 The future

Not a happy birthday

In March 2017 the EU will mark the sixtieth anniversary of the signing of the Treaty of Rome which established the European Economic Community from which it has evolved. Ten years earlier – on the fiftieth anniversary – there was a very great deal to celebrate; the infant organisation had expanded to cover nearly the whole of the European continent, bringing peace, prosperity, democratic values and the rule of law in its wake, and setting an example to the rest of the world on how to resolve disputes by negotiation rather than force. The celebrations did not last for long. The recession of 2008 and its long aftermath put the future of the eurozone in peril. The Russian interventions in Georgia and Ukraine, the plight of Greece, the turmoil in the Middle East and the subsequent migration crisis, the terrorist attacks in Paris and Brussels and the election of authoritarian governments in Poland and Hungary which challenged many of the principles of the Union, all posed problems which the EU, and its member states, were ill-prepared to meet.

If the fiftieth birthday was a celebration of the EU's transformation of its periphery, its next anniversary will be defined by fear of how the periphery is changing Europe. The refugee crisis may be more threatening than the euro crisis because it reaches deep into national politics bringing questions of identity, culture and sovereignty to the fore. All this caused the Hungarian-American financier and philanthropist George Soros, whose charitable foundations had done much to spread support for European values in post-Soviet states both within and without the Union, to declare in an interview with the *New York Review of Books*, in February 2016, that 'the EU is on the verge of collapse'. Perhaps Soros is over-stating the risk, but unless the Union successfully confronts its manifold challenges, it will face a sad and debilitating decline.

After the referendum

In June 2016, British electors vote in a referendum on whether or not the UK should remain in the EU, on the basis of the deal approved at the meeting of the European Council on February 18th–19th 2016. Not everybody would accept that it will be a 'win-win' situation for both Britain and the EU if voters choose to remain, but it will assuredly be a 'lose-lose' one if they decide to quit. Not only Britain would be diminished by the loss of its main economic partners and in many other ways, but the EU too would carry significantly less weight in the world without one of its three most powerful members. It too would have many painful adjustments to make. Some EU enthusiasts might view it as a gain to lose a half-hearted and often obstructive member state, and it is true that closer integration might be possible without the British, but the net effect of Brexit on the EU would be strongly negative. Whether the UK is in or out, a future two-speed Europe seems highly likely.

The eurozone

Fears that the eurozone might implode as a consequence of the economic recession after 2008, and particularly because of the collapse of the Greek economy have – so far – proved unfounded, but few economists are confident that it can survive indefinitely without fundamental reform. New crises will come, from outside the EU or within, and unless eurozone countries find a better response than the deflationary policies which – at German insistence and in parallel to those applied in Britain by chancellor George Osborne – they have followed in recent years, there is little prospect of sustained economic growth. Without such growth it will be difficult indeed to reverse the steady decline in enthusiasm for the Union in virtually all member states as recorded in opinion polls (notably the EU's own Eurobarometer, which has measured public opinion in all member states since 1973).

This decline has been accompanied by the rise of anti-EU parties, both of the right and the left, across much of the European Union. The Front National in France, Podemos in Spain, the Five Star Movement in Italy, Pegida and Alternative für Deutschland in Germany, Geert Wilders' Freedom Party in the Netherlands, Jobbik in Hungary, Syriza in Greece, the Danish People's Party, the Sweden Democrats and the Finns Party (previously the True Finns) have little in common, except for hostility to the EU. In Britain, their counterpart is UKIP, but in addition the Conservative Party, where probably a majority of members and a large phalanx of Tory MPs are eurosceptic or even europhobic, appears vulnerable to a takeover by anti-Europeans. The Liberal Democrats and the Labour Party remain pretty firmly in the pro-EU column, but their influence on events is sharply reduced, the former by their virtual wipe-out in the 2015 general election, the latter by its choice of a leader widely viewed as unelectable.

Leadership crisis

Europe as a whole is suffering from an acute crisis of leadership, and there is a growing conviction that the current generation of national leaders has failed to match the vision and determination of their post-war predecessors: Jean Monnet and Robert Schuman, Konrad Adenauer, Alcide de Gasperi, Altiero Spinelli, Paul-Henri Spaak and several others. Their successors have been far less willing to subjugate often very trivial national interests to the general good of the Union, and more interested in grandstanding than in making difficult decisions. What leadership there has been has most often been the result of the current French and German leaders coming together and convincing or shaming their colleagues to follow their lead. This was particularly notable during the eras of Helmut Schmidt and Valéry Giscard d'Estaing and, to a lesser degree, of Helmut Kohl and François Mitterrand. The Franco-German partnership has continued, but in more recent years has tended to run out of steam, with Angela Merkel being left virtually alone to assume responsibility, both during the economic recession and the acute migration crisis of 2015–16. In fact the paradox of German power is that many other EU member states called for German leadership while the German chancellor was a reluctant hegemon; but as soon as she showed leadership she found many other European capitals refusing to follow, while at home her popularity sharply declined in her own party and country.

The periphery

Many future threats to the EU are likely to come from its periphery. The refugee crisis – which began in 2015 – continues. More than a million people claimed asylum in Germany alone in 2015 and many more will follow in 2016. The flows of people coupled with security fears after the Paris and Brussels terrorist attacks and a lack of solidarity in EU member states are putting pressure on the EU's border-free travel and leading to sharp divisions amongst member states.

Europe's fears of migration and ISIS have become entangled with its steadily deteriorating relationship with Vladimir Putin's Russia following his annexation of Crimea in 2014. The EU member states have so far stuck together to maintain sanctions on Russia but much more economic assistance should be forthcoming to help Ukraine defend itself against unremitting pressure from Russia. In general, the EU countries must strive for absolute unity in confronting Russia, rather than allow themselves to be picked off one by one, as in the past, over bilateral deals with Russia concerning energy supplies and pipeline agreements.

The wider world

In the wider world, too, the EU needs to strengthen its position. Over the next decade China is likely to emerge as the largest economy in the world, and there are signs that it is using its enormous market to rewrite the rules of the global economy and deal with other countries from a position of strength. So far, EU member states have been so keen to burnish their bilateral political relationships with Beijing and attract investment that they have squandered much of the influence they could have had by adopting common positions.

One way of strengthening the EU's hand is to deepen the transatlantic relationship. In July 2013 negotiations began to create a Transatlantic free trade area, known as the Transatlantic Trade and Investment Partnership (TTIP). The twelfth round of these negotiations was completed in Brussels in February 2016, but they are expected to carry on for at least another 4–6 years. Serious objections have been made to some of its provisions by trade unions, charities, NGOs, environmental groups and others. But if their objections can be satisfactorily met, there is no doubt that it will be of immense benefit to citizens on both sides of the Atlantic. It should be a priority objective of the European Union to bring this about.

G3 or G2?

More than half a century ago, Paul-Henri Spaak, a former Belgian prime minister and foreign minister, reportedly said of the original six members of the EEC: 'We are all small countries now – but not all of us realise this'. In the second decade of the twenty-first century this has become a truism, and former 'great powers', such as France and Germany, are increasingly aware of their limited clout in the world, unless they act together under the umbrella of the EU. This is equally true of the UK, which risks becoming even less influential if it continues to be only a 'semi-detached' member of the EU, or votes to leave altogether. The recession of 2008–09, and the subsequent arrival of China as the second largest economy in the world and a fast-growing military power, has underlined the increasing marginality of Europe and has led to talk of a future G2, in which the United States and China will effectively jointly determine the fate of the world. It need not happen. As the former UK foreign secretary, David Miliband, said in a speech in Warsaw in June 2009:[1]

> The question for all Europeans is whether we want to be players or spectators in the new world order. Whether we want to support the US in promoting our shared values – of freedom and liberty, peace and prosperity – or stand aside and let others shape our 21st century for us. If we want to avoid a so-called G2 world, shaped by the US-China relationship, we need to make G3 cooperation – US, China and the EU – work.

This will require the EU member states to work much more closely together than in the past at least in the international sphere – and a disciplined curbing of both national and personal egos. The peoples of Europe should expect nothing less.

Note

1 Quoted in Charles Grant, *Is Europe doomed to fail as a power?*, London, Centre for European Reform, 2009.

Appendices

Appendix 1 Basic statistics of the member states

Table 1A, which has been compiled mostly from information supplied by the EU's Statistical Office (Eurostat), contains comparative data on the 28 member states. The figures refer to 2014, except for per capita GDP which are for 2013.

Table 1A

	Pop. (million)	Total area (km2)	GDP per head PPS (% of EU average)	Real growth rate (%)	Youth unemployment rate (%)	Employment rate (%)	Inflation (%; 2005 = 100)
Austria	8.6	83,858	128	2.0	10.2	74.6	1.5
Belgium	11.2	30,528	119	1.3	22.4	67.2	0.5
Bulgaria	7.2	110,994	45	1.5	23.0	63.5	−1.6
Croatia	4.2	58,594	61	−0.4	46.3	57.2	0.2
Cyprus	0.8	9,251	89	−2.5	33.9	67.2	−0.3
Czech Republic	10.5	78,865	82	2.0	14.5	72.5	0.4
Denmark	5.7	43,098	124	1.3	11.2	77.3	0.3
Estonia	1.9	45,227	73	2.9	14.4	73.3	0.5
Finland	5.5	338,150	113	−0.7	21.1	73.3	1.2
France	66.4	549,087	107	0.2	24.6	69.6	0.6
Germany	81.2	357,031	122	1.6	7.4	77.3	0.8
Greece	10.8	131,857	73	0.7	51.1	52.9	−1.4
Hungary	9.8	93,034	66	3.7	18.9	63.0	0.0
Ireland	4.6	70,295	130	5.2	21.9	65.5	0.3
Italy	60.8	301,323	99	−0.4	42.0	59.7	0.2
Latvia	2.0	64,589	64	2.4	18.2	69.7	0.7
Lithuania	2.9	65,300	73	3.0	18.5	69.9	0.2
Luxembourg	0.6	2,586	257	4.1	23.5	71.1	0.7
Malta	0.4	316	86	4.1	11.1	64.8	0.8
Netherlands	16.9	35,518	131	1.0	11.9	76.5	0.3

(Continued)

Table 1A (Continued)

	Pop. (million)	Total area (km2)	GDP per head PPS (% of EU average)	Real growth rate (%)	Youth unemployment rate (%)	Employment rate (%)	Inflation (%; 2005 = 100)
Poland	38.6	312,685	67	3.3	22.0	64.9	0.1
Portugal	10.4	91,909	79	0.9	33.3	65.4	−0.2
Romania	19.9	238,391	55	2.9	23.6	64.7	1.4
Slovakia	5.4	49,033	82	2.5	19.1	67.2	−0.1
Slovenia	2.1	20,373	75	3.2	26.9	65.0	0.4
Spain	46.4	504,890	94	1.4	51.7	58.6	−0.2
Sweden	9.7	449,974	127	2.3	22.4	79.8	0.2
United Kingdom	64.8	244,101	109	2.9	16.1	74.8	1.5
EU–28	**508.2**	**4,433,353**	**100**	**1.4**	**21.4**	**68.4**	**0.6**

Source: Eurostat.

Appendix 2   Presidents of the High Authority, the Commission and the European Council

Presidents of the High Authority of the European Coal and Steel Community (ECSC)

(merged with the European Commission on July 1st 1967)

1952 Jean Monnet
1955 Rene Mayer
1958 Paul Finet
1959 Piero Malvestiti
1963 Dino Del Bo

Presidents of the Commission of the European Atomic Energy Community (Euratom)

(merged with the European Commission on July 1st 1967)

1958 Louis Armand
1959 Etienne Hirsch
1962 Pierre Chatenet

Presidents of the European Commission

(and since 1967 of the combined European Communities)

1958 Walter Hallstein
1967 Jean Rey
1970 Franco-Maria Malfatti
1972 Sicco Mansholt
1973 Francois-Xavier Ortoli
1977 Roy Jenkins

1981 Gaston Thorn
1985 Jacques Delors
1995 Jacques Santer
1999 Romano Prodi
2004 Jose Manuel Barroso
2014 Jean-Claude Juncker

Presidents of the European Council

2009 Herman Van Rompuy
2014 Donald Tusk

Appendix 3 The European Commission, 2014–19

Jean-Claude Juncker (Luxembourg)	President
Frans Timmermans (Netherlands)	First Vice-President – Better Regulation, Interinstitutional Relations, Rule of Law and Charter of Fundamental Rights
Federica Mogherini (Italy)	Vice-President – High Representative for Foreign Affairs and Security Policy
Kristalina Georgieva (Bulgaria)	Vice-President – Budget & Human Resources
Andrus Ansip (Estonia)	Vice-President – Digital Single Market
Maroš Šefčovič (Slovakia)	Vice-President – Energy Union
Valdis Dombrovskis (Latvia)	Vice-President – Euro & Social Dialogue
Jyrki Katainen (Finland)	Vice-President – Jobs, Growth, Investment and Competitiveness
Günther Oettinger (Germany)	Digital Economy & Society
Johannes Hahn (Austria)	European Neighbourhood Policy & Enlargement Negotiations
Cecilia Malmström (Sweden)	Trade
Neven Mimica (Croatia)	International Cooperation & Development
Miguel Arias Cañete (Spain)	Climate Action & Energy
Karmenu Vella (Malta)	Environment, Maritime Affairs and Fisheries

Vytenis Andriukaitis (Lithuania)	Health & Food Safety
Dimitris Avramopoulos (Greece)	Migration, Home Affairs and Citizenship
Marianne Thyssen (Belgium)	Employment, Social Affairs, Skills and Labour Mobility
Pierre Moscovici (France)	Economic and Financial Affairs, Taxation and Customs
Christos Stylianides (Cyprus)	Humanitarian Aid & Crisis Management
Phil Hogan (Ireland)	Agriculture & Rural Development
Jonathan Hill (UK)	Financial Stability, Financial Services and Capital Markets Union
Violeta Bulc (Slovenia)	Transport
Elżbieta Bieńkowska (Poland)	Internal Market, Industry, Entrepreneurship and SMEs
Vĕra Jourová (Czech Republic)	Justice, Consumers and Gender Equality
Tibor Navracsics (Hungary)	Education, Culture, Youth and Sport
Corina Crețu (Romania)	Regional Policy
Margrethe Vestager (Denmark)	Competition
Carlos Moedas (Portugal)	Research, Science and Innovation

Appendix 4 The Directorates-General and Services of the European Commission

The commission is divided into departments and services. The departments are known as Directorates-General (DGs). Each DG deals with a specific policy area. The commission services deal with more general administrative issues or have a specific mandate, for example fighting fraud or creating statistics. There are 33 DGs and 11 services.

Directorates-General (DGs)	Services
Agriculture and Rural Development	Central Library
Budget	European Anti-Fraud Office
Climate Action	Commission Data Protection Officer
Communication	European Political Strategy Centre
Communications Networks, Content and Technology	Historical archives
	Infrastructures and Logistics – Brussels
Competition	Infrastructures and Logistics – Luxembourg
Economic and Financial Affairs	Internal Audit Service
Education and Culture	Legal Service
Employment, Social Affairs and Inclusion	Office for Administration and Payment of Individual Entitlements
Energy	Publications Office
Environment	
Eurostat	
Financial Stability, Financial Services and Capital Markets Union	

Health and Food Safety
Humanitarian Aid and Civil Protection
Human Resources and Security
Informatics
Internal Market, Industry,
   Entrepreuneurship and SMEs
International Cooperation and
   Development
Interpretation
Joint Research Centre
Justice and Consumers
Maritime Affairs and Fisheries
Migration and Home Affairs
Mobility and Transport
Neighbourhood and Enlargement
   Negotiations
Regional and urban Policy
Research and Innovation
Secretariat-General
Service for Foreign Policy Instruments
Taxation and Customs Union
Trade
Translation

Appendix 5 Addresses of main EU institutions and specialised agencies

Institutions

European Parliament

Secretariat
Centre Europeen, Plateau du Kirchberg
L-2929 Luxembourg
Tel. +352 43001
Website: www.europarl.eu

Council of the European Union

General Secretariat
Rue de la Loi 175
B-1048 Brussels
Belgium
Tel. +322 2856111
Website: www.consilium.europa.eu/en/home/

European Commission

Rue de la Loi 170
B-1049 Brussels
Belgium
Tel. +322 2991111
Website: www.ec.europa.eu/index_en.htm

Court of Justice of the European Union

Boulevard Konrad Adenauer
L-2925 Luxembourg
Tel. +352 43031
Website: www.curia.europa.eu/

European Court of Auditors

12 rue Alcide de Gasperi
L-1615 Luxembourg
Tel. +352 43981
Website: www.eca.eu

European Economic and Social Committee

Rue Belliard 99
B-1040 Brussels
Belgium
Tel. +322 5469011
Website: www.eesc.europa.eu/

Committee of the Regions

Rue Belliard 101
B-1040 Brussels
Belgium
Tel. +322 2822211
Website: www.cor.europa.eu/

European Investment Bank

100 boulevard Konrad Adenauer
L-2950 Luxembourg
Tel.+352 43791
Website: www.eib.org

European Central Bank

Sonnemannstrasse 20
D-60314 Frankfurt am Main
Germany
Tel. +49 69 13440
Website: www.ecb.int

European Ombudsman

1 avenue du Président Robert Schuman
CS 30403
F-67001 Strasbourg Cedex
France
Tel. +33 3 8817 2313
Website: www.ombudsman.europa.eu/en/

European Data Protection Supervisor

Rue Wiertz 60
B-1047 Brussels
Belgium
Tel. +322 2831900
Website: www.edps.europa.eu

Agencies

European Centre for the Development of Vocational Training (Cedefop)

123 Europe
GR-57001 Thessaloniki
Greece
Tel. +30 2310 490111
Website: www.cedefop.europa.eu

European Foundation for the Improvement of Living and Working Conditions (Eurofound)

Wyattwille Road
Loughlinstown
Dublin 18
Ireland
Tel. +353 1 2043100
Website: www.eurofound.europa.eu

European Environment Agency (EEA)

Kongens Nytorv 6
DK-1050 Copenhagen K
Denmark
Tel. +45 33 367100
Website: www.eea.europa.eu

European Training Foundation (ETF)

Villa Gualino
Viale Settimio Severo 65
I-10133 Turin
Italy
Tel. +39 011 6302222
Website: www.etf.europa.eu

European Monitoring Centre for Drugs and Drug Addiction (EMCDDA)

Praça Europa 1
Cais do Sodré
P-1249-289 Lisbon
Portugal
Tel. +351 21121 0200
Website: www.emcdda.europa.eu

European Agency for the Evaluation of Medicinal Products (EMEA)

30 Churchill Place
Canary Wharf
London E14 5EU
UK
Tel. +44 20 3660 6000
Website: www.ema.europa.eu

Office for Harmonisation in the Internal Market (OHIM)

Avenida de Europa 4
E-03008 Alicante
Spain
Tel. +34 96 5139100
Website: oami.europa.eu

European Agency for Safety and Health at Work (EU-OSHA)

12 Santiago de Compostela
E-48003 Bilbao
Spain
Tel. +34 944 358 400
Website: www.osha.europa.eu

Community Plant Variety Office (CPVO)

3 boulevard Maréchal-Foch
F-49101 Angers Cedex 02
France
Tel. +33 2 4125 6400
Website: www.cpvo.europa.eu

Translation Centre for the Bodies of the European Union (CdT)

Bâtiment Drosbach
12E rue Guillaume Kroll
L-1822 Luxembourg
Tel. +352 42 17111
Website: www.cdt.europa.eu

European Union Agency for Fundamental Rights (FRA)

Schwarzenbergplatz 11
A-1040 Vienna
Austria
Tel. +43 1 580300
Website: fra.europa.eu

European Agency for Reconstruction (EAR)

Egnatia 4
GR-54626 Thessaloniki
Greece
Tel. +30 2310 505100
Website: www.ear.europa.eu

European Food Safety Authority (EFSA)

Via Carlo Magno 1A
I-43126 Parma
Italy
Tel.: +39 0521 036 111
Website: www.efsa.europa.eu

The European Union's Judicial Cooperation Unit (Eurojust)

Maanweg 174
NL-2516 AB Den Haag
Netherlands
Tel.: +31 070 4125000
Website: www.eurojust.europa.eu

European Maritime Safety Agency (EMSA)

Praça Europa 4
1249-206 Lisbon
Portugal
Tel. +351 21 1209 200
Website: www.emsa.europa.eu

European Aviation Safety Agency (EASA)

Ottoplatz 1
D-50679 Cologne
Germany
Tel. +49 221 8999 000
Website: www.easa.europa.eu

European Union Agency for Network and Information Security Agency (ENISA)

Science and Technology Park of Crete (ITE)
Vassilika Vouton
700 13 Heraklion
Greece
Tel. +30 2814409710
http://www.enisa.europa.eu

Appendix 6 Party groups in the European Parliament

The elections for the European Parliament are contested in each member state by the main national political parties. Within the parliament, however, the elected members have joined together in trans-national groups, and they sit in these groups rather than in national delegations, inside the chamber. As described in Chapter 8, there are currently 8 of these, as well as some 15 MEPs who have declined to join any group and who sit as non-affiliated independents. The current legislature runs from 2014 to 2019.

In early 2016, the cross-border groups each had the following number of MEPs shown in Table 6A.

Table 6A Cross-border groups

Cross-border groups	Number of MEPs
European People's Party (EPP)	216
Socialists and Democrats (S&D)	190
European Conservatives and Reformists (ECR)	75
Alliance of Liberals and Democrats for Europe (ALDE)	70
European United Left/Nordic Green Left Group (GUE/NGL)	51
Greens/European Free Alliance (Greens/EFA)	50
Europe of Freedom & Democracy (EFD)	45
Europe of Nations and Freedom (ENF)	38
Unattached members (NI)	15
TOTAL	**750**

Source: European Parliament.

Table 6B shows the breakdown of group numbers by member state.

Table 6B Political groups in the European Parliament, January 2016

	EPP	S&D	ECR	ALDE	GUE/ NGL	Greens	EFD	ENF	NI	Total
Austria	5	5	–	1	–	3	–	4	–	18
Belgium	4	4	4	6	–	2	–	1	–	21
Bulgaria	7	4	2	4	–	–	–	–	–	17
Croatia	5	2	1	2	–	1	–	–	–	11
Cyprus	2	2	–	–	2	–	–	–	–	6
Czech Republic	7	4	2	4	2	–	1	–	–	20
Denmark	1	3	4	3	1	1	–	–	–	13
Estonia	1	1	–	3	–	1	–	–	–	6
Finland	3	2	2	4	1	1	–	–	–	13
France	20	13	–	5	4	6	1	20	3	74
Germany	34	27	8	4	8	13	–	–	2	96
Greece	5	4	1	–	6	–	–	–	5	21
Hungary	12	4	–	–	–	2	–	–	3	21
Ireland	4	1	1	1	4	–	–	–	–	11
Italy	15	31	2	–	3	–	17	5	–	73
Latvia	4	1	1	1	–	1	–	–	–	8
Lithuania	2	2	1	4	–	1	1	–	–	11
Luxembourg	3	1	–	1	–	1	–	–	–	6
Malta	3	3	–	–	–	–	–	–	–	6
Netherlands	5	3	2	7	3	2	–	4	–	26
Poland	23	5	19	–	–	–	1	2	1	51
Portugal	7	8	–	2	4	–	–	–	–	21
Romania	12	15	1	3	–	–	–	1	–	32
Slovakia	6	4	3	–	–	–	–	–	–	13
Slovenia	5	1	–	1	–	1	–	–	–	8
Spain	17	14	–	8	11	4	–	–	–	54
Sweden	4	6	–	3	1	4	2	–	–	20
UK	–	20	21	1	1	6	22	1	1	73
Total	216	190	75	70	51	50	45	38	15	750

Source: European Parliament.

Appendix 7 Overseas links with the EU

Table 7A The 79 ACP states

African		Caribbean	Pacific
Angola	Liberia	Antigua & Barbuda	Cook Islands
Benin	Madagascar	Bahamas	Federal States of
Botswana	Malawi	Barbados	Micronesia
Burkina Faso	Mali	Belize	Fiji
Burundi	Mauritania	Cuba*	Kiribati
Cameroon	Mauritius	Dominica	Marshall Islands
Cape Verde	Mozambique	Dominican	Nauru
Central African	Namibia	Republic	Niue
Republic	Niger	Grenada	Palau
Chad	Nigeria	Guyana	Papua New Guinea
Comoros	Rwanda	Haiti	Solomon Islands
Congo (Brazzaville)	São Tomé & Príncipe	Jamaica	Timor Leste
Congo (Kinshasa)	Senegal	St Kitts & Nevis	Tonga
Côte d'Ivoire	Seychelles	St Lucia	Tuvalu
Djibouti	Sierra Leone	St Vincent & The	Vanuatu
Equatorial Guinea	Somalia	Grenadines	Western Samoa
Eritrea	South Africa*	Suriname	
Ethiopia	Sudan	Trinidad & Tobago	
Gabon	Swaziland		
The Gambia	Tanzania		
Ghana	Togo		
Guinea	Uganda		
Guinea Bissau	Zambia		
Kenya	Zimbabwe		
Lesotho			

Note: * Qualified membership.

Overseas Countries and Territories (OCTs)

Denmark
Special relationship
Greenland

France
Territorial collectives
Mayotte
St Pierre & Miquelon
Overseas territories
New Caledonia & dependencies
French Polynesia
French Southern & Antarctic Territories
Wallis & Futuna Islands

Netherlands
Overseas countries
Netherlands Antilles (Bonaire, Curacao, St Martin, Saba, St Eustace)
Aruba

UK
Overseas countries and territories
Anguilla
British Antarctic Territory
British Indian Ocean Territory
British Virgin Islands
Cayman Islands
Falkland Islands
Southern Sandwich Islands & dependencies
Montserrat
Pitcairn Island
St Helena & dependencies
Turks & Caicos Islands

Appendix 8 The Maastricht, Amsterdam, Nice and Lisbon treaties

The *Treaty on European Union* was approved at the Maastricht European Council on December 9th and 10th 1991, and signed in Maastricht on February 7th 1992. After ratification by the 12 national parliaments, it came into force on November 1st 1993. The treaty, which is divided into six parts, and a long list of annexes and protocols, consists principally of amendments to the Rome treaty, in whose text it was incorporated. The main provisions of the Maastricht treaty are as follows:

1   The commitment of the Community to the achievement of economic and monetary union (EMU), including a single currency administered by a single independent central bank. This was to be achieved in three stages. The third stage, to start no later than January 1st 1999, committed those countries which fulfilled four specific criteria – relating to inflation, budget deficits, exchange rates and interest rates – to proceed to the adoption of a common currency. A protocol provided that the UK would not be obliged to enter the third stage of EMU without a separate decision to do so by its government and parliament.

2   The development of common foreign and defence policies, with defence issues initially subcontracted to the Western European Union, whose membership would be opened to all EC member states.

3   The introduction of union citizenship, defining the rights and obligations of nationals of the member states. These include freedom of movement, right of residence, the right to vote and stand as a candidate at municipal and European elections, and shared diplomatic protection outside the union.

4   EC powers in areas such as education and vocational training, trans-European networks, industry, health, culture, development cooperation and consumer protection were confirmed or extended.

5   The establishment of a Cohesion Fund to transfer resources from the richer to the poorer member states.

6   The strengthening of judicial, immigration and police cooperation between member states, largely on an intergovernmental basis.

7   An agreement by 11 member states, excluding the UK, to use EC machinery to implement measures arising from the Social Charter of 1989 concerning the protection of workers' health and safety, working conditions, information and consultation of workers, equal opportunity and treatment, and the integration of persons excluded from the labour market.

8   Institutional changes, including an extension of the legislative powers of the European Parliament, the increase in the commission's term of office from four to five years and the granting to the Court of Justice of the right to impose fines on member states for failing to implement its judgments.

The *Treaty of Amsterdam* was approved at the Amsterdam European Council on June 16th and 17th 1997, where it was signed on October 2nd 1997. It is divided into 6 sections and 19 chapters, with a substantial number of protocols, annexes and declarations. It consists mainly of amendments to the previous treaties, and was incorporated in the text of the Rome treaty when it was ratified by the European Parliament and the 15 member states. It came into effect on May 1st 1999. Its main provisions are as follows:

1   Free movement of persons, asylum, immigration, the crossing of external borders and judicial cooperation in civil matters are brought within the Community framework (i.e. transferred from Pillar Three to Pillar One).

2   The Schengen Agreement, on opening internal borders, is also brought within the Community framework.

3   The Protocol on Social Policy (the Social Chapter) is incorporated into the treaty and will apply to the United Kingdom and to all future entrants.

4   An employment chapter is added to the Treaty.

5   The provisions for a common foreign and security policy are strengthened, the Secretary-General of the Council of Ministers will become the high representative for the CFSP and will form a 'troika' with the presidents of the council and the commission.

6   The European Parliament's powers are extended, giving it the right to co-decision with the Council over the majority of EU legislation.

7   Qualified majority voting in the Council of Ministers is extended to include research, employment, social exclusion, equal opportunities and public health.

8   The role of the president of the commission is upgraded. His or her appointment will need to be approved by the European Parliament and their assent will be needed for the appointment of the other members of the commission.
9   A new 'flexibility' clause is added, enabling groups of member states to use the EU institutions to cooperate more closely (enhanced cooperation) on specific areas not within the exclusive competence of the EU.

The Treaty of Nice was approved at the Nice meeting of the European Council on December 11th 2000 and signed there on February 26th 2001. Its main purpose was to provide for institutional changes within the EU to pave the way for the expected entry of a substantial number of member states during the first decade of the twenty-first century. Parts of the treaty were due to come into effect only in 2005, with the remainder following ratification by the 15 member states and the European Parliament. A referendum in Ireland on June 7th 2001 resulted in a 'no' vote of 53.87 per cent compared with 46.13 per cent 'yes'. A further referendum in Ireland, in October 2002, reversed this verdict by 62.89 per cent to 37.11 per cent, enabling the treaty to come into effect on February 1st 2003. Its main provisions are as follows:

1   A reweighting of votes in the Council of Ministers to strengthen the position of the larger member states when new members, which are mostly small, join the Union.
2   The larger member states will give up their right to a second member of the commission. When EU membership reaches 27 or more, member states will no longer have an automatic right to nominate commissioners, who will be allocated on a rotation system in which all states, large or small, will be treated equally.
3   The number of seats in the European Parliament, both for the existing member states and for the 12 countries negotiating membership, is determined, giving a total maximum number of MEPs of 732. Membership numbers for other EU institutions are also agreed.
4   Qualified majority voting in the Council of Ministers is extended to 30 more Articles of the Treaty of Rome, including notably the appointment of the president of the commission. The European Parliament's powers of co-decision are extended to ten more Articles.
5   Minor changes are made to the powers of the Court of Justice and the European Central Bank.
6   The scope of the 'flexibility' clause of the Amsterdam treaty is extended.
7   There are new provisions for the implementation of the European Security and Defence Policy.

The *Treaty of Lisbon* took effect on December 1st 2009, after being signed in the Portuguese capital in December 2007. It was designed to replace the Treaty establishing a Constitution for Europe (TCE), which had been approved by the European Council in June 2004 and would have come into force on November 1st 2006, had it not been rejected in referendums in France and the Netherlands in May and June 2005. The Lisbon treaty incorporates most provisions of the TCE. It does not do so in a coherent way. It adopts the same approach as the previous amending treaties, (Maastricht, Amsterdam, etc.), modifying and updating individual articles in the earlier treaties and adding new ones. Each treaty is illegible by itself to a lay reader. Only the consolidated treaty text produced by the Council of Ministers (see Chapter 3) provides a read-through 'clean' version, setting out the sum of the successive revisions of the Rome treaty in one document. But the Council of Ministers produces the consolidated texts for information only. They have no legal validity.

The Lisbon treaty formally renamed the Treaty of Rome as the 'Treaty on the Functioning of the European Union' (TFEU). The main changes brought about by Lisbon are in the following areas:

More democracy and openness

- A new citizens initiative means that one million people, out of the EU's population of 500 million, from a given number of member states can petition the European Commission to bring forward new policy proposals.
- The Council of Ministers will now meet in public when considering and voting on draft laws.
- The Treaty increases the number of areas where the European Parliament shares decision-making with the Council of Ministers.
- National parliaments will have greater opportunities to make a direct input into EU decision making. A new early-warning system gives national parliaments the right to comment on draft laws and to check that the EU does not overstep its authority by involving itself in matters best dealt with nationally or locally.
- In the Council of Ministers, qualified majority voting will be extended. Rules for qualified majority voting (QMV) will be simplified in 2014. From then on, the complex weighting of national votes disappears. To be adopted under QMV, decisions taken in the council will need the support of 55 per cent of the member states, representing at least 65 per cent of the European population.
- Further policy areas may in future be decided by majority voting, but important areas such as taxation and defence will continue to require a unanimous vote.

Institutional changes

- A new position of High Representative for Foreign and Security Policy/Vice-President of the Commission will be created in order to promote EU action on the international scene and to be better able to defend its interests and values abroad, speaking with one voice whenever possible. The high representative will also head the EU's new European External Action Service (EEAS).
- The European Council will elect its own president for a maximum period of five years. This will give the EU a public face at the highest level, making the EU's actions more visible and consistent.
- The President of the Commission will henceforth be 'elected' by the European Parliament, on a proposal from the European Council.
- The Lisbon treaty formalises the position of the European Central Bank by making it an institution of the European Union.

Foreign security and defence policy

- Lisbon spells out more clearly the EU's role in the area of common foreign and security policy. Decisions on defence issues will continue to need unanimous approval of the 28 member states.
- It extends the EU's role to include disarmament operations, military advice and assistance, and helping to restore stability after conflicts.
- It also creates the possibility of enhanced cooperation between member states which wish to work together more closely in the area of defence. The Lisbon treaty provides that member states will make available to the EU the civil and military capability necessary to implement the common security and defence policy and sets out the role of the European Defence Agency.
- It introduces a solidarity clause (of a voluntary nature) when a member state is the victim of a terrorist attack or a natural or man-made disaster.

Justice and crime

- The treaty contains provisions strengthening the EU's ability to fight international cross-border crime, illegal immigration, trafficking of people, arms and drugs. The roles of the European Parliament and the Court of Justice are strengthened and decision-making will be speeded up via more qualified majority voting.
- These new provisions respect the different legal systems and traditions of member states.

- Exceptionally, Ireland and the United Kingdom, with their common law system and non-participation in Schengen, will have a special arrangement allowing them to decide on a case-by-case basis whether to participate in legislation in this area (an 'opt-in').

Human rights

- Lisbon recognises the rights, freedoms and principles set out in the Charter of Fundamental Rights and makes the charter legally binding.
- The treaty will also allow the EU to accede to the European Convention on Human Rights. The convention, and the European Court of Human Rights which oversees it, are the foundations of human rights protection in Europe.

Who does what

The Lisbon treaty abandons the short-lived three-pillar power structure invented by the Maastricht treaty, largely because it no longer corresponded to the realities of European decision-taking. The new treaty clarifies in turn the powers belonging to the EU, those belonging to member states, and those powers which are shared. It sets out the limits on the EU's powers more clearly than before. A basic rule is that the EU will only be able to exercise those powers that have been conferred on it by the member states. It must respect the fact that all other powers rest with the member states. Thus:

- The EU has exclusive charge over areas such as competition rules, monetary policy of the euro area and the common commercial policy.
- Member states have primary responsibility in fields such as health, education and industry.
- The EU and the member states share competence in areas such as the internal market, agriculture, transport and energy.

Find out more

Inevitably the Lisbon Treaty is a lengthy document – over 300 pages in the consolidated version, including annexes and protocols. The full consolidated text is available online at http://eur-lex.europa.eu/legal-content/EN/TXT/PDF/?uri=CELEX:12012E/TXT&from=EN [accessed March 17 2016].

Appendix 9 Chronology of major events concerning the European Union

Table 9A

1945	May	End of second world war in Europe.
1947	June	United States launches Marshall Plan to aid European reconstruction.
1948	April	Creation of the Organisation for Economic Cooperation (OEEC) to coordinate Marshall Plan assistance.
1949	April	North Atlantic Treaty signed, creating NATO.
1950	May	French foreign minister, Robert Schuman, proposes the pooling of French and West German coal and steel resources in a community open to other West European nations.
1951	April	Belgium, France, Italy, Luxembourg, the Netherlands and West Germany sign the Treaty of Paris, setting up the European Coal and Steel Community (ECSC).
1952	May	The same six countries sign a treaty to establish a European Defence Community (EDC), with a common European army.
	August	The ECSC established, with its headquarters in Luxembourg.
1954	August	French parliament refuses to ratify the EDC treaty, which is immediately abandoned.
1955	June	Negotiations begin at Messina for the creation of a European Common Market.
1957	March	Two treaties signed in Rome, setting up the European Economic Community and Euratom, by the six members of the ECSC.
1958	January	The EEC and Euratom treaties come into effect. The EEC Commission is established, with its headquarters 'provisionally' in Brussels.
1960	January	The Stockholm Convention established the European Free Trade Association (EFTA), linking the UK, Austria, Denmark, Norway, Portugal, Sweden and Switzerland.
	December	The OEEC is wound up and replaced by the Organisation for Economic Cooperation and Development (OECD).

(*Continued*)

Table 9A (Continued)

1961	May	EFTA established, with its headquarters in Geneva.
	July	The EEC signs an association agreement with Greece.
		Ireland applies for EEC membership.
	August	Denmark and the UK also apply for membership.
	November	Membership negotiations open in Brussels.
1962	April	Norway applies for EEC membership.
1963	January	President de Gaulle vetoes UK membership; the other applicant states suspend their applications. Franco-German Treaty of Cooperation signed.
	July	Yaoundé Convention, providing for economic aid and trade concessions to 17 African states, formerly colonies of EEC countries, is signed in the capital of Cameroon.
	September	The EEC signs an association agreement with Turkey.
1964	July	Common Agricultural Policy (CAP) takes effect.
1965	June	EEC in crisis as France begins seven-month boycott, refusing to be out-voted on issues it considers of great importance.
1966	January	France resumes its active membership, after negotiation of the 'Luxembourg compromise', under which important issues are, in effect, to be decided by unanimity, irrespective of the provisions of the Rome treaty.
1967	May	Denmark, Ireland, Norway and the UK make second application to join the EEC. In view of de Gaulle's continued hostility, the applications are left on the table.
	July	The EEC is merged with the ECSC and Euratom to form a single European Community (EC).
1968	July	All internal tariffs removed within the EC, which establishes a common external tariff (CET).
1969	December	France's President Pompidou agrees with other EC leaders at a 'summit' meeting in The Hague to consider an enlargement of EC membership.
1970	June	Entry negotiations open with the four applicant states.
1972	January	Treaties of Accession signed between the EC and Denmark, Ireland, Norway and the UK.
	July	Free trade agreements signed with the six EFTA states which did not apply to join the EC.
	September	Norway turns down EC membership in a referendum (46% for, 54% against).
1973	January	Denmark, Ireland and the UK become full members of the Community.
	May	Norway signs free trade agreement with the EC.
1974	April	At request of the new UK Labour government, a 'renegotiation' of the membership terms begin.
1975	February	First Lomé Convention, replacing the Yaoundé Convention of 1963, is signed, giving economic aid and trade concessions to 46 African, Caribbean and Pacific (ACP) states.

(*Continued*)

Table 9A (Continued)

	June	Referendum in the UK shows a 2:1 majority in favour of staying in the EC. Greece applies for EC membership.
1977	*March*	Portugal applies for membership.
	July	Spain applies for membership.
1979	*March*	European Monetary System (EMS) established.
	June	First direct elections to the European Parliament.
	December	Row over UK budget contribution to EC at the Dublin summit when Margaret Thatcher demands 'my money back'.
1980	*May*	Provisional solution to UK budget problem, intended to last for three years.
1981	*January*	Greece becomes member of the EC.
1984	*June*	Second direct elections to European Parliament. Fontainebleau summit agrees on reducing the UK budget contribution and on increasing the EC's financial resources.
1985	*January*	Jacques Delors becomes president of European Commission.
	June	At Milan summit agreement is reached on seven year timetable to remove 300 barriers to the internal market, according to a programme devised by a British commissioner, Lord Cockfield. An intergovernmental conference is also appointed to consider amendments to the Rome treaty.
	December	The intergovernmental conference produces the Single European Act, a series of treaty amendments designed to speed up decision-making, especially on internal market measures. It is signed by all member states.
1986	*January*	Spain and Portugal become members of the EC.
1987	*April*	Turkey applies to join the EC.
	July	The Single European Act comes into force.
1988	*February*	Delors I package, which sets the guidelines for expanding EC budgets, but with tighter control over agricultural spending, over the five years 1988–92, agreed.
1989	*June*	Third direct elections to European Parliament. Austria applies to join the EC.
	July	G7 summit asks EC to coordinate western aid to Poland and Hungary. This aid is extended to other east European countries, and negotiations follow to conclude trade and association agreements with the former Soviet 'satellites'.
	November	Breach of the Berlin Wall heralds the collapse of communism in eastern Europe.
	December	Negotiations begin between the EC and EFTA states to form a European Economic Area (EEA).
1990	*July*	Capital movements liberalised throughout the Community. Madrid summit conference approves a plan to introduce economic and monetary union in three stages, with Margaret Thatcher reserving the UK position. Cyprus and Malta apply for EC membership.

(Continued)

Table 9A (Continued)

	October	German unification: former East Germany joins EC, as integral part of West Germany.
	December	Two intergovernmental conferences, on economic and monetary union and on political union respectively, begin work. Rome EC summit approves food aid and technical assistance programmes for the Soviet Union.
1991	July	Sweden applies for EC membership.
	September	Following the failed Soviet coup, EC mission visits the former Soviet Union and the newly independent Baltic states to discuss an enhanced aid programme. EC-sponsored peace conference opens in Yugoslavia.
	November	Agreement reached to set up EEA on January 1st 1993.
	December	Maastricht summit agrees Treaty on European Union. This includes detailed arrangements for single currency to be in force no later than 1999, with an opt-out provision for the UK, and for gradual progression towards a common foreign and security policy.
1992	February	Delors II package proposes increasing EC budget by 30% over five years.
	March	Finland applies for EC membership.
	May	Switzerland applies for EC membership.
	June	Denmark rejects Maastricht treaty in referendum. Jacques Delors is reappointed for two more years, from January 1993, at Lisbon summit. Reform of CAP narrowly agreed by Council of Ministers.
	December	Switzerland turns down EEA in a referendum. Edinburgh summit adopts reduced Delors II budget package, and sets up European Investment Fund.
1993	February	Entry negotiations begin with Austria, Finland and Sweden.
	April	Negotiations begin on accession of Norway.
	May	In second referendum the Danish people vote in favour of the Maastricht treaty.
	July	Adoption of the TACIS programme of technical assistance to the independent states of the former Soviet Union.
	August	After many delays, the UK ratifies the Maastricht treaty.
	October	Germany, the last state to do so, ratifies the Maastricht treaty after a court challenge fails.
	November	Maastricht treaty comes into force: the European Community becomes the European Union.
	December	Brussels summit approves an action plan on growth, competitiveness and employment. Uruguay round of GATT negotiations successfully concluded in Geneva.

(*Continued*)

Table 9A (Continued)

1994	*January*	EEA agreement takes effect, linking the EU and five EFTA members, excluding Switzerland and Liechtenstein.
	March	Accession negotiations successfully completed with Austria, Finland, Norway and Sweden.
	June	Fourth direct elections to the European Parliament. Partnership and Cooperation Agreement signed with Russia at Corfu summit.
	July	Jacques Santer nominated commission president to succeed Jacques Delors.
	November	Norway rejects EU membership in referendum.
1995	*January*	Austria, Finland and Sweden join the EU. New Santer Commission takes office. Pact on Stability in Europe between the EU and the states belonging to the Organisation on Security and Cooperation in Europe (OSCE) signed in Paris.
	April	Liechtenstein accedes to the EEA.
	May	Commission produces white paper to prepare the countries of central and eastern Europe for membership of the EU.
	July	EU member states sign convention establishing Europol (the European Police Office). First EU ombudsman, Jacob Söderman, elected.
	November	Euro-Mediterranean ministerial conference at Barcelona adopts declaration on future relations, including financial aid and progress towards free trade areas, between EU and 12 Mediterranean states.
	December	EU and the United States sign a new transatlantic agenda and joint action plan. Customs union between Turkey and the EU approved by European Parliament. Madrid summit confirms introduction of a single currency on January 1st 1999. During the year Bulgaria, Estonia, Latvia, Lithuania, Romania and Slovakia apply for EU membership.
1996	*January*	Czech Republic applies for EU membership.
	March	Intergovernmental conference to review the Maastricht treaty and to prepare for further enlargement opens in Turin. EU bans UK beef exports, but offers financial aid to help combat BSE outbreak. The UK begins systematic policy of non-cooperation in effort to secure the lifting of the ban.
	June	The UK ends non-cooperation after EU stipulates conditions for the eventual lifting of the ban. Slovenia applies for EU membership.
	October	EU emphatically rejects the extra-territorial provisions of the Helms-Burton Act regarding trade with Cuba, and threatens counter-measures against the United States.

(*Continued*)

Table 9A (Continued)

	December	Dublin summit agrees on stability pact to impose economic and financial disciplines on member states joining the single currency in preparation for scheduled launch in 1999.
1997	May	Newly elected Labour government in UK announces 'fresh start' in relations with EU, and ends British opt-out from the Social Chapter.
	June	Signing of the Amsterdam Treaty, containing modest amendments to Rome and Maastricht treaties.
	July	Commission adopts 'Agenda 2000' policy statement, preparing for further EU enlargement, and setting long-term targets for financial and agricultural reforms.
	December	At Luxembourg summit the way is cleared for membership negotiations to begin in March 1998 with Cyprus, the Czech Republic, Estonia, Hungary, Poland and Slovenia.
1998	May	Agreement is reached at special Brussels summit for 11 member states to participate in a single currency from January 1st 1999. Wim Duisenberg is appointed as the first president of the European Central Bank. At EU-US summit President Clinton agrees to ask Congress to exclude the EU from sanctions under the Helms-Burton Act.
	September	Malta reactivates its application for EU membership.
	December	European Parliament refuses to approve final accounts of the 1996 budget, precipitating a crisis with the commission.
1999	March	Entire Santer Commission resigns to avoid vote of censure by the Parliament. At Berlin summit Romano Prodi is nominated to succeed Santer. Summit also approves budget perspectives for 2000–06.
	May	Treaty of Amsterdam comes into force. Foreign ministers propose a stability pact for south-east Europe, following the Kosovo conflict.
	September	New commission, led by Romano Prodi, takes over.
	October	Special summit meeting on justice and home affairs calls for the creation of an area of 'freedom, justice and security' within the EU.
	December	Helsinki summit decides to open accession negotiations with Bulgaria, Latvia, Lithuania, Malta, Romania and Slovakia.
2000	March	Special Economic Summit in Lisbon inaugurates a ten-year programme to make the EU 'the most competitive and dynamic knowledge-based economy in the world'.
	September	Denmark votes in referendum by 53.3% to 46.7% not to adopt the euro.

(Continued)

Table 9.A (Continued)

	October	Convention draws up a draft Charter of Fundamental Rights for the EU.
	December	European Council in Nice agrees treaty amending the Union's institutional provisions to facilitate the entry of up to 12 new member states.
2001	January	Greece becomes the twelfth country to join the euro.
	June	Irish referendum rejects Nice treaty (53.87% to 46.13%).
	December	Laeken summit adopts wide-ranging proposals to combat terrorism in the wake of the September 11th attacks on the United States. It also establishes a Convention on EU reform and a possible EU constitution.
2002	January– February	Euro notes and coins replace national currencies in the 12 member states of the euro zone.
	July	The treaty establishing the European Coal and Steel- Community expires after 50 years. Its residual duties and obligations are transferred to the EU.
	October	A second Irish referendum accepts the Nice treaty by 62.89% to 37.11%.
	December	Copenhagen summit completes accession negotiations with ten candidate countries, paving the way for a 25-member EU from May 1st 2004. It agrees target dates for Bulgaria and Romania for 2007, and that opening negotiations with Turkey should be decided in December 2004.
2003		Nine candidate countries approve their membership terms by referendums, while Cyprus ratifies its acces- sion treaty by a unanimous parliamentary vote.
	February	Nice treaty comes into effect. Croatia applies for EU membership.
	June	Convention on a European constitution completes its work and presents a draft to the Thessaloniki summit, which passes it on to an intergovernmental conference.
	September	Swedish referendum rejects the euro by 56% to 44%.
	December	The IGC presents a revised draft of the constitution to a summit which fails to agree, largely because of disagreement over proposed voting weights in the Council of Ministers.
2004	February– March	The Commission adopts EU financial perspectives for 2007–13. Former Yugoslav Republic of Macedonia applies to join EU.
	May	Ten new countries – Cyprus, the Czech Republic, Estonia, Hungary, Latvia, Lithuania, Malta, Poland, Slovakia and Slovenia – join the EU, bringing membership to 25.

(*Continued*)

Table 9A (Continued)

	June	European Council approves the draft Treaty establishing a Constitution for Europe (TCE). Jose Manuel Barroso named as new Commission president.
	November	The Barroso Commission takes over until January 2010.
2005	March	Summit meeting agrees to ease the provisions of the Stability and Growth Pact, redefine the objectives of the Lisbon strategy, and water down the proposed directive to liberalise the provision of cross-border services.
	May–June	French and Dutch voters reject the TCE in referendums, by respectively 55% to 45% and 62% to 38%.
	December	European Council agrees the EU's financial perspective for 2007–13.
2006	January	Slovenia joins euro.
	June	Tenth European Development Fund, covering 2007–13 and totalling €22 billion, agreed for ACP countries.
2007	January	Bulgaria and Romania become members of the EU.
	March	Berlin Declaration on the 50th anniversary of the signing of the Rome treaty.
	December	Treaty of Lisbon signed.
2008	January	Cyprus and Malta join euro.
	June	Irish referendum rejects Lisbon treaty (53.4% to 46.6%).
	August	President Nicolas Sarkozy negotiates ceasefire in Russo-Georgian war.
	September	US bank group Lehmann Brothers collapses, sparking biggest global economic and financial crisis since the 1930s.
	December	European Council agrees to coordinate national measures to combat the recession. Montenegro applies to join the EU.
2009	January	Slovakia joins the euro.
	April	Albania applies to join the EU.
	June	Iceland applies to join the EU.
	September	Jose Manuel Barroso appointed for a second five-year term as president of the commission (2009–14).
	October	In second referendum, Irish approve Lisbon treaty (67.1% to 32.9%).
	November	Herman Van Rompuy appointed as permanent president of the European Council, and Catherine Ashton as high representative for foreign and security policy.
	December	Treaty of Lisbon comes into force. Serbia applies to join the EU.
2010	February	EU heads of government hold the first of a series of crisis and semi-crisis meetings running over five weeks to handle Greece and Eurozone recession.

(Continued)

Table 9A (Continued)

	May	First Greek bailout of €110 billion in exchange for spending cuts and tax hikes.
		Eurozone government heads agree deeper fiscal consolidation and better budget surveillance to defend euro.
	November	European Council agrees Irish bailout worth €85 billion after property bubble burst. The bailout ended in 2013.
	December	'Enhanced cooperation' procedure used for first time, involving civil law issues of cross-border divorce and custody of children.
2011	January	Estonia adopts the euro as its currency.
		Three new supervisory authorities introduced for banking, insurance and pensions, and securities' markets.
	March	France and UK co-sponsor UN Security Council resolution on no-fly zone in Libya. Germany abstains in SC vote.
	May	Portugal bailout agreed worth €78 billion. The procedure ended in 2014.
	July	Second Greek bailout agreed for €40 billion. Private investors take a 50% haircut on their Greek assets.
		Eurozone countries sign a treaty to create a European Stability Mechanism with €500 billion for countries in need.
	November	Former head of Bank of Italy, Mario Draghi, becomes president of the European Central Bank.
	December	UK premier David Cameron vetoes new fiscal compact-treaty at European Council. Other leaders sign inter-governmental treaty to get round UK obstructionism.
2012	January	Fiscal compact is formally adopted as an intergovernmental treaty and domiciled in Luxembourg.
	March	Bailout of €100 billion agreed for Spanish banks.
	October	European Stability Mechanism enters into force.
	December	European Union is awarded Nobel Peace Prize.
2013	January	Fiscal compact becomes operational. It imposes budget disciplines and imposes automatic penalties.
	March	EU governments agree €10 billion bailout for Cyprus in exchange for bank restructuring.
	July	Croatia joins EU as 28th member.
	November	Tension with Russia rises as Ukraine decides at last minute not to sign extensive partnership deal with EU.
	December	Council of Ministers adopts medium-term EU budget guidelines for 2014–20.
2014	January	Latvia joins euro as eighteenth member.
		EU foreign ministers suspend some sanctions against Iran following international deal on its nuclear programme.

(Continued)

Table 9A (Continued)

	March	EU foreign ministers impose sanctions on Russia following incursions into Ukraine and annexation of Crimea.
	April	Council of Ministers adopts Single Resolution Mechanism as second pillar of European banking union.
	May	Elections to the European Parliament for 2014–19 legislature.
	June	Following vote Jean-Claude Juncker is appointed president of the incoming European Commission. Partnership agreements are signed with Georgia, Moldova and (with a new government in office) Ukraine.
	August	Donald Tusk and Federica Mogherini appointed respectively President of the European Council and High Representative for foreign and security policy.
	October	European Council agrees ambitious greenhouse gas reduction targets for 2030 to stay ahead in global climate change negotiations.
	December	Tusk replaces Herman Van Rompuy as president of European Council.
2015	January	Lithuania joins euro as nineteenth member.
	March	Iceland withdraws its application to join the EU.
	May	Conservative party wins outright victory in UK elections, confirming a commitment to hold in/out referendum on EU membership by end-2017.
	June	Council of Ministers and European Parliament agree to end all roaming charges on mobile phones by 2017.
	July	Third bailout agreed for Greece.
	September–December	Overwhelmed by refugee inflows first from North Africa and then from Syria, the EU tries to build capacities to handle inflows in Greece and Italy to process refugees and share them among member states. It has also contributed €1 billion to the UN and €3 billion to Turkey in burden-sharing costs.
2016	February	European Council and UK premier David Cameron agree a modest EU reform package to put to British voters in a referendum to be held on June 23rd 2016.

Suggestions for further reading

There is a vast literature on the EU, much of it of a highly specialist nature. The European Commission itself produces a stream of pamphlets and documentation of various kinds, much of which is available (often free of charge) from the information offices of the EU in London, Edinburgh, Cardiff and Belfast. There are similar offices in all the capital cities of member states, as well as in other major centres including New York, Washington, New Delhi, Ottawa and Canberra. Most EU publications, including all official documents, are accessible online at https://publications.europa.eu [accessed March 18th 2016].

Among the more significant books addressed to general readers in the recent past, the following may be mentioned.

Adams, M. *et al.*, *Judging Europe's Judges*, Hart Publishing, London, 2015.
Bainbridge, T, and Teasdale, A., *The Penguin Companion to European Union*, 4th edition, Penguin Books, London, 2012.
Charter, D. *Europe: In or Out?*, Biteback, London, 2014.
Dinan, D., *Europe Recast: A History of European Union*, Palgrave Macmillan, Basingstoke, 2004.
Grant, C., *Delors: Inside the House that Jack Built*, Beasley, London, 1994.
Green, S., *The European Identity: Historical and Cultural Realities We Cannot Deny*, Haus Books, London, 2015.
Hix, S., *The Political System of the European Union*, Macmillan, London, 2005.
Hix, S., *What's Wrong with the European Union and How to Fix it*, Polity Press, London, 2008.
Leonard, D. and Leonard, M. (eds), *The Pro-European Reader*, Palgrave Macmillan, London, 2001.
Leonard, M., *Why Europe will Run the 21st Century*, Fourth Estate, London, 2005.
MacShane, D., *Brexit*, I.B. Tauris, London, 2015.
Marquand, D., *The End of the West: the Once and Future Europe*, Princeton University Press, Princeton, 2012.
Nugent, N. and Rhinard, M., *The European Commission*, Palgrave Macmillan, London, 2015.

Owen, D., *The UK's In–Out Referendum*, Haus Books, London, 2015.

Peet, J. and La Guardia, A., *Unhappy Union*, The Economist in association with Profile Books, London, 2014.

Pinder, J. and Usherwood, S., *A Very Short Introduction to the European Union*, 3rd edition, Oxford University Press, Oxford, 2016.

Rifkin, J., *The European Dream*, Polity Press, London, 2004.

Siedentop, L., *Democracy in Europe*, Columbia University Press, New York, 2001.

Soros, G. with Schmitz, G.P., *The Tragedy of the European Union: Disintegration or Revival?*, Public Affairs, New York, 2014.

Wall, S., *A Stranger in Europe: Britain and the EU from Thatcher to Blair*, Oxford University Press, Oxford, 2008.

Westlake, M., *The Council of the European Union*, 2nd edition, John Harper Publishing, 2004.

Young, H., *This Blessed Plot: Britain and Europe from Churchill to Blair*, Macmillan, London, 1998.

Other sources of information

There are a number of think tanks, based either in London or Brussels, whose websites include a mass of news and views about the European Union, often revised on a daily basis. They include the following:

Bruegel, Director: Guntram B. Wolff, rue de la Charité 33, 1210 Brussels (website available at Bruegel.org [accessed March 18th 2016]).

Centre for European Policy Studies (CEPS), Director: Daniel Gros, Congresplaats 1, 1000 Brussels (website available at ceps.eu [accessed March 18th 2016]).

Centre for European Reform (CER), Director: Charles Grant, 14 Great College Street, London, SW1P 3RX (website available at www.cer.org.uk [accessed March 18th 2016]).

European Council on Foreign Relations (ECFR), Director: Mark Leonard, 7th Floor, King's Buildings, 16 Smith Square, London SW1P (website available at www.ecfr.eu [accessed March 18th 2016]).

European Policy Centre (EPC), Chief Executive: Fabian Zuleeg, 14–16 rue du Trône, 1000 Brussels (website available at http://epc.eu [accessed March 18th 2016]).

Royal Institute of International Affairs (Chatham House), Director: Robin Niblett, 9–10 St. James's Square, London, SW1 (website available at www.chathamhouse.org [accessed March 18th 2016]).

Finally, the most comprehensive daily reports and analyses of EU and related events are freely accessible on the website of the independent news agency, Euractiv (www.euractiv.com [accessed March 18th 2016]).

Index